MW01015165

Communication

SHRK™

A Human Communication Guide

Travice Baldwin Obas, MEd

Penny Joyner Waddell, EdD

Kendall Hunt

publishing company

Cover designed by Cassandra West

publishing company

www.kendallhunt.com
Send all inquiries to:
4050 Westmark Drive
Dubuque, IA   52004-1840

Copyright © 2018 by Kendall Hunt Publishing Company

ISBN 978-1-5249-3818-5

All rights reserved. No part of this publication may be reproduced,
stored in a retrieval system, or transmitted, in any form or by any means,
electronic, mechanical, photocopying, recording, or otherwise,
without the prior written permission of the copyright owner.

Published in the United States of America

Logo and Book Cover Design
Created by
Cassandra West, Graphic Artist

E-mail: Cwest@SpeechShark.com

"YOU DO NOT HAVE TO BE GREAT TO START, BUT YOU HAVE TO START TO BE GREAT!"

Zig Ziglar

LET'S GET STARTED!

Table of Contents

Learn about the foundations of communicating effectively with others and how to confidently deliver a message.

Unit #1: Foundations of Communication   1

Chapter 1 Foundations of Communication 3

Chapter 2 Communication and You 19

Chapter 3 Communication and Culture 27

Unit #2: Communication Elements   37

Chapter 4 Communication and Language 39

Chapter 5 Communication and Listening 51

Chapter 6 Nonverbal Communication 65

Unit #3: Interpersonal Communication   83

Chapter 7 Interpersonal Communication Foundations 85

Chapter 8 Interpersonal Communication Conflict 103

Unit #4: Communication in Groups and Teams   111

Chapter 9   Communication in Groups and Teams 113

Chapter 10   Problem-Solving in Groups and Teams. 131

Chapter 11   Professional Communication. 139

Unit #5: Public Communication   153

Chapter 12   Communication and Public Presentation 157

Chapter 13   Presentation Types and Delivery. 175

Chapter 14   Planning and Organizing the Presentation 227

Chapter 15   Presenting and Rehearsing the Presentation 277

Works Cited 327

Index 331

Photo Credits 341

Meet the SpeechSharks!

Travice Baldwin Obas
TObas@SpeechShark.com

Dr. Penny Joyner Waddell
PWaddell@SpeechShark.com

With years of experience as public speaking coaches and human communication instructors, Travice Baldwin Obas and Dr. Penny Joyner Waddell teamed up to write a guidebook designed to help with understanding basic human communication. They also have authored a public speaking workbook, *SpeechShark,* published by Kendall Hunt. The *SpeechShark* workbook is a companion book for the SpeechShark app, a speechwriting tool to help novice and experienced speakers plan, write, rehearse, and present professional speeches.

Human communication can be quite daunting, but with the practical approach in this *Guide to Human Communication,* Obas and Waddell are able to give tips and instructional content which makes even the most complex communication skills understandable.

Both authors are available as speakers separately or as a team for conferences, conventions, and professional development opportunities. Topics include: Overcoming the Fear of Public Speaking, PREP for Impromptu Speaking and Interviews, Planning a Speech, Understanding Nonverbal Communication, Creating and Using Effective Visual Aids, Managing a Tech Team, Adding Movement and Energy to Presentations, Dealing with Conflict, and more!

App Development Team

Contributing developers: Marcus Smith, Maurice McFarlane, Cassandra West, and Charles Hardnett.

Marcus Smith is a developer for both Android and iOS versions of SpeechShark. He started his education at Gwinnett Technical College in the Game Development program; then graduated from Kennesaw State University as a Software Engineer. He has worked on several group projects experienced with mobile platforms and web APIs, as well as principles of software design, also as QA analyst identifying software defects and recommending improvements. Don't let his serious expressions fool you! In his free time, he is often working on small fun mobile projects, practicing for casual video game tournaments, and re-watching favorite TV shows like *Game of Thrones.*

Maurice McFarlane, when not perfecting his serious face, spends time doing copious amounts of push-ups in inappropriate places, sipping Earl Grey tea, and coding iOS applications as part of the SpeechShark development team. An accomplished applications developer and karaoke singer, includes adventures working with Tier 1-2 retailers (many of which you have probably shopped with) on Point-of-Sale system customizations, building custom APIs for payment devices, and implementing P2Pe/EMV solutions. Adventures consist of bar hopping, purchasing Udemy tech courses in an effort to, as he puts it, ". . . become one with the machine," binging on One-Punch-Man, hanging with his homies, and preparing for the inevitable coming of the Sharknado.

Cassandra West is the graphic designer for SpeechShark. Her expertise includes brand identity, corporate presentations and campaigns, web collaboration, UI design, package design, book cover/layout design, and more. Cassie has worked with many of the top companies in the Atlanta area and a few outside the state of Georgia. This talented designer is a wonderful combination of beauty and brains with a side of pizazz! Her smile is infectious and her artistic flair, along with a positive outlook on life, makes her a shark you will always want to have around!

Charles Hardnett is the project manager and senior developer for SpeechShark. His career includes a vast array of experiences as a computer science professor and researcher, software developer, educational administrator, and software architect. He has worked on projects involving the development of compilers for high-performance computing, access and switching for telecommunications, web applications for a variety of domains, and mobile applications for entertainment, productivity, and education. A fun fact about Charles is that he is a certified wedding and party DJ.

Preface

Several years ago, I had the inspiration to develop a speech writing app that would help students and business leaders to write speeches. Through many years as a speech instructor and speech coach, I learned that when people say they have a fear of public speaking, it is more a fear of not knowing what to say. Speakers that have a clear message and a plan for the points they will cover will take time to rehearse and incorporate trained tech support to make the presentation shine. Through this experience, they realize they have cured their own "fear of public speaking" or speech anxiety. The SpeechShark app was developed to be a tool for speakers to help organize thoughts and put content into a package that would be well received by any audience. The next page contains instructions for using the SpeechShark app and we invite you to give it a try!

With the help of a talented app design team, SpeechShark, the app, was born! Charles Hardnett, project manager, worked closely with Maurice McFarlane (IOS Specialist) and Marcus Smith (Android Specialist). Cassandra West (Graphic Artist) designed the SpeechShark icon, logo, and colors used within the app along with the cover for this Communication Shark and the SpeechShark book. My job as the app designer was to provide the idea storyboards, the plan that a speech should follow, and to troubleshoot content issues that would rise to the surface. You've heard the saying, "It takes a village to raise a child," well I can tell you, it takes a dedicated team to build an app. This is not as easy as it looks and I am sure this team became quite frustrated with me on many occasions as I was asking them to help develop the app while all of them were working other full-time jobs! True to the SpeechShark theme, they threw themselves one hundred percent into the turbulent waters and assumed the sharky attitudes that made this dream a reality. Over the past few years, I have lovingly referred to my friends as "The Sharks." Before this project, I might have considered sharks as cold, bloodthirsty predators in the ocean. Now, I have a true respect for a species that remains in constant motion, never vulnerable, with armor-plated skin and with a reputation of power and skill not held by many!

Since that time Travice Obas and I worked together to write an instructional guidebook for public speaking as a companion to the app. We named the book SpeechShark and we've heard from hundreds of students who say that the SpeechShark book and the SpeechShark app have helped tremendously when planning, preparing, and presenting speeches in a public setting. Since we were able to help so many people with the SpeechShark guide, we decided to branch out and write *Communication Shark, a Guide for Human Communication*. This new book focuses on the foundation of communication and includes interesting aspects such as communication and you, culture, language, listening, nonverbal, interpersonal, group and team communication, problem-solving, and conflict management.

Speakers are not sharks, like vicious man–eaters; instead, they are a focused species with a key role to communicate with others. Communication may happen one-on-one, in pairs, a group, or to an audience of hundreds. Instead of an ocean, communicators navigate stages and platforms. Instead of sharp, pointed teeth, they use their intelligence and problem-solving and decision-making skills to strategize and create a calculated plan for success. To humans, communication should not be a large, deep abysmal pit, but an opportunity for us to go deeper!

Did you know that a group of sharks is called a shiver? Have you ever walked on to a stage to make a presentation or tried to get the nerve to speak one-on-one to your boss or to a new friend and felt a shiver of excitement or anxiety? Now, perhaps you are understanding why we have taken on the title of SpeechShark for the app, for the SpeechShark book, and also for the Communication Shark book. These instructional guides have been published by Kendall Hunt Publishing Company and are available as hard-copy or e-books. Kendall Hunt realized that an app as effective as SpeechShark would also benefit the public if accompanying guidebooks were available. It has been a pleasure to work with them on this project.

~Penny Joyner Waddell, EdD

How Do I Use the SpeechShark App?

Did you purchase the SpeechShark app? Excellent! If not, visit our Web site at www.SpeechShark.com to see a demonstration. The app is available for Android users in **GooglePlay** and for iOS users in the **Apple Store**. Using the app means you are on your way to creating effective and exciting speech presentations for your audience! Click on your SpeechShark app and let's get started!

Here are steps to follow:

1. Open the SpeechShark app.
2. Select "Home" to see options to create speeches, manage speeches, or select preferences.
3. If you want to create a NEW speech, select "Create Speeches."
4. A page will open that asks about the purpose of your speech. Read through each type of speech and choose the type that works best for your purpose. If you need more information about each type of speech, simply "LONG PRESS" the speech type to receive a brief tutorial regarding the speech. A "SHORT PRESS" of the speech type will take you directly to the next step in creating a speech.
5. Answer each prompting question using a complete sentence. Use correct grammar and spelling as this information will automatically begin building a speech outline.
6. Take your time and work through each step—one at a time—answering each prompting question, and when finished touch the "Continue" bar.
7. SpeechShark takes all of the guesswork out of crafting an effective speech, but it is up to you to answer the prompts, keep the purpose of your speech as your goal, and consider who will be listening to your speech. What does your audience need to know? What does your audience WANT to know? What can you do and say to connect with the audience and engage them?
8. As you have answered all of the questions, you will notice that SpeechShark will then deliver a full written outline that you can print, share, or e-mail. Additionally, you will see that SpeechShark will automatically generate three note cards that can be used for notes on your phone or tablet/iPad. This will make you a Card Shark because instead of standing in front of your audience with awkward 5x7 note cards, your notes are easily accessed using your electronic device and are available with a simple swipe.
9. Once the speech has been written, you can always retrieve it by going back to the "Home" file on the SpeechShark app and selecting "Manage Speeches." Every speech you craft will be stored there in a file with the "TITLE" that you give to the speech.
10. You, too, can be a **SpeechShark**!

Acknowledgments

Deep appreciation is extended to the following: Co-author, Penny Joyner Waddell; the dedicated members of the SpeechShark app design team: Charles Hardnett, Maurice McFarlane, Marcus Smith, and Cassandra West; the publishers and editors of Kendall Hunt; and most importantly, support from my family, colleagues, and friends.

Communication SH🦈RK™

Unit #1:

Foundations of Communication

Communication Foundations

Communication and You

Communication and Culture

Key Terms to Know

Chapter 1—Communication Foundations

- Channel
- Communication
- Competent Communicator
- Context
- Dyad
- Environment
- Feedback
- Group Communication
- Interpersonal Communication
- Intrapersonal Communication
- Linear Communication Model
- Mass Communication
- Message
- Noise
- Public Communication
- Receiver
- Sender
- Social Media
- Transactional Communication

Chapter 2—Communication and You

- Empathy
- Identity Management
- Organization
- Perceived Self
- Perception Checking
- Public Self
- Self-Concept
- Self-Esteem
- Self-Fulfilling Prophecy
- Self-Serving Bias
- Stereotyping

Chapter 3—Communication and Culture

- Co-Culture
- Collectivistic
- Culture
- Ethnicity
- Ethnocentrism
- High Context
- Individualistic
- Low Context
- Power Distance
- Prejudice
- Race

Chapter One

Communication Foundations

In this chapter:

Communication Basics

Communication Models

Types of Communication

Functions of Communication

Communication in Everyday Life

Communication and Social Media

Competent Communication and Social Media

Communication Competence

COMMUNICATION BASICS

Defining communication can present a challenge, as it reflects a variety of meanings based on context. Since this is a course focused on understanding the fundamentals of human interaction and behavior, **Communication is defined as a process of utilizing messages to generate meaning through human interaction.** The meaning that is generated is accomplished through a variety of contexts. Meaning can be evaluated through vocal methods, written messages, use of visual imagery, in addition to how we listen, read, and interpret messages.

What success you achieve in your personal, professional, or educational lives is indicative of how effectively you communicate. When you are able to communicate effectively with others, relationships are more defined and rewarding. Communication skills, such as speaking, listening, and problem-solving are identified as integral skills necessary in order to compete in our society.

Having effective communication skills can assist you with being perceived as a dynamic communicator, a person who has knowledge, talents, and personality that make you stand out from others. According to the National Association of Colleges and Employers, there are several key attributes employers seek when looking for the perfect employee (NACE). As we cover Human Communication Skills, we note that Problem-Solving Skills, Written Communication Skills, Verbal Communication Skills, and Interpersonal Skills are high on the list. Problem-Solving is the most sought after skill with "82.9%" of all employers putting this as the top skill they seek. Next on the list are Written Communication Skills with "80.3%," and Verbal Communication Skills with "67.5%" of employers noting the importance. Employers also rank Interpersonal Skills at "54.7%," which means they are looking for employees who relate well to each other (NACE).

There are other skills that employers seek, but when talking about communication skills, we can see that Human Communication Skills are necessary for good business as well as good relationships. Learning to communicate more effectively will help you improve your relationships with others, including in the workplace.

If you are wondering about your own skills for the workplace, please complete the evaluation on the next page. If you feel there are areas to improve, get started! You can be a Communication Shark!

HOW ARE YOUR SKILLS?

Name: _____ Date: _____

Complete the following evaluation to become aware of your own employability skills.

Skill	Excellent	Good	Average	Fair	Poor
Problem-solving skills					
Ability to work in a team					
Communication skills (written)					
Leadership					
Strong work ethic					
Analytical/quantitative skills					
Communication skills (verbal)					
Initiative					
Detail-oriented					
Flexibility/adaptability					
Technical skills					
Interpersonal skills (relates well to others)					
Computer skills					
Organizational ability					
Strategic planning skills					
Creativity					
Friendly/outgoing personality					
Tactfulness					
Entrepreneurial skills/risk-taker					
Fluency in a foreign language					

1. Where are your strong areas? _____

   _____

   _____

2. What areas need work? _____

   _____

   _____

COMMUNICATION MODELS

To better understand the nature of communication, researchers utilize communication models. In this section, we will cover the two models most used. Models of communication can interpret the process of communication as a way to simplify the complex interactions of elements in order to clarify relevant relationships and perhaps predict outcomes.

Communication Models accomplish the following goals:

- Identify basic components in the communication process
- Show how the components relate and interact with each other
- Help explain why communication succeeds or fails

The first communication model is the linear communication model. This model shows the function of communication in only one direction.

LINEAR COMMUNICATION Model

SENDER ENCODES → Channel → MESSAGE → Channel → DECODES RECEIVER

A sender creates a message and sends that message through a channel to the receiver, who is the person who decodes and receives the message. The channel is represented as the method we utilize to express the message.

TRANSACTIONAL COMMUNICATION Model

The second model we will discuss is the transactional communication model. Communication in real time is complex and simultaneous, as we are continuously exchanging verbal and nonverbal messages.

The **Sender and Receiver** have an important function in the model of communication, as they are both the encoder (sender) and the decoder (receiver) of messages. The communication source creates a message intended to produce a desired response. This message has no meaning until it has reached the receiver, who interprets and evaluates the message. This process of sending and receiving messages formulates communi-

cation. To communicate with others, you encode your ideas into verbal and nonverbal messages (codes) and send those messages to generate meaning. Decoding is the process of converting that message into information that can be understood. The **channel** is represented as the method we utilize to express the message. In this model, the concept of feedback and the elements of noise are explored as they impact the flow of communication. **Feedback** is defined as a response that can be seen, heard, or felt in either a verbal or non-verbal method. You provide feedback when you nod, smile, frown, or laugh. In addition, showing levels of interest such as asking questions or other types of appropriate behavior are important to ensuring your intended message was received. Expert communicators work to interpret feedback, to ensure they are achieving their purpose, otherwise they adjust the message. **Noise** is defined as anything that can prevent a message from being received. Noise can be either internal or external. External noise includes physical elements in the environment that interfere with effective communication. Examples may include traffic/honking, a difficult accent, high/low pitch, warm/cold environment, odors, or types of designs/colors used to communicate a message. Unlike external noise, internal noise is a mental distraction you experience while processing a message. Internal noise consists of thoughts, feelings, and attitudes that inhibit the ability to understand a message as it was intended. If you are preoccupied with your own personal thoughts, you can misinterpret information. This model reflects this process in a variation of contexts. **Context is identified as the environment or setting in which the communication occurs.** Choosing particular environments can determine whether or not an intended message is accurately received. For example, if you choose to deliver sensitive information in a context that is open, such as a classroom, you change the way in which the message is interpreted.

The Transactional Model of Communication, as you can see, is more complex than the Linear Model of Communication. Here is a diagram to help:

	Noise	**Noise**	**Noise**	
COMMUNICATOR	Channels	Messages	Channels	**COMMUNICATOR**
(Sends and Receives)	⟷		⟷	(Sends and Receives)
Encodes/Decodes	**Noise**	**Noise**	**Noise**	Encodes/Decodes

TYPES OF COMMUNICATION

Let's consider the types of communication that we use on a daily basis: Intrapersonal Communication, Dyadic Interpersonal Communication, Group Communication, Public Communication, and Mass Communication.

Intrapersonal Communication

Do you ever consider how you process internal thoughts? We call this **intrapersonal communication, which is defined as "communication with yourself."** The way in which we mentally process information has a direct impact on how we interact with others. Understanding that "voice in your head" is imperative to understanding how to communicate internally.

Dyadic/Interpersonal Communication

Communication researchers have identified the act of two humans interacting as a dyad. This is the term that is often utilized in research of human beings communicating in various communication contexts. Most commonly, the term used to describe **human behavior and interaction between two individuals is referred to as interpersonal communication**, "inter" (meaning between) and "personal" (meaning person to person). Individuals interact by using verbal and nonverbal messages to generate meaning for the purpose of maintaining a relationship.

Group Communication

When the parameter of communication between two individuals expands, we refer to that as group communication. **Group communication must include at least three individuals, in which the foundation is to accomplish a task or goal.** Groups may vary in size and scope, and we will discuss those aspects in the chapters focused on group communication.

Public Communication

To reflect the identification of a public presentation made in front of an audience, **public communication was formed to showcase the balance between a speaker delivering remarks and an audience providing limited feedback**. In the chapters describing public speaking, we will discuss the most effective ways for public speakers to communicate, through careful preparation and delivery of information.

Mass Communication

When messages are expanded to large audiences through a variety of contexts, including print, electronic, social media, and so forth, we define that form of communication as mass communication. **Mass communication has the ability to provide information and disseminate messages in an expansive way to instantly connect with audiences.**

FUNCTIONS OF COMMUNICATION

Communication is a fundamental element that we as human beings need in an effort to survive. If you reflect on Abraham Maslow's Hierarchy of Needs, you will see that communication satisfies many of our needs. The five needs shown by Maslow can be broken down into four primary functions: physical, identity, social, and practical needs. We'll take these one at a time to help explain this.

Physical Needs

Did you know that evidence suggests that we as humans are dependent on other human beings to foster our physical health? Consider the stories you may have read about a spouse dying, and soon after the other spouse passes away due to the incomparable loss of that loved one.

Maslow's Hierarchy of Needs

Identity Needs

In addition to survival needs, communication serves as a way in which we learn about who we are, based on our interactions with others.

Social Needs

Just as communication can assist us with defining who we are, it may also connect us to others. In the movie, *I Am Legend,* starring Will Smith, you watch the deterioration of the character, as he is isolated as the only human being left alive, having only his dog as a companion.

Practical Needs

We have focused on the physical, mental, and social benefits of communication; however, in a practical sense, communication allows us to be effective in our everyday interactions. Consider the difficulty in placing an order in a drive-through, or not being able to ask for what you need, provide information about a task, and so forth.

COMMUNICATION IN EVERYDAY LIFE

As we reflect on communication across the decades, we can certainly identify the dramatic changes and challenges technology and social media have played a role in shaping current communication.

With the shift of technology infused within the foundations of our human interactions, we have to ask whether or not these communication tools make our communication lives better or more efficient. What are the drawbacks of these elements on human interaction?

Early communication was limited to face-to-face, and storytelling was how knowledge and information was passed down from generation to generation. As time progressed, we began to utilize what many of you today call *snail* mail and also telegraph messages to connect with each other. With the inventions of radio, telephones, and television, information became more accessible and altered the scope of how humans interacted. In current society, the convergence of technology and digital platforms serves with the most significant impact on how we communicate on a daily basis. These include e-mail and social media along with information and communication based on the Internet.

Graph of Accelerating Pace of Communication Technology

Digital Age

Phones, Radio, Television

Face-to-Face
Storytelling
Telegraph
Mail

COMMUNICATION AND SOCIAL MEDIA

Social Media consists of the use of digital technology and channels to interact with a limited group of receivers.

In a world where social media rules the communication game, we have to ask why we use it. Some of us simply use it for information access. Others use it to keep up with friends, family members, or to initiate romantic relationships. There is also the aspect of establishing our professional identity online. And lastly, we simply utilize social media for our own enjoyment.

Reasons We Use Social Media	Details
Information	To gain knowledge or content
Personal Relationships	To maintain connections with others
Identity Management	To observe behaviors to validate personal choices
Entertainment	To share interests or activities

How do you use social media? Do you find yourself Facebook messaging your friends to ask them to meet you for dinner or do you still text or call them on the phone? If you are using social media outlets as a way to maintain or grow personal relationships, you might find that it is hard to truly connect with a screen between the two of you. Often words written may be misunderstood without the nonverbal cues that go along with a personal conversation. According to Albert Mehrabian's theory of communication, the written

word only compromises 7% of the total communication we use. I guess that is why so many people include emojis along with their texts and Facebook posts! Does this look familiar?

Hi Friend!☺ *I haven't heard from you in a while.*☺ *Does this mean you are mad at me?*☹ *Would you mind if I gave you a call* ☎ *to say Hello!*✋ *Check one:* ☒ *or* ☑

COMPETENT COMMUNICATION AND SOCIAL MEDIA

What Are the Best Practices?

- Channel/Medium
- Cautious Posting
- Considerate/Civil
- Privacy
- Safety

With social media technology changing rapidly, there are always adjustments needed to maintain effective communication in an online world. It is imperative to consider the elements above when posting information online.

To evaluate your own use of social media for communicating, use the following table:

Questions to Ask:	Yes	No
Is this the most appropriate channel or medium for me to communicate?		
What are the potential drawbacks or issues that could arise in me posting, liking, or sharing information?		
Am I considerate and exercising civility with the information that I choose to convey?		
What concerns or issues of privacy need to be considered?		
How am I safeguarding the safety of myself and others?		

COMMUNICATION COMPETENCE

It is important to distinguish that although we all have the ability to communicate, it does not ensure that we are conducting that communication in an appropriate manner. What constitutes an effective communicator? In my years as a communication scholar, I have consistently referred to an effective communicator as an individual that develops competence in their ability to communicate with others.

Competent Communicator: A person who has knowledge, skill, and motivation to do what is appropriate, effective, and ethical in any situation.

Although there is not one way to communicate, certainly having comprehensive knowledge of what you are communicating is critical. In addition, you must develop a skill set that will help deliver your messages effectively; that requires skill. Lastly, you must be motivated and have the desire to be a competent communicator. Once those elements are in alignment, you will know what is appropriate, effective, and ethical in any communication scenario you find yourself.

HOW DO YOU USE SOCIAL MEDIA?

Name:_____ Date:_____

Answer the following areas truthfully to evaluate your own use of social media. If you don't recognize the icon, chances are you are not using that form of social media.

Social Media	Twice a Day	Once a Day	Twice a Week	Once a Week	Twice a Month	Once a Month	Almost Never	Never

You won't fear a shark attack when you keep your eyes open and are prepared for whatever comes your way! Some refer to shark movements as a feeding frenzy. Truthfully, it is no frenzy at all, but a graceful ballet in which the sharks are fast and swim confidently toward their goal. You can do this too! Be a Communication Shark! Use this section to test your skills and understanding.

Foundations of Communication

1. What is the definition of communication?

   _____

   _____

2. Provide THREE key attributes that employers seek in potential employees.

   _____

   _____

3. What model of communication demonstrates communication in only one direction?

   _____

   _____

4. Who is the person that originates the message?

   _____

5. Who is the person who decodes (interprets) the message?

   _____

6. How does the sender know if the intended message was received?

   _____

   _____

7. What is communication with one's self?

_____

_____

8. Please provide a definition of dyadic or interpersonal communication.

_____

_____

9. What is the purpose of group communication?

_____

_____

10. What type of communication instantly connects messages to the audience?

_____

_____

11. What are the FOUR functions of Maslow's Hierarchy of Needs?

_____

_____

12. What are TWO of the early forms of communication technology?

_____

_____

13. What are the FOUR methods or reasons why we utilize social media?

_____

_____

14. Please provide the best practices to consider when engaging with social media.

_____

_____

15. Please provide the THREE key elements in the definition of a competent communicator.

_____

_____

Shark Bites

This activity will help you analyze your personal dependence on technology to improve communication skills.

Social Media Detox

Consider a twenty-four-hour social media detox. For twenty-four hours, eliminate Twitter, Facebook, Instagram, Snapchat, and so forth. Keep a journal/diary of your experience and answer the following questions:

1. What do you discover about yourself?

2. Do you manage to get more accomplished throughout your day?

3. What are your thoughts about "missing out" on things going on in the world and with your family or friends?

4. Which social media format did you miss the most?

5. Which social media format did you miss the least?

6. After going through the twenty-four-hour detox, did you make any decisions to change, alter, or omit the use of any of your social media formats?

Chapter Two

Communication and You

In this chapter:

Communication and Self-Concept

Perception

Communication and Identity Management

COMMUNICATION AND SELF-CONCEPT

As we learn more about communication, the most vital aspect is our understanding of ourselves; and how our concept of self will shape our interactions and experiences with others.

The most simplistic definition of **self-concept is the way that we view or see ourselves**; however, that term incorporates the perceptions that we hold about ourselves and also characteristics that other people have told us about ourselves.

Ask yourself the following questions:

- Who are you?
- What makes you, *YOU*?
- What are the beliefs that you have about yourself?

Generally, people respond with their name, age, ethnic background, gender, religious affiliation, occupation and roles they play (sister, wife, friend, etc.). They also incorporate adjectives that perhaps describe their personality or physical attributes. When you look in the mirror, past the aesthetics, who are you? Our programmed beliefs dictate the perception we hold about ourselves, which in turn influences esteem, self-worth, and happiness.

Programming of our self-concept begins in childhood. Generally, in the first six years of existence our brains absorb, record, and believe what we are told about ourselves. From birth, our socialization process is determined and we develop a social mask and behave based on norms. We adopt cultural, political, and gender norms of society. We embrace the ideals of our parents, peers, and social media expectations to fit in and be accepted; meanwhile, our authentic self remains in the shadows.

What if who you thought you were was all wrong? Often, we don't even realize who we are meant to be, because we become consumed with living out someone else's ideals of who we are. Concept of ourselves is not inherently authentic. To transform the outside, we must understand how to transform who we are on the inside.

In order to evolve into the best version of ourselves, we must understand who we really are and who we are designed to become. We must question our thoughts and beliefs.

We must understand personality traits transmitted through our culture or genetics. Also, look at signature traits, talents, and character strengths.

The denial of self-expression often leads to detrimental effects on our health. If we are always trying to be "normal," we may not realize our true potential. When we are forced to be something we are not, we take on a distorted persona that we create, and that does not always align to our true inner self.

HOW WE VIEW OURSELVES

Self Distortions	Self-Fulfilling Prophecy
The tendency to distort what happens to you and how you feel about a variety of experiences.	A prediction you make that you cause to happen or become true.
Self-concept has the powerful ability to shape our present life and influence future behaviors.	Two aspects of self-fulfilling prophecy: (1) The expectations that influence our behavior and (2) when expectations predict actions.
Having a realistic or distorted self-concept impacts us and those around us (friends, co-workers, significant others).	Positive or negative attributes of self-fulfilling prophecies can influence behavior and its potential to shape who we are as communicators.

PERCEPTION

We have discussed the power of self-concept and its impact on the understanding of ourselves. Now, let's explore the correlation of our self-concept and how it impacts our view of others and the world around us.

Perception is defined as: **The process you use to *select, organize,* and *interpret* sensory stimuli in the world around us.** Given the number of stimuli that we are exposed to, we must make decisions regarding stimuli with which we direct our focus.

The process of perception can be defined in three simple steps:

1. Selection   Using our senses to notice and choose from many stimuli

- Once we have selected what stimuli to focus on, we must arrange the information in a way that makes sense.

2. Organization   Sorting selected stimuli into messages

- How do we organize our perceptions? The most common method includes a combination of a physical role, interaction, and psychological constructs.

3. Interpretation   Interpreting the meaning of messages

- We have selected and organized our perceptions, and lastly, we must provide an interpretation. How do these reflections determine what we notice about others?

There are factors that influence and alter the accuracy in depicting perception. We should combat biases and common perceptual tendencies that influence accuracy in our perception of others.

An ideal perspective for managing your perceptions is to conduct a perception checking process. Conduct the following:

- Describe the behavior you observed.
- Create possible interpretations of behavior.
- Ask for clarification about interpretations.

Source: Waddell

This tool works effectively in our understanding of others and creates a sense of cooperation when determining our interpretations and behaviors.

COMMUNICATION AND IDENTITY MANAGEMENT

We rely on communication strategies to influence how others view us. This is defined as **identity management**.

To better understand the concept of identity management, we must identify what "selves" are at the focal point. First, we will discuss the self that closely reflects our self-concept. We will refer to this self as the *perceived self,* **the person we think we are when we assume no one else is watching**.

The other self we will identify is the *presented self,* **the person that we publicly showcase to those around us**.

The process of identity management can occur in various levels of self-presentation, due to the nature of multiple identities that we manage. Our ability to manage these identities becomes critical to how we are perceived.

Self-Presentation: Our ability to observe and control how you express yourself verbally and nonverbally when interacting with others.

Individuals who monitor and analyze their behaviors and adapt their communication accordingly are perceived as competent in their identity management. Why should we be concerned about managing our identities? Social rules and norms often dictate societal expectations, so why bother trying to create a desired impression of ourselves? In any communication situation we find ourselves in, it is imperative that we choose the most appropriate way to act. Impression management allows you to determine what *self* is the most appropriate to reveal.

You won't fear a shark attack when you keep your eyes open and are prepared for whatever comes your way! Some refer to shark movements as a feeding frenzy. Truthfully, it is no frenzy at all, but a graceful ballet in which the sharks are fast and swim confidently toward their goal. You can do this too! Be a Communication Shark! Use this section to test your skills and understanding.

Communication and You

1. How is self-concept defined?

   _____

   _____

2. Who determines your self-concept?

   _____

   _____

3. What are the additional influential factors of our self-concept?

   _____

   _____

4. What are the THREE steps of the Perception Process?

   _____

   _____

5. What are the steps to ensure accuracy in our perceptions?

   _____

   _____

6. What is a self-fulfilling prophecy?

_____

_____

7. How do social rules and norms influence self-esteem?

_____

_____

8. What is identity management?

_____

_____

9. What is our perceived self?

_____

_____

10. What is our presented self?

_____

_____

11. How would you define self-presentation?

_____

_____

Shark Bites

Self-Concept and Perception Exercise

With the opportunity to take a closer look at yourself, you have hopefully gained a greater understanding of how you see yourself and how you present yourself to others. Based on this new understanding, I would like for you to help us know you better. For this assignment, you will need to use both your analytical and creative skills. You have the task of selecting an animal, object, or color, and use it to tell us more about you. Develop a comparison between yourself and that animal, object, or color in at least *two* distinct ways. Only one way may be a physical comparison (tall, pretty, muscular, etc.), and at least one must deal with your personality.

Animal/Object/Color	Physical Comparison	Personality Comparison

Chapter Three

Communication and Culture

In this chapter:

Understanding Culture

Communication and Co-Cultures

Dimensions of Culture

Intercultural Communication Strategies

UNDERSTANDING CULTURE

As communicators, we are more connected with individuals from similar cultures and backgrounds. The diversity that we experience can produce benefits, but also potential challenges with communication. In the next section, we will explore the effects culture has on our ability to communicate effectively.

How would you define culture? What about *sub-sets* of culture? Below are working definitions that help create the framework.

- **Define Culture:** A learned set of interpretations about beliefs, values, traditions that affect the behaviors of a group of people.
- **Define Co-Culture:** Co-cultures exist within the mainstream society, yet remain connected to each other through cultural heritage.

COMMUNICATION AND CO-CULTURES

How we view ourselves and how we relate to others is generated from our cultural and co-cultural identities. Our ethnicity (the region of the world that we come from), age, religious affiliation, and sexual preferences shape our cultural identity.

What is Ethnicity? Varying definitions exist; however, it generally places an identification of an individual to a group based on culture, religion, or nationality.

Communicating in a Multicultural Environment

It is important to understand and overcome potential pitfalls in understanding others.

- **Ethnocentrism:** Is defined as belief that your culture is superior to others. This belief often leads individuals of that culture thinking that they are entitled to certain privileges and rights that are not provided to others.
- **Stereotyping:** Stereotypes are generalizations about a group of individuals that are often exaggerated or oversimplify characteristics of a group. These generalizations often lead to perceptions (good or bad) that overlook how individuals should be identified and affect how we interact and understand others.
- **Prejudice:** Is defined as an attitude based on little or no direct experience with that individual or group. Stereotypes can often lead to prejudice, when you make a judgment about someone prior to getting to know them. The word prejudice has two facets: *pre,* meaning before, and *judice,* meaning judge.
- **Discrimination:** Is how we act out or express prejudice. Often when we discriminate, we exclude individuals from opportunities granted to other individuals. Discrimination can be represented in various forms that create inequity in employment opportunities, work promotions, and access to housing and educational resources. These forms of intolerance create disparity across ethnic, racial, religious, gender, sexual orientation, age, disability, and physical appearance. When restriction of rights or opportunities from particular groups exists, communication can break down and interactions with others can be damaged.
- **Racism:** Correlates the impact of ethnocentrism, stereotypes, prejudice, and discrimination. It reflects an attitude or intention to inflict harm based on superiority of their race over others.

DIMENSIONS OF CULTURE

According to Geert H. Hofstede, *Cultural Dimension* is a learned set of shared interpretations about beliefs, values, norms, and social practice that affect the behaviors of a relatively large group of people. There are five dimensions with which you should be aware. They are individualism versus collectivism, low versus high power, masculine versus feminine, low versus high context (uncertainty avoidance), and short-term time versus long-term time. All five are different but have their place as we discuss culture and how it affects our own communication skills. We will offer examples of countries where you might find these specific types of cultures, but in our diverse world, it is important to remember that although these dimensions are noted for other cultures, the people who come from these cultures could be your next-door neighbor. Understanding where your friends, co-workers, and neighbors are from will help you to also understand their culture. The result is that you will do a much better job communicating with a person or family when you understand their culture (Hofstede).

Individualism vs. Collectivism

Individualism	"I" is important: Independence Personal achievement
	Examples: USA, Australia, Great Britain, Canada
Collectivism	"We" is important: Group identity Group achievement
	Examples: Guatemala, Ecuador, Panama, Venezuela

Low vs. High Power

High Power	*Inequalities:* Between people Between roles
	Examples: Malaysia, Slovakia, Guatemala, Panama
Low Power	*Equality:* Between people Between roles Interdependence
	Examples: Austria, Israel, Denmark, New Zealand

Masculine vs. Feminine

Masculine	*Descriptors:* Assertive, Decisive, Dominant Gender roles are separated
	Examples: Slovakia, Japan, Hungary, Austria
Feminine	*Descriptors:* Nurturing and cooperative Gender roles overlap
	Examples: Sweden, Norway, Latvia, The Netherlands

Low vs. High Context—Uncertainty Avoidance

High Context	*Communication:*
	     Messages are implied
	     Messages are more nonverbal
	
	 Examples:
	 Chinese, Japanese, Native American, African American, Latino

Low Context	*Communication:*
	     Messages are explicit
	     Messages are more verbally direct
	     Messages are more objective
	
	 Examples: German, Swiss, Scandinavian, Canadian

Short-Term Time vs. Long–Term Time

Short-Term	*Descriptor:*
	     Adhere to schedules
	     Adhere to deadlines
	
	 Examples: Pakistan, Nigeria, Philippines, Canada

Long-Term	*Descriptor:*
	     Not obsessed with schedules
	     Not obsessed with deadlines
	
	 Examples: China, Hong Kong, Taiwan, Japan, Jamaica

Here is another way to look at cultural dimensions. Where do you find yourself in this mix? Do you feel more comfortable communicating with people who share your same culture? Do you enjoy working with people from various cultures? Before we can understand someone else, we need to first understand ourselves, our own perceptions, beliefs, and values.

The next section will give you tips and tools to help you be a more effective communicator with people who are outside of your culture and perhaps even your comfort zone.

INTERCULTURAL COMMUNICATION STRATEGIES

It is imperative to practice communication strategies that enhance our ability to respect, understand, and adapt to other cultures. While practicing, remember that you should have a good understanding of other cultures so that you can choose a strategy that works best.

One good rule is to avoid judging others until you understand the full story. We call this strategy **mindfulness** because this means you are fully aware of the present moment without making judgments.

Of course, the opposite is true when you rush in to judge or perceive situations without understanding the full story. We call this strategy **mindlessness** and you will find this occurs as you allow narrow categories and false judgments to become habits of thought and behavior.

Here are three simple tips to help you communicate more effectively with people who do not share your personal culture:

- **Be Mindful** and fully aware of the present moment without making hasty judgments about others.
- **Adapt to Others** and accommodate your conversations and speech behaviors to the norms of individuals from different cultures.
- **Engage Others** and spend time and energy interacting with individuals from other cultures.

While we do not share the same culture with everyone we meet, we do share some of the very same traits. Realizing this will also prove that in the long run, we actually have more in common with people from various cultures than we differ.

It can be easy to focus on the differences in culture; however, it is worth noting the elements of communication that we share.

- We **smile** when happy
- We **wave** as a greeting
- We **laugh** when amused
- We **blush** when embarrassed
- We **cry** when sad or in pain
- We **frown** when concerned or not at ease
- We **adopt a fetal position** when cold, dejected, or feeling hopeless
- We **shrug** when expressing "I don't know"
- We **slump** when tired or dejected
- We **stand straight** when confident or alert

Take a look at the examples. Can you identify with these traits?

Traits We All Share

Frown

Smile

Fetal Position

Blush

Laugher

Sadness

You won't fear a shark attack when you keep your eyes open and are prepared for whatever comes your way! Some refer to shark movements as a feeding frenzy. Truthfully, it is no frenzy at all, but a graceful ballet in which the sharks are fast and swim confidently toward their goal. You can do this too! Be a Communication Shark! Use this section to test your skills and understanding.

Communication and Culture

1. How is culture defined?

     _____

     _____

2. What is ethnicity?

     _____

     _____

3. How would you define co-culture?

     _____

     _____

4. Please provide TWO examples of co-culture.

     _____

     _____

5. How is prejudice defined?

     _____

     _____

6. What is ethnocentrism?

_____

_____

7. What are TWO examples of stereotypes?

_____

_____

8. What dimension(s) of culture focus on *I versus Group* dynamic in the approach?

_____

_____

9. What cultural dimension perceives the woman as nurturing and modest?

_____

_____

10. How do we demonstrate mindfulness when interacting with others from different cultures?

_____

_____

Shark Bites

Cultural Awareness Checklist

Instructions: Answer the following questions with the very first thought that comes to your mind. This will help you to understand your own cultural awareness. There are ten questions posted here. If you answer NO to five or more questions, you may need to re-evaluate your own cultural sensitivity.

Questions to Consider:	Yes	No
Do you speak another language fluently?		
Can you understand another language?		
Have you ever traveled to another country?		
Do you attend a multicultural church or religious organization?		
Do you work with a diverse group of people?		
Have you participated in a study abroad program?		
When planning events or parties, do you invite a variety of cultures?		
My best friend or significant other is from a different culture?		
Does your college or institution host events that appeal to a multicultural audience?		
Are you more comfortable with people who are of your own culture?		

1. What have you learned about your own cultural awareness?

2. What plans do you have to improve your own cultural awareness?

Communication SH RK™

Unit #2:

Communication Elements

Communication and Language

Communication and Listening

Nonverbal Communication

Key Terms to Know

Chapter 4—Communication and Language

- Albert Mehrabian's Communication Model
- Communication
- Communication Barrier
- Connotative Language
- Denotative Language
- Gender
- Language
- Linguistics
- Nonverbal Communication
- Semantics
- Sex
- Slang
- Verbal Communication

Chapter 5—Communication and Listening

- Active Listening
- Appreciative Listening
- Communication
- Critical Listening
- Decoding
- Empathetic Listening
- Encoding
- Feedback
- Informative Listening
- Noise

Chapter 6—Nonverbal Communication

- Action Language
- Adaptors
- Affect Displays
- Appearance
- Artifactual
- Chronemics
- Cultural
- Emblems
- Expectancy Violation Theory
- Eye Contact
- Gender
- Gestures
- Haptics
- Illustrators
- Intimate Distances
- Kinesics
- Nonverbal Communication
- Object Language
- Olfactory
- Paralinguistics
- Personal Distances
- Poise
- Posture
- Primary Territories
- Professional
- Proxemics
- Public Distances
- Public Territories
- Regulators
- Relational
- Secondary Territories
- Sign Language
- Smiling
- Social Distances
- Territoriality

Chapter Four

Communication and Language

In this chapter:

Nature of Language

Power of Language

Language Miscommunication and Barriers

Gender, Culture, and Language

NATURE OF LANGUAGE

Whether face-to-face, using Skype, telephone, e-mail, texts, Messenger, Twitter, Facebook, or any other version of electronics, communication happens as we send and receive messages, interpret meanings, and respond accordingly.

Verbal communication happens through **language** and is actually the smallest part of the communication process. The Communication Model developed by **Albert Mehrabian** almost fifty years ago is still being used to illustrate that only 7% of communication involves words, 38% involves the way we say the words, and 55% involves what we see as body language (Mehrabian).

Language is used for communication but involves the meanings of words and phrases which scholars often label as semantics. When you are discussing the meaning of a word, you are talking about **semantics** and that is an element of **linguistics** also known as language. So, if someone asks you "What is language?" you can answer that by saying language is a system that we use for communicating that involves words. Not so difficult, right?

This next area may prove to be harder to understand as we cover denotative and connotative language. The truth is that words do not always have just one meaning. Actually, most of the words we use have many different meanings and are defined as either denotative or connotative. As we explore **denotative language**, we realize that this is a word that is defined exactly as it is shown in the dictionary. An English instructor I had one time explained that if a word is denotative, you could bet that it is found in the dictionary as a definition. Here is an example: the definition of an apple is a round fruit grown on a tree that has thin red or green skin. Yes, that is a basic definition and exactly the definition of an apple. However, if you say that your daughter is the "apple of my eye," you are not talking about fruit any longer. This is when the word—apple—becomes **connotative language**. When we use expression in language, the meaning of the word can change depending upon the connotation in which the word was said. One thing to always keep in mind is that you should use denotative language if you want to make sure there are no misunderstandings because negative connotations toward a great word can often result in disastrous results.

Language can be **verbal** or **nonverbal**. For example, the sending and receiving of language using a computer, reading it from a book as you are doing now, e-mails, texts, Facebook posts, and so much more involves the written language (nonverbal); whereas the spoken language is verbal. Understanding the nature of language is understanding that meaning is derived from so much more than the words used. Signals and symbols are both evident as sounds have meaning, just as much as meaning is derived from words. Verbal sounds include laughing, crying, sighing, and others which communicate meaning.

POWER OF LANGUAGE

"Sticks and stones may break my bones, but words will never hurt me." That is an old adage that has been repeated over and over through the years. Parents will repeat the rhyme to soothe the feelings of their child after hurtful words were exchanged on the playground. As a parent, I also found myself saying this to my own child who was hurt by something someone said to her at school. Even as I was saying the rhyme, I realized that the saying just isn't true at all and wondered why any of us ever used it!

The truth is, words have a power to heal, motivate, and encourage. Words also can be harmful. While they will not break bones, they most certainly

can break a heart. Harsh words can break a spirit and they can break down dreams by lowering a person's self-esteem. Yes, there is a power in language. Speakers have a responsibility to use the power of language for good.

We cannot discuss the power of language without also recognizing that the power is in the use of language. Having a good command of language means that the speaker has a good understanding of how to use language effectively and how to organize meaning to share a message through language. You've also heard about the Power of Persuasion. Again, it is the effective use of language that can persuade someone to change the way they think of something or at the very least to be motivated to think differently about a topic for which they have developed an understanding.

Your instructor may use the power of language as she shares information regarding assignments due and testing to be completed. The power of language is not the sole responsibility of the speaker, but it is how the speaker uses language. This power can belong to anyone who has a good command of the language for which they are speaking.

LANGUAGE MISCOMMUNICATION AND BARRIERS

In order to communicate, we need language. When people can't communicate, we have a barrier to communication. This might happen due to impairments such as vocal or hearing difficulties, but even those without such issues may find themselves in situations where they misunderstand or misinterpret meanings of a message being sent. In this section, we will cover several different types of language miscommunications and barriers.

Speaking another language makes it difficult to use language with others who do not share the same understanding of the language. There is a story in the Bible, Genesis Chapter Eleven, that illustrates the difficulty of trying to communicate with people who speak other languages. During that time, all of the people spoke one language. Together, the people decided to build a giant tower tall enough to reach God in the heavens. According to the story, God looked down upon these people and decided that their efforts were not healthy for them. He decided to divide the people into different linguistic groups with many different languages so that they could not understand and communicate with each other. The building ceased as the communication barrier caused such trouble that orders were not followed and the plans could not be shared. The streets were in chaos as one would try to speak to the other, but the language coming from his mouth was not understood. People would go from one to another trying to communicate with no success. Needless to say, the building project stopped and never went further.

Language miscommunication and **barriers** also create conflict between genders, cultures, and political and religious views. Accents and dialects differ between people who have the same language but come from different parts of the country. Although their base language may be the same and is easily recognized and communicated, there will be times when the different accents or meanings may create misinterpretations and that of course leads to barriers.

Recently, I was visiting London, England, and asked for a biscuit only to find out that they thought I meant a cookie. I'm from Georgia in the United States, so I was really asking for a soft buttery baked piece of bread and definitely did not mean that I wanted a cookie. Of course, I took the cookie and said, "Thank you" with a smile because I did learn that good manners are good no matter the language or the meanings of language.

Have you seen the movie, *Pitch Perfect*? In the movie there is a girl in the singing group that never speaks above a whisper throughout most of the movie. The others could never hear her enough to understand what she was trying to communicate and that is another excellent example of a language barrier; although it may be a bit different from other language barriers. If the people to whom you are speaking are not able to hear your message, then you have a **communication barrier**.

Slang words are often used in certain cultural situations and are effective within the group; however, using the same slang words outside of your cultural group will result in strange stares and looks of confusion. Leave the jargons and slang language at home when out in public so that your message can be understood by others. Barriers are also evident when people use a poor word choice or sarcasm to convey meanings. Often a poor word choice will send a negative message that may be miscommunicated. This also is a type of language barrier that may send a completely different message than the one you intend to send.

My dear husband is quite the dinosaur and he was texting, believe it or not, to one of his friends. The friend responded LOL (Laugh Out Loud) and my husband was laughing because he thought his friend was having trouble spelling a word on his phone. Yes, even texting can cause language barriers.

Now that you know the many different types of language miscommunication and barriers, try to consider how you are communicating so that you are not guilty of saying one thing and meaning another.

GENDER, CULTURE, AND LANGUAGE

Do male sharks and female sharks communicate the same way? Do sharks communicate between various species of underwater creatures? You may be wondering what this has to do with you. What about the differences humans see in culture? How does that affect communication? Could age be part of culture? Does a young man communicate to another young man the way he communicates to his grandpa? Does the grandma communicate differently to her grandbabies than she does to her older grandchildren?

No matter the situation, you will find the topic of gender and communication or culture and communication are addressed. Communication between genders and cultures will always be a hot topic. In the next couple of sections, we will address this issue and share information regarding how communication varies. Understanding why there are differences can help us personally and professionally.

It has been said that gender is responsible for shaping how communication is created and viewed. Watch any commercial on television and think for a moment how the path for the advertisement is changed depending upon if it is intended for male or for female audiences. Watch the same commercial and consider how they use female characters or how they use male characters to entice you to purchase their products. Before taking a basic human communication course, you might have never stopped to look at a commercial based on gender or wondered how the copywriter thought carefully while crafting the commercial just to get YOUR attention. Interesting, right?

Although this type of stereotyping has been around for years, the changes we have seen lately regarding the nature of the relationship between gender and culture stereotyping as it relates to role changes in society are quite evident. Stereotyping is found in relationship roles, but also in occupational status, politics, and religion. All of these involve communication and that, of course, involves language.

As you consider this, you will develop an appreciation for the complicated ways that gender and culture influence your own personal views of masculinity and femininity. This certainly shows up in relationships between men and women, whether we consider the relationship as romantic, friendly, or professional.

Do you find that some instructors react differently to male or female students? When you are in a club or business meeting, does the director of the meeting react differently to questions from men rather than the way they react to questions from women?

Do you also notice the differences in reactions regarding various cultures? As we speak about culture differences, understand that we are talking about more than race. Cultural differences are found between genders, age groups, interest groups, nationalities, experiences, political differences, religious differences, and the list goes on. As I get older, I realize there are communication issues found between people who work in various careers, too! For example, at a grammar school gathering, there are moms who are working full-time while raising a family and there are moms who do not have a full-time career. There are moms who homeschool their

children and moms who look forward to sending their children to school each day on a big, yellow school bus. They are all still communicating but it is HOW they are communicating that holds the biggest fascination. Do you notice that the various cultures (working or non-working) seem to gravitate toward each other? When searching for a room-mom, will the instructor ask the working mom for help or the non-working mom? Are there dads in the same gathering? Does the dad get asked to volunteer to help? Communication can be more complicated than we think, especially when we add gender and culture to the equation.

Socially, we see the gender culture is not as expected and women can choose to be welders, mechanics, doctors, lawyers, judges, and construction workers. On the other hand, men can choose to be nurses, chefs, teachers, and administrative assistants.

As you look into the value of studying communication as it relates to gender and culture, you might discover something about yourself and how you alter your own ideas regarding the gender or culture with whom you are communicating.

Does your own communication style conform to prevailing cultural attitudes for gender? If so, you might find yourself working to strengthen your personal effectiveness as a communicator. Our world is becoming more diverse; therefore, it is vital that we understand how our communication skills may change depending upon various genders and cultures.

Let's take a quick look at the difference between gender and sex. **Gender** is socially constructed whereas **sex** is based on biology. They tend to go together, but all men are not masculine and all women are not feminine. This makes the two terms, gender and sex, inconsistent. The term, gender, can refer to feelings, roles, and identities whether they are externally obvious or internalized.

We are born as either male or female (sex), but we can take on masculine or feminine (gender) roles. By definition, **gender** is learned. We teach our little boys not to cry and to be tough. We dress our little boys in blue jeans and sports shirts. Consequently, they develop masculine traits as they learn to be strong, ambitious, successful, and in control of their feelings. In the same manner, we teach our little girls to wear lace and to act like a little lady. Yes, we want our daughters to be strong, ambitious, successful, and in control of their feelings, too, but they are also allowed a soft side and encouraged to lean on their male counterpart for support and to solve problems.

The answer to this madness is to learn to communicate effectively for everyone and to not change our message depending upon the gender or culture. Men and women can both be nurturing, loving, and strong, sensible, hardworking, capable people.

Culture consists of practices that reflect a particular social order with regard to values, meanings, behaviors, and expectations. Gender is part of culture. Have you ever been to dinner with a person of the opposite sex and notice that the check is almost always presented to the man? Women get maternity leave as a normal practice, but does the father get paternity leave?

Communication is a process as you have learned earlier in this chapter. Communication is systemic and language involves symbols. It takes both in order for us to send and receive messages to and from each other. As we consider HOW we communicate and what meanings we attach to messages received, we also are aware of the systems involved in which contexts affect the meaning of the messages. How things are said in the context of the situation are just as important as what is being communicated. This is the primary reason for us to take a deeper look at the impact gender and culture play in the communication process.

So, what have we learned? Sex is biological, but gender is social. Culture refers to practices and structures dictated in a social environment for identities and behaviors of males and females. Communication is a process by which we share a message or participate in a human interaction using symbols for language that need to be understood through contexts.

You won't fear a shark attack when you keep your eyes open and are prepared for whatever comes your way! Some refer to shark movements as a feeding frenzy. Truthfully, it is no frenzy at all, but a graceful ballet in which the sharks are fast and swim confidently toward their goal. You can do this too! Be a Communication Shark! Use this section to test your skills and understanding.

Communication and Language

1. What is the breakdown of Albert Mehrabian's Communication Model?

   _____

   _____

2. What is language?

   _____

   _____

3. Define semantics:

   _____

   _____

4. What is language miscommunication?

   _____

   _____

5. When are slang words used?

   _____

   _____

6. What is the difference between verbal and nonverbal communication?

_____

_____

7. List four values which are practices involved with culture:

_____

_____

8. What is the difference between gender and sex?

_____

_____

9. Define communication:

_____

_____

10. What is the difference between denotative and connotative language?

_____

_____

Shark Bites

Let's work on Denotation and Connotation. The best way to remember this is to know that D stands for Dictionary and Definition. In other words, the denotated word is the Definition you find in the Dictionary! Connotation is the word based on feelings or emotions. It can be that the same word could have a positive, negative, or neutral meaning depending on the connotation. Ready for some fun? Grab a partner and work together on the following words. I'll supply the neutral word and you can show the positive or negative connotation of the word. The first one is an example.

Neutral—Denotation	Positive—Connotation	Negative—Connotation
Buck Definition: male deer	Strong young man	"Buck" the system
Assertive Definition:		
House Definition:		
Request Definition:		
Dog Definition:		
Horse Definition:		
Protest Definition:		
Request Definition:		
Economical Definition:		
Snake Definition:		
Woman Definition:		

Shark Bites

Continued . . .

Now, let's take a look at a way to help you practice what you have learned about nonverbal communication.

- Pair up in groups of two.
- Each group will be noted as Partner #1 and Partner #2.
- Partner #1 will read the script shown below and as the script is read, Partner #2 will attempt to communicate a response, but without words (nonverbally).
- Following the activity, ask the partners to reverse roles so that Partner #2 reads the script and Partner #1 will communicate the response without words.

Script A:

1. Has anybody seen my phone? I just had it, but now I can't find it.
2. What does it look like?

1. It's an iPhone with a red and black cover.
2. Where did you have it last?

1. I had it in here just a few minutes ago.
2. Did you look in your pocket?

1. No, but I'll check (checks all pockets).
2. Well, is it there?

1. What is the rush?
2. No, rush, I just have other things to do than to find YOUR phone!

Script B:

1. Would you like to go to lunch with me?
2. I am kind of hungry, where are you going?

1. I thought about going someplace quick that wouldn't take too much time.
2. That sounds good to me. Do you have a car or will we walk?

1. Let's walk. It's pretty outside and a great day to stretch your legs.
2. OK, but where do you want to go?

1. How about the burger place across the street?
2. No, I ate there yesterday and it wasn't that great. Do you like sushi?

1. Sure, there's a sushi place about two blocks away.
2. Hey, wait for me . . .

Chapter Five

Communication and Listening

In this chapter:

Value of Listening   Challenges in Listening

Process of Listening   Types of Listening

Misconceptions of Listening   Listening Strategies and Support

VALUE OF LISTENING

Consider how sharks find their prey. They do this using sensory receptors found along the sides of their bodies. These receptors perform much like our ears. They feel vibrations or movement in the water around them with these receptors and respond to the message received.

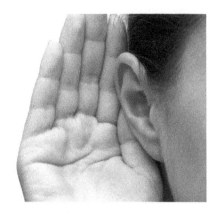

Communication Sharks also use sensory receptors to navigate communication waters to detect and gather information from that which we hear. **We listen!** Some of us are better listeners than others. You will also find that at times you may be a better listener than you are at other times. What we hear is often influenced by the amount of distractions that interfere with content being delivered. Instead of hearing a full sentence spoken to us, we might only hear bits and pieces of that sentence and decode the message into something that is not what the speaker intended. It happens all of the time. Business deals, marriages, and friendships are often broken because of this breakdown in communication. Become a better listener and you will be a more effective employee, a better marriage partner, and a more reliable friend.

PROCESS OF LISTENING

To understand the process of listening, it is important to first understand how listening fits into **Communication**, a process in which ideas or information are transmitted, shared, or exchanged. In other words, you can communicate through various methods that are verbal and nonverbal: writing, speaking, art, music, movement, food, clothing, e-mails, videos, gifts, and the list goes on. More information about verbal and nonverbal communication can be found in this book. Verbal communication is transmitted as we listen to hear content shared.

First, the speaker decides to send a message. Before sending the message, the speaker encodes the message and content they plan to send. **Encoding** is a process by which a person derives meaning and understanding. It may involve finding a common understanding to develop a deeper understanding of the point or topic. Many speakers find that conducting research or speaking to someone with experience about the topic will help them develop a deeper understanding of the topic.

Once the speaker has a good understanding of the content, the speaker delivers the message to the audience. Each rhetorical situation is different; therefore, the speaker needs to consider many factors when deciding how to deliver the message. Finding common ground between the speaker and the audience, emphasizing the sharing of an idea with the audience, and determining an effective approach, will help the speaker to achieve the intended goal.

As we speak about an audience for the listener, we need to realize that the audience may be one person or many people. The audience receives the message, but the message may be distorted according to distractions in the surrounding area or by preconceived ideas and opinions of each audience member. As the audience receives the message, they decode what they have heard and understood before sending verbal and/or nonverbal feedback to the speaker. **Decoding** is a process by which we translate or interpret the content into meaning. The decoding process can be altered depending upon "noise" in the environment. **Noise** can be defined as distractions in the speaking environment, but also can include preconceived notions, opinions, and ideas. Sometimes feedback is verbal, but many times the feedback to the speaker is nonverbal. Feedback helps the speaker to know if the content delivered has been effectively decoded and received. In order to have feedback, the receiver (audience) will need to listen.

Here is a diagram showing how it might look:

Now that you have a better understanding of the communication process, let's look at the process of listening. This will look a good bit like the communication process described earlier but removes the speaker from the equation so that we can focus on the individual's listening responsibilities. The listening process requires the listener to receive, understand, remember, evaluate, and respond.

The Listening Process:

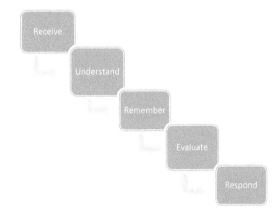

MISCONCEPTIONS OF LISTENING

Receive: There is a great deal of difference between listening and hearing. Listening is a choice we make. It is an active skill that requires the listener to focus on the message, *receive* content so that the message can be understood, remembered, and evaluated in order for the listener to elicit an appropriate and effective response.

Without any effort, you can hear something; however, it takes a conscious effort to listen. Hearing is a physical process that occurs as sound waves vibrate against our eardrums. Then, that sound moves to our brain where it is decoded into a message or response.

Perhaps this table will make this clearer for you:

Listening	Hearing
Activity	Process
Learned Skill: Can be taught and learned	Response to stimuli: Involuntary
Active: Requires the listener to be engaged, encode/decode, and respond	Passive: Requires no action on the part of the listener
Choice: Requires focus and attention	Continuous: If no hearing loss, hearing is ongoing
Message or content is consciously received and message gets a response	Sound is received, but will not always elicit a response

Effective speakers are great listeners! They must listen to discover what is needed by their potential audience and then they go the extra mile to research main points within the content to provide their audience with credible information.

To receive the full message being sent, the listener should resist distractions and devote complete attention to the message.

Since listening is the most important communication activity, it is important to also recognize the benefits of effective listening skills. These include listening to learn about a topic, listening to relate to others, listening to show concern, listening to influence others to change attitudes, and listening for enjoyment.

Auditory signals account for verbal messages, but nonverbal messages often send a strong, clear message. As a rule, we believe what we see before we believe what we hear.

CHALLENGES IN LISTENING

The listener's challenge is to receive the message and avoid distractions that often change the meaning of the message. If distractions are prevalent, the listener can try to space himself closer to the speaker or remove the distractions. For example, the listener shows he is actively receiving the message by putting down the phone, turning off music, and positioning himself so that he is facing the speaker to show active listening skills. Here is your challenge: understand, remember, evaluate, and respond. Let's look at each one for more clarity.

Understand: Once the message has been received, the listener needs to confirm an understanding of the message. Verbal and nonverbal cues should be considered during this phase of the listening process.

The listener should first review verbal communication received and ask questions that are necessary to clarify understanding of the message. Avoid judging the speaker and try to see the message from the speaker's point of view. Paraphrase content heard in order to confirm a clear understanding between the listener and the speaker.

Nonverbal communication received will include vocal cues as well as visual cues. For example, you can often hear in someone's tone whether they are happy, unhappy, anxious, scared, or joyful. Visual cues will include how the speaker is standing/sitting, what they are doing with their hands and feet, how they greet you, what they wear, gestures, smiling, head nods, and postures.

Remember: Let's be honest, we do not all have memories like an elephant, but once we receive a message, it is important to remember the message. People have different strategies for remembering things. The old-fashioned way of remembering things was to take notes, but now that we have such incredible phones, we find ourselves opening the reminder or notes app on our phones and jotting down messages. We can also use the recording feature on our phones to record the entire conversation or speech in order to retrieve it at a later time.

If your phone isn't handy, you might try to identify key words or ideas that are received in the message, paraphrase (repeat to the speaker) the message, understood, and recount the message to someone else. As you repeat or recount the message, your brain will be hearing the message a second time through your own verbalization. This will also help you to remember key facts in order to reconstruct the message at another time.

Evaluate: When a message is shared, the speaker is usually trying to accomplish a particular purpose. The listener will evaluate the purpose while hearing the message. Is the purpose to inform, entertain, persuade, motivate, or is the speaker merely looking for approval, affirmation, or your opinion? We evaluate the message depending on cues sent by the messenger. Verbal and nonverbal cues once again play a big part of our receiving, understanding, and remembering the message.

It is the evaluation part of this process that can be the most difficult challenge as many listeners' biggest mistake comes when we try to make judgments prior to hearing the full message. With this in mind, resist the temptation to evaluate the message until there is a complete and thorough understanding of the message. Resist thinking ahead of the speaker to anticipate what may be upcoming.

Another challenge is realizing that we often make evaluations based upon our own prejudices, biases, or opinions that might change the meaning of the message.

Respond: Feedback can often happen as we are hearing the message and again later with a response made after the message was received.

During the receipt of the message, the listener should respond by using active listening skills: smiling, head nodding, and attention to the message. Empathetic listening involves seeing the other person's point of view. This also results in a response that shows the listener as responsive and supportive or not.

The listener can make verbal responses during the message delivery to show understanding or the lack of understanding. Questions sent in response to the message are used to seek clarification or to show agreement.

If you are looking for advice regarding how to respond to a message, Communication Sharks will tell you that it is always best to be honest. The person who is sharing a message deserves to expect honest responses from the listener, even if the listener does not agree with the message. Deliver the response in good taste and take the speaker's point of view into consideration.

TYPES OF LISTENING

Active Listening: Listen to understand. Determine if nonverbal cues sent by the speaker mirrors the speaker's message. Position your body so that your shoulders are facing the speaker, body posed forward, and use positive head nods and smiles to send a nonverbal cue that you are actively listening to the speaker.

Critical Listening: Resist outside noises and distractions to use critical listening skills. This involves looking past a speaker's distracting behavior and the environmental distractions that are around you. Avoid concentrating on yourself and your own feelings/perceptions. Instead, concentrate on the speaker and the message being delivered.

Empathetic Listening: Try to see the speaker's point of view, even if you do not share the speaker's views. We often find ourselves in diverse audiences and it is imperative that we actively try to understand the speaker's message and offer positive nonverbal cues in support for the speaker.

Informative Listening: Taking notes during a speech will help you to use informative listening skills. Make notes of the main points, research, or data presented, and examples that are especially interesting to you. Even if your colleague is speaking to you about an issue, take notes about the issue and show active listening skills with strong body posture.

Appreciative Listening: This is my favorite type of listening skill. As we show enjoyment of a speaker and their content, we exhibit appreciative listening. Send nonverbal cues that you are listening and enjoying the speech. This is important and also helps the speaker to be less anxious due to the positive nonverbal cues sent during the speech.

LISTENING STRATEGIES AND SUPPORT

What keeps us from being good listeners?

In the earlier section, we discussed "noise" that can be distracters during communication. Let's spend time now exploring these distracters in more detail. They include things we hear, see, do, know, and perceive/feel. These distracters are all prevalent whether we are in a public speaking situation or a private conversation. I'm sure you will be able to relate to all of these.

Things we hear: Have you ever tried to talk to someone in a crowded restaurant and the environmental noise surrounding you was so loud that you couldn't carry on a cohesive conversation? This could be anything from background music, other people's conversations, dishes rattling, glasses clinking, to chairs scraping on the floor. Extraneous noise can make it difficult to enjoy the person with whom you are sharing dinner. Do unusual accents cause you to reflect on how the speaker is pronouncing or saying a certain word resulting in misunderstanding content that was being shared? Perhaps you are visiting with friends during a "play date" with your children and you are trying to listen while your friend tells you about an issue she is having with her phone company, but you are also trying to tune in to the chatter going on with the children. Chances are you didn't hear your friend's entire story and you also did not gather the full meaning of the tug-of-war going on with the children. You may be hearing lots of sounds, but are you really listening?

Things we see: Often, we have trouble focusing on a message if things we see are interfering with the message. It could be a glare off the windshield of a car parked outside, the speaker's choice of clothing, decorations on the stage, or other people in the audience. I am sure this distraction is something with which all of you can identify.

Things we do: What are your own listening habits? Do you have a tendency to tune out of conversations while you check your text messages, Facebook, or Twitter? Are you completing a sentence on your computer while a colleague is trying to tell you about a problem they are having in their department? Does the heavy cologne worn by the speaker distract you from listening to the content? Do you anticipate how you will respond before your speaker finishes his/her sentence? What poor listening habits do you have that might keep you from actively listening?

Things we know/don't know: Have you ever been confused by meanings of words and spent the next few minutes trying to decide the meaning of the word or correct pronunciation of the word instead of listening to the message? Do you wonder, "How is that spelled?" or look up the meaning on your phone? Do you find yourself pondering over incorrectly cited research or questioning facts offered by the speaker?

Too many facts presented during a speech can also cause us to miss the speaker's main point because we are too focused on details. These things can prevent us from active listening.

Things we perceive/feel: Illness, pain, hunger, anger, extreme happiness, or exhaustion can keep us from hearing all that is being said to us. Negative attitudes, prejudices, beliefs, or feelings toward a topic can cause us to lose our desire to actively listen as a topic is presented. We are more critical of speakers who have views which differ from our own. Consequently, we will receive less of the intended message that we would have heard if we listened with an open mind. Likewise, we might listen closer to those who speak about a topic with which we agree. To become better listeners, resist positive or negative distractions, focus on verbal and nonverbal messages, try to see the speaker's point of view, take notes, and concentrate on active listening.

WHAT TYPE LISTENER ARE YOU?

Instructions: Evaluate the following by answering the questions truthfully as you are at this time. Later, take the same evaluation to see if you can notice improvements. When finished, tally your score using the key found at the end of the evaluation.

Questions:	Never 1	Rarely 2	Sometimes 3	Often 4	Always 5
1. I pay attention to the speaker.					
2. I can ignore distractions during the speech.					
3. I can listen to a speaker's ideas without letting my ideas/opinions get in the way.					
4. I can ignore distracting personal habits of the speaker (throat-clearing, movements, note cards).					
5. I take notes to organize the speaker's main points.					
6. During the speech, I am thinking of questions to ask about ideas I do not understand.					
7. I can understand the meaning of unknown words from the balance of the speaker's message.					
8. I can separate fact from opinion, without it being verbally cited.					
9. I can tell the difference between important and unimportant details.					
10. I do not recognize unsupported points that a speaker makes.					
11. I agree and respect that others have differing points of view.					
12. I evaluate the speaker and the content of the speech.					
13. I identify specific words or phrases that impress me as I listen.					
14. I get caught up in the story or poem the speaker shares.					
15. I put what I hear into my own words so that I can recount it to others.					
16. I listen to what the speaker is saying and try to feel what the speaker feels.					
17. I find hidden meanings revealed by subtle verbal and nonverbal cues.					
18. I check my cell phone for text messages and e-mails while listening to a speech.					
19. In a casual setting, if the speaker is struggling to explain something, I step in and assist.					
20. When people speak to me, I give head nods and verbal confirmations like, "OK" or "Yes."					
Calculate Score by Adding Points					

Due to many different types of situations and speaker variables, responses to this questionnaire may not always reveal the same results. However, this assessment should give an idea of your average listening skills. **Circle the evaluation that corresponds with your score.**

15–30—POOR—Continue work to improve your listening skills; 31–70—AVERAGE—But, you need to set your goals higher; 70–100—GOOD—Never stop working to be a better listener

You won't fear a shark attack when you keep your eyes open and are prepared for whatever comes your way! Some refer to shark movements as a feeding frenzy. Truthfully, it is no frenzy at all, but a graceful ballet in which the sharks are fast and swim confidently toward their goal. You can do this too! Be a Communication Shark! Use this section to test your skills and understanding.

Communication and Listening

1. What are the six steps found in the communication process?

   _____

   _____

2. What happens through the encoding process?

   _____

   _____

3. What happens during the decoding process?

   _____

   _____

4. What is noise?

   _____

   _____

5. Describe feedback.

   _____

   _____

6. Is listening an activity or a process?

_____

_____

7. Is hearing an activity or a process?

_____

_____

8. Is listening a learned skill or an involuntary response?

_____

_____

9. What distracters can keep us from receiving communication signals sent our way?

_____

_____

10. List the five types of listening skills:

_____

_____

11. What is active listening?

_____

_____

12. What is critical listening?

_____

_____

13. What is empathetic listening?

_____

_____

14. What is informative listening?

_____

_____

15. What is appreciative listening?

_____

_____

16. What type listener are you (Poor, Average, Good)?

_____

_____

17. What are the steps in the listening process?

_____

_____

18. What are your own listening habits?

_____

_____

19. What type of things (perceive/feel) may affect how we listen?

_____

_____

20. How do things you do not know influence your ability to listen?

_____

_____

Shark Bites

The Communication Shark Listening Challenge

One of the biggest challenges in communication can start with poor listening skills. The average person speaks about 150 words per minute. However, we are able to hear about 1,000 words per minute. To build awareness of the listening process described in this chapter, choose four groups of three to five people and follow the directions listed.

Challenge #1

Begin by giving each group a different specific topic (great movies, favorite song, favorite food, best holiday of the year, traditions for birthdays/anniversaries).

- Ask all groups to talk about their topic at the same time for three minutes and as loudly as they can.
- After time is up, ask how many people were listening to their own group speaking while also eavesdropping on the conversation of the group closest to them. What did they hear?
- Brainstorm effective ways to focus on what is being said within your group.

Challenge #2

Begin the group topic conversations again (great movies, favorite song, favorite food, best holiday of the year, traditions for birthdays/anniversaries), but this time, practice some of these tips in a real conversation.

- Pay attention to the body language and spoken words of the speaker. Also, focus on intonation, pace, rate, volume, and pitch. How can the speaker help the audience to be more effective listeners?
- Avoid thinking ahead about how you are going to respond while another person is speaking.
- Interact with the speaker that lets her know you are fully engaged in what she is saying.
- Focus on not interrupting or finishing the other group member's sentence.
- Listen before thinking of how to respond.
- Stop the group conversations and as a combination of all groups, discuss what was heard; discuss what was confusing; and discuss which conversation you would rather have joined.

Chapter Six
Nonverbal Communication

In this chapter:

Characteristics of Nonverbal Communication

Influences of Nonverbal Communication

Functions of Nonverbal Communication

Understanding Space, Place, Time, Touch, and Smell

Types of Nonverbal Communication

Improving Nonverbal Competence

Context and Setting

CHARACTERISTICS OF NONVERBAL COMMUNICATION

Have you ever made an assumption based upon what you saw without ever hearing the full story? If your answer is yes, then you are in good company. Most of us will believe what we see before we believe what we hear. Communication that does not involve sound is **nonverbal communication** and makes up for the largest majority of all we communicate.

We send nonverbal messages and cues all day long every day. It can be the way you give someone a side-look when you question their motives, a wink or a smile, even the type clothing you wear sends a very clear and unspoken message. To have a good understanding of nonverbal communication, we realize that many different channels are used, but they all boil down to three simple languages: sign language, action language, and object language.

Sign language is used as we gesture to replace words. We often use this type of language to further explain things when words do not seem to be enough. When describing a fish to his sister, John said, "You wouldn't *believe* how *big* this fish was!" As he was talking to his sister, his hands were showing the size of the huge fish that he saw. The sister heard his words, but she was able to envision the actual size of the fish by watching her brother's hands. We use this type of nonverbal communication on a regular basis and some people will tell you that they can't talk if their hands are tied.

Action language involves movements that we use to supplement words and to share emotion. Someone who is walking confidently with head and chin up, shoulders straight, and a look of purpose in their step is using action language to show confidence. In the reverse, if someone walks in with shoulders hunched over, head drooped, and head nodding from left to right slowly, we get the cue that this person is not very happy about something. Further communication will tell us why the person is unhappy, but we get a clear message from the beginning that something is not right!

Object language is the intentional or unintentional use of objects to communicate. This may include types of clothing, shoes, jewelry, hair styles, or even the type car you drive. All of these objects communicate loudly something about YOU. Several years ago, my grown daughters were going wedding dress shopping with a friend. As they were leaving to go, I commented how they were all so beautifully dressed and how I usually went shopping in my blue jeans and t-shirt. The girls told me that when they go shopping dressed up, they get better service from the people working in the shops than if they are wearing their knock-around clothes. Being a curious person, I tried it out during my last shopping trip and the girls are right! I received much better service when my object language met with my budget. So, what does this say about the young man walking down the street with his pants sagging below his pants line? I'll let you answer that question!

One aspect of object language is called **artifactual communication**. This is the way we use our own appearance as a way to communicate nonverbally who we are. Clothing styles, the type of materials, the color of garments, and how we wear the clothing speaks volumes about us.

My daughter just graduated from the University of Georgia and was more than happy during the winter months to wear her UGA hoody to classes. Wearing the sweatshirt showed her pride in the college and a nonverbal cue that she was a proud student. Last week as our new semester began on the campus where I teach college, a young man came to class wearing all bright green articles of clothing: pants, shirt, shoes, bookbag, and jacket. As we were getting to know each other on the first day, he was sending a very clear nonverbal cue that his favorite color was green. Even his sunglasses had green frames. Artifactual communication goes further than clothing choice and colors, but also in the way we decorate our homes and the color of our cars!

Regardless of whether we are using sign language, action language, or object language, we all need to channel these cues through one direction or another using our bodies. We do this in two basic ways. The first is with movements we make with our bodies and the second involves the appearance our bodies communicate to others.

INFLUENCES OF NONVERBAL COMMUNICATION

Using our hands, face, and body gestures, we send communication cues. Consider how we lift a hand to wave hello to a friend. While this accompanied with a great big smile is a universal signal in the United States, it can also send a completely different message without the smile and may be read as saying no or stop.

A "thumbs-up" will mean you did a great job to one culture but means something entirely different in other cultures. Posture, Poise, and Gestures are also ways we use our body to send nonverbal cues.

Posture sends a non-verbal cue about how you feel about yourself. Not only will good posture show self-confidence, but it has a positive effect on your breathing patterns and the way you project as you speak. Good posture also lends itself to effective movements and gesturing during the speech. Have you ever heard someone tell you to "Stand tall"? Hold your chin up, keep your eyes focused and take your place among great leaders who know what it takes to deliver a strong message. As you go into a room, walk with a positive purpose to let others know that you are ready and prepared.

Poise is displayed with how you carry your body. Are you comfortable in your own skin? Shoulders should be up and eyes looking at your audience to display positive self-confidence. People who walk in looking at the floor and with shoulders drooping will send a negative non-verbal cue about themselves and their speech topic. Instead, walk confidently smiling at others and letting them know you are happy to see them. Avoid leaning against furniture or walls, shifting from one foot to the other, adjusting your clothing or hair, handling notes, or putting your hands in your pocket. All of these negative behaviors will send negative non-verbal cues to your audience and will be evidence of a poor self-image and lack of confidence in yourself. When all eyes are on you, make sure you are communicating through nonverbal cues that will increase your credibility.

Gestures are the ways you use your hands, body, and facial expressions to communicate. I've often had students ask, "What should I do with my hands when speaking?" My advice is to get immersed in your topic so that you do not think about your hands and body. When you do this, you will have more natural and meaningful gestures. Don't put your hands in your pockets, clench them in front of you, or hold them behind you. These movements send a nega-

tive non-verbal cue. Gestures should not seem rehearsed but should enhance your delivery and make visual points about things you are describing. They should be natural movements. The important thing is to make sure your gestures mirror the message you are sending.

The study of gestures using face and body movements is called **kinesics** and through this study we have learned there are six ways we use our bodies to send cues: adaptors, affect displays, emblems, illustrators, regulators, and appearance. Some of these are intentional and others are unintentional, some are positive and others are negative, yet all send a message.

Adaptors are unusually unintentional forms of nonverbal communication. These gestures are used when we straighten our collars, adjust a skirt, or move the hair from our eyes. You'll also notice this when people take off their glasses to think before responding to a question. Folding arms in front of your chest or holding clasped hands in front of your body are adaptors and send a nonverbal cue.

Affect Displays are the easiest to spot because this is where we use our faces for smiling and frowning. The smile could be a genuine smile or a sarcastic smile, but they both send a message. Smiling is a non-verbal cue that says, "I am happy to be here!" A genuine smile will send a positive message. As you smile, you will be pleased to notice that others will also smile at you. This reciprocal smile will help you not be as nervous as you might be without positive nonverbal cues.

General body movements showing stress or extreme happiness are also affect displays. Have you ever seen someone who is completely relaxed? The look on his face along with the positioning of arms and legs can show complete relaxation. The same is true when you see someone under a great deal of stress. The stress is seen in furrowed eyebrows, pursed lips, but also in the manner in which they hold their hands and use general body movements of tight or jerky motions.

Emblems are movements or gestures that take the place of words. The waving "hello," making the thumbs-up sign, the distinct head nod to indicate a yes or no response, the thumb and forefinger in a circle to indicate you are OK with something, and folding hands for prayer are all good examples. I'm sure you can think of others to add to this list.

Illustrators are the way we use our bodies to gesture and indicate directions: right, left, up, down, over, under, close, or distant. We might use our head, eyes, or one of our limbs (legs, arms, or hands).

Regulators are used during communication with others to show interest or to motivate the speaker to continue speaking or to give room for you to speak. These are usually unintentional movements but can also be intentional. For example, when listening to their young teenager explaining a situation, the parents may use a regulator (smile, head nod, leaning forward) to show that they are listening and encouraging the teenager to continue with the story. **Head Tilting and Head Nodding** is a non-verbal cue which lets you know if the person to whom you are speaking comprehends your point or if they still might have questions.

Appearance tells a great deal about us. Are you young, old, female, male, fit, or unfit? Do you take care to make sure clothes fit properly, are pressed, and clean? What type clothing do you wear? What type bag do you carry? Your **General Appearance** is a large part of your communication. Even when you are not speaking, you are communicating to others around you. **Physical Appearance** during a speech presentation sends a positive or negative message about the speaker's credibility. For most speaking occasions, it is important to dress as if you are going to a job interview. Business or business casual dressing for a speech is always preferred. Occasionally, speakers may dress according to the topic they are presenting. For example, if you are giving a speech about cooking, you might wear a chef's hat and apron. But for the most part, your audience will appreciate the fact that you took time to dress professionally for the speech. Blue jeans and a t-shirt that says, "BITE ME," may not be the best choice if you want your audience to take you seriously. Overly bright outfits or unusual styles or garments that do not fit properly can be distracting. While it may be appropriate to show tattoos or piercings, if your speech topic is about tattoos or piercings, it is a better idea to avoid clothing that flaunt these. Have you ever heard "You only get one chance to make a first impression"? What message are you trying to send? Dress the part, Communication Shark! These same tips work whether you are speaking one-on-one with a friend, business acquaintance, or to a group of people at work. Be aware of your appearance because your appearance is speaking volumes about you!

We can't complete this section without also discussing eye contact. Speakers are always told to have strong eye contact because it allows the speaker to connect with whom they are speaking. While this is true for speakers with large audiences, it is also true when we are speaking one-on-one or in small groups. Notice eye contact the next time you are speaking with someone. Did they have strong eye contact or weak eye contact? Did their pupils dilate while you were speaking to them?

Eye contact promotes goodwill and a connection with the others. It also helps you appear more credible and knowledgeable about the topic you discuss. This is how you connect with others and have them invest in your topic. Avoid gazing at any one person or group of people for too long at a time. Share your eye contact and your attention with everyone in your group as you speak.

FUNCTIONS OF NONVERBAL COMMUNICATION

The functions of nonverbal communication involve the way we combine verbal and nonverbal cues to send messages and communicate with others. In the chapter about verbal communication, we shared the research conducted by Albert Mehrabian that shows only 7% of communication involves words, 55% involves body language, and 38% involves how we say the words. While this continues to be a point of contention for some, and many people have tried to say the percentages could not be true, subsequent research has revealed much of the very same data. It is the intonation of the voice that includes tone, volume, pitch, pace, rate, and color that influences the 38% Mehrabian detailed. If you were to add the 7% and the 38% together that involves language—the words and how the words are said—the figure is still smaller than the communication we see from body language. Integrating the two forms of communication, verbal and nonverbal, helps us to receive messages or cues by what we hear and also by what we see. In other words, nonverbal cues are used to enhance, alter, complement, contradict, or accent verbal messages that are delivered.

UNDERSTANDING SPACE, PLACE, TIME, TOUCH, AND SMELL

Now, it is finally time to talk about one of the nonverbal communication cues that I find most fascinating and that is **proxemics**. This is the study of spatial distances and reveals so much about your feelings of the people with whom you are around. We send spatial cues to show whether we are comfortable or uncomfortable with the space placed between us and the person speaking. Have you ever noticed a person back up when you move in to speak to them? If they do this, you might be moving into their personal space.

There are four distances that we will explore: **public, social, personal,** and **intimate distances**. Without going further, you already know that there are certain people that you will allow to be closer to you than others. My students can stand a bit closer to me than a stranger, but my children and husband can be even closer. Whether you know it or not, you have an invisible wall that surrounds you. If someone stands a bit too close to that wall, you will find yourself backing up to position your wall for a comfortable distance. This diagram will help you to understand this better:

Intimate

Personal

Social

Public

Distance	Size of Space	When Used
Intimate	0–18 inches	Reserved for family and spouse
Personal	18 inches to 4 feet	Within arm's reach . . . Can touch only if you extend arms
Social	4–12 feet	Conducting business or visiting at a gathering
Public	12–25 feet	Shopping or public area Close enough to see, but can take defensive action if threatened

Public Space is the space 12 to 25 feet away from others. It is appropriate to move closer to others when visiting or making a particular point, but advisable not to stay too close to any person for too long of a period. If you do, you will notice that it will make the other person nervous. If there is a table in front and you move closer to the table, the audience member may move their personal items closer to them and away from you. If you see this, take the cue that you are too close and back away.

Social Space allows you to get just a little closer. This is the space that others are most comfortable with when working with a co-worker or customer and is usually about 4 to 12 feet.

Personal Space allows someone to get closer, but not closer than 18 inches to 4 feet. This area is usually reserved for friends or family members.

Intimate Space is the closest and is usually 18 inches or less away and usually involves touching the person next to you. This area is reserved for very close family members and also a romantic partner. With intimate space, we usually allow someone there for a short period of time but will expect that same person to move to the personal space area at a certain point. We often will allow someone in the intimate space for a quick hug or to bid farewell, but also expect them to move back to the personal or social space once the hug is over.

As we conclude this section about proxemics, remember these designated spaces are the standards we recognize most often in the United States; however, they can change due to diverse cultures and circumstances. In all cases, whether speaking to an audience or speaking one-on-one to another person, be sure to read carefully the non-verbal cues being sent. Space distances with one person or a group of people may be altered according to that person or group's comfort level.

While we are talking about space, we should also cover **territoriality** which is the way we view our own space and/or objects. These can be broken down into three general areas: primary, secondary, and public.

Primary Territories are things or spaces we own or possess. This can be any number of objects such as your shoes, purse, hair, or your bank account, but can also extend to your apartment, family, and friends. **Secondary Territories** are spaces that you occupy or to which you are assigned, but do not necessarily belong to you. For example, your home town, school, or church are primary territories. If you sit in the second row— piano side—at church every Sunday morning, you may consider the seat as your territory and you might not appreciate someone else sitting in what you consider to be *your seat*. **Public Territories** are spaces that can be used and are open to everyone. An example of this would be a zoo, theme park, or beach. While the beach may be your very favorite beach in the world, it is still considered public territory because any number of people may visit the area and it is not designated for any one group of people.

The **Expectancy Violation Theory**, proposed by Judee K. Burgoon almost fifty years ago, covers how we perceive our territory and how we respond when someone violates our own expectations. According to Burgoon, we all have expectations of other's behaviors. When someone violates our own social norms or expectations, it can cause us to perceive that person in a positive or negative light. Any number of nonverbal communication factors come into play through this theory and involve space, time, objects, and behaviors. Would you like to hear a couple of examples?

Consider a situation where you and about a thousand other people are standing in line to purchase tickets for a P!nk concert. People are standing within 4–6 inches of each other and no one thinks this is odd. However, if you are at a grocery store at 11:00 a.m. on a Tuesday morning and there are only about six customers in the store, you would think it quite odd if one of the other customers comes to the produce aisle and stands less than one foot away from you without speaking. That is because of social norms. In a crowded line, you would

expect someone to stand closer to you than is normally expected, but in an empty grocery store, you may become nervous or uneasy if another customer intruded upon your personal space.

Another situation may involve nonverbal cues sent through clothing choices. For example, if you are on the basketball court with your friends shooting free throws, you would expect all of your friends to be wearing casual or athletic clothing. What would you think if someone walked on to the court wearing a tuxedo and decided to join in? Would you think that was odd? It actually depends on the situation. If it happened that the person in a tuxedo was your coach and on his way to his wedding, you would probably throw the ball to him and stand back to watch him perform a jump stop after receiving the pass, pivot around to square up to the basket, and then score points from the shot and from your friends watching! I'm sure that shot would be met with lots of high fives and handshakes! On the other hand, if the person in a tuxedo was a complete stranger, you and your friends might give him the once-over and then look at each other to question his motives. Be sure to check out Shark Bites at the end of this chapter to try some activities to help you conduct your own Expectancy Violation Theory experiments. You might have fun with this but be careful so that you don't make someone mad!

Chronemics is the study of how we use time to communicate. If you arrive early or if you arrive late, you are sending a non-verbal cue about your time and the time of those who are expecting you.

I'm sure all of you have a friend who constantly arrives late for all functions. In fact, you might even find yourself telling this friend the event begins thirty minutes to an hour prior to the time it actually begins, just so they will arrive in time. If your friend constantly arrives late, they are sending you a message that their time is more valuable to them than your time. This is true for personal events and for professional events. They are being rude to you. Don't forget it!

If someone always arrives a few minutes early or on time, this means that they honor your time and they value you and the event. This is a non-verbal form of communication that many people dismiss, but the way you handle this will determine how others consider you in the long run.

Why are time restraints important when presenting a speech? When asked to present a speech, always ask the host about the time limit for your speech. Often other points of interest are included during the gathering and your speech will be just one portion of the event. Whether you are the keynote speaker or a support speaker, timing is extremely important so that the event planner can keep the event moving according to a planned schedule. If your speech is longer than needed, the entire event may run overtime.

A good rule to follow is to meet the minimum time limit, but not go over the maximum time limit. A 4–6-minute speech should last five minutes. A 20–30-minute speech should last 25 minutes. It is always preferred to end your speech just short of the maximum time limit to keep your event host happy!

Your SpeechShark app has a built-in timer to help you stay on time! Just dial in the time that you have been asked to speak and the app will give you a visual reminder of the time left! The screenshot to the right will show what this looks like in your app. If a speech is designed to last 8–10 minutes, we suggest you dial in 9 minutes as your max time. This gives you a little cushion to make sure you do not go over the time limit.

Haptics is the study of communicating through touch. This happens when we shake hands with a colleague, share a friendly pat on the back, or hug a family member. We send non-verbal communication through touch.

When interviewing for a job position, it is almost always expected for the interviewee to shake the hand of the interviewer when thanking the person for the meeting and for the opportunity to speak about the job. The way you shake someone's hand sends a nonverbal cue about you and your credibility. Most of the time, people will use their right hands for a handshake. Just a word of caution, make sure you are sensitive to the way the other person shakes your hand so that you can match the touch. This is one way to make sure your handshake is not too weak or too strong so that you do not send the wrong message.

Complex emotions are obvious through our own use of touch during communication. For example, when speaking to a child, the mother may touch her child's shoulder or head to help calm the child. When communicating to strangers, it is doubtful we touch at all. Touching may enhance messages sent or emotions we feel during communication. Culture plays an important part with touch and we should always be mindful of cues the recipient sends to us to let us know if a touch is welcomed or not.

Olfactory Communication is another type of nonverbal cue that is quite interesting and involves taste and smell. We think of this type of communication primarily with animals, but it is also important to humans. This afternoon as my family came home for our weekly gathering, my daughters said they could smell the lovely meal cooking in the oven before they ever opened the front door. This smell triggers happy memories for my family and has them thinking not only about the smell of dinner cooking, but also the taste which never changes from one cooking to the next. Hopefully by using the scent and flavors, I was able to send a positive nonverbal cue that our family gathering would once again be a special time.

Smells can send positive or negative nonverbal cues. Have you ever been in the room with someone who wore too much cologne? If you have allergies the scent could have caused health as well as sensory reactions, but more often than not heavy scents are not pleasant. As with any form of nonverbal communication, use caution to make sure you are sending the right type of cue to others.

TYPES OF NONVERBAL COMMUNICATION

As we discussed the characteristics, influences, and functions of nonverbal communication, we also have covered most of the types of nonverbal communication. But just to make sure you understand the types, we will list them again: kinesics, paralinguistics, haptics, proxemics, chronemics, territoriality, artifactual, and olfactory.

Types of Nonverbal Communication	Area	Definition
Kinesics	Body	The use of facial and body language to communicate.
Paralinguistics	Vocal	The nonverbal aspect of speech that involves sound but not words.
Haptics	Touch	The use of touch to communicate feelings, intentions, behaviors, and attitudes.
Proxemics	Space	The use of space and distance to communicate relationships between people.
Chronemics	Time	The use of time and how you communicate to others by the way you organize and react to time.
Territoriality	Territory	The use of ownership to a space, objects, or persons to communicate.
Artifactual	Object	The use of objects (color, clothing, cars, homes, decorations, etc.) to communicate.
Olfactory	Smell	The use of scent and taste to communicate a wide variety of messages.

TYPES OF NONVERBAL COMMUNICATION WORKSHEET

Name: _____Date: _____

Complete the missing areas:

Types of Nonverbal Communication	Area	Definition
Kinesics		The use of facial and body language to communicate.
Paralinguistics	Vocal	
		The use of touch to communicate feelings, intentions, behaviors, and attitudes.
Proxemics	Space	
Chronemics		The use of _____ and how you communicate to others by the way you _____ _____.
		The use of ownership to a space, objects, or persons to communicate.
Artifactual	Object	
Olfactory		The use of _____ and _____ to communicate a wide variety of messages.

IMPROVING NONVERBAL COMPETENCE

We've probably shared just enough information here about nonverbal communication that you are nervous and now wondering what you should do to improve your own nonverbal communication skills. You may also be wondering if you are correctly reading other people's nonverbal communication cues. Here are some simple tips:

1. **Watch and Learn:** Pay attention to everything you see. Consider eye contact, body movements, posture, gestures, and object usage. As you watch others and recognize nonverbal communication cues, you will also become more aware of your own nonverbal communication cues. Increase your awareness of messages YOU send and also remember the connotation in which messages are sent or received. Look for multiple cues and avoid evaluating harshly based upon one cue.

2. **Listen and Learn:** Vocal tones can paint a clear picture. Whether happy or sad, the tone in your voice will affect the message you communicate or the message you hear. Listen carefully and as you do, you will notice that you also begin to have stronger eye contact with others. Consequently, you will hear and see nonverbal cues that might go unnoticed by others.

3. **Use Eye Contact:** The best way to connect with others is through good eye contact. Avoiding eye contact sends a message that you are not telling the truth or that you are trying to hide something. If your eye contact is too piercing, that also sends an intimidating and negative cue. Good eye contact is a happy mix of direct eye contact and sharing eye contact with others, but is comfortable when you spend only four to five seconds of direct eye contact with each person.

4. **Match Cues to Meanings:** We believe what we see before we believe what we hear. Are the cues matching the message being sent? Subtle nonverbal cues will tell the true story. Make sure your story is true before you tell it. If you don't, your nonverbal cues will tell it all.

5. **Consider the Message:** Consider the situation in which the message is being delivered. Match the nonverbal cues to the message and remember that there are often situations around that can alter the intended meaning. Avoid misreading signals or over-reading into things. The more aware you are of nonverbal communication, the better you will become reading the signals, understanding the cues, and getting to the true message.

6. **ASK Questions:** A friend once told me that ASK stands for Actively Seeking Knowledge. I liked that acronym and wanted to share it with you. If you see something but feel like you might be getting mixed signals due to nonverbal communication cues, then speak up! ASK! You can rephrase the message or ask if you have the correct understanding.

The more experience you get with identifying nonverbal messages, the better you will become at picking up on cues being sent. You will improve your own competence with sending nonverbal messages and also with interpreting nonverbal messages. Here is the secret: people who are good listeners are also very good with understanding and interpreting nonverbal messages. Good listeners have better eye contact than poor listeners. Along with the good eye contact, you will be seeing signals that others may miss.

CONTEXT AND SETTING

In this chapter, we have covered many aspects of nonverbal communication as it pertains to relational, professional, cultural, and gendered contexts.

Relational: As we take time to learn more about nonverbal communication, we find that it can help improve the relationships we have with others, whether family, friends, or co-workers. This occurs because we are able to encode and decode messages appropriately reading the nonverbal cues sent and received. We learn to read others' cues and, consequently, we develop a better understanding of when it is appropriate to express emotions or share thoughts and when it is not appropriate. As a result, our social networks expand and the relationships we have become stronger.

Professional: It is no secret that employers are seeking employees with effective communication skills. Employers want to know that their employees can communicate with customers, co-workers, and the administration. Contradictory or mixed messages in the workplace can lead to lack of job satisfaction and may affect performance evaluations. More than ever, it is important that we have a clear understanding of verbal and nonverbal communication cues so that we are able to be more effective in the workplace. Being able to encode and decode messages is the point that may make or break a career.

Cultural: Being sensitive to cultures different from our own and working to communicate effectively to everyone we meet will help us become better communicators and better people. Understanding nonverbal behaviors of people from other cultures can only be positive as we will be working with all types of people in our future. Being aware of eye contact, space, and touch may be the very thing that helps us to get along with people that may have a culture different from our own. Knowing whether to shake hands, bow, or nod, could be the difference between closing a deal or closing a door. Before meeting with others from a different culture, be sure to spend a little time understanding their nonverbal cues.

Gender: Men and women are more similar than you may think when it comes to nonverbal communication, but there are differences to note. Women tend to use more gestures, but men use larger gestures. Since women tend to orient their bodies directly toward the body of the person with whom they are speaking, they tend to send and receive nonverbal messages better than men. That is because women tend to have better eye contact than men. The biological difference between men and women account for the differences involved with vocal pitch and with volume. Spatially, men tend to take up more room than women and ironically enough women are more comfortable in crowded rooms than men. Both genders want to socialize and present themselves in a positive manner. Generally speaking, nonverbal cues from men and women tend to be somewhat similar. Understanding the differences between the way that men and women use nonverbal communication is important and should be evaluated carefully.

You won't fear a shark attack when you keep your eyes open and are prepared for whatever comes your way! Some refer to shark movements as a feeding frenzy. Truthfully, it is no frenzy at all, but a graceful ballet in which the sharks are fast and swim confidently toward their goal. You can do this too! Be a Communication Shark! Use this section to test your skills and understanding.

Nonverbal Communication

1. What is nonverbal communication?

   _____

   _____

2. When do we use sign language?

   _____

   _____

3. Give three examples of object language that you are using right now:

   _____

   _____

4. What is the difference between posture and poise?

   _____

   _____

5. Describe an adaptor that YOU use and would like to eliminate from your habits:

   _____

   _____

6. Why is eye contact a good nonverbal cue?

   _____

   _____

7. List the four distances that are part of proxemics:

   _____

   _____

8. What is the difference between proxemics and haptics?

   _____

   _____

9. What are the eight types of nonverbal communication?

   _____

   _____

10. List and describe two things that you can do to improve your nonverbal competence:

    _____

    _____

Shark Bites

After reading this chapter and gaining a better understanding regarding the Expectancy Violation Theory, let's try a couple of activities to help you experiment with this theory firsthand. After each of the experiments, draw a diagram of the elevator and note where people were standing. Answer the questions asked and share your answers with a friend.

Experiment #1:

Go to a large building that has lots of activity. This could be a busy office building or hotel. Make your way to the elevator. Push the button to go UP and observe the following:

1. How many people enter the elevator while you are there?

2. Which direction do they face when entering the elevator? Do they face the back wall or do they turn and face the door?

3. Where do they stand when entering the elevator? Notice and chart which people go to the very back or which people stand nearest the door.

4. How do the people stand if the elevator is full?

5. How do the people stand if the elevator is empty except for you and the one person?

6. Are they holding anything in their hands? If so, what do they do with the objects while on the elevator?

7. Where are they looking? Do they make eye contact with the other people on the elevator? How long do they maintain the eye contact? Do they look at the floor numbers showing on the monitor?

Shark Bites

Now, let's make this more interesting!

Experiment #2:

Go to a large building that has lots of activity. Get back on the elevator. Push the button to go UP, stay near the door, but turn and face the back wall (don't cheat – don't turn around to face the door) and observe the following:

1. How many people enter the elevator while you are there?

2. How do they react when they see you facing the back wall?

3. Where do they stand when entering the elevator?

4. Do they also face the back wall or do they turn to face the door?

5. Do they look at you to figure out what you are doing?

6. When you look directly at them, do they avert the gaze to look at the floor, check their watches, look at the panel with the floors indicated, or get angry with you?

7. How do the people stand if the elevator is full? Do they stand near you or far away from you?

8. How do the people stand if the elevator is empty except for you and the one person?

9. Do people tend to get off at the very next floor instead of staying for the floor they need?

10. Are they holding something (purse, phone, book) in their hands? If so, what do they do with the objects in their hands?

11. Where are they looking? Do they make eye contact with you or with the other people on the elevator?

12. How long do they maintain the eye contact? Do they look at the floor numbers showing on the monitor?

This was interesting, right? Perhaps it was also a bit uncomfortable. Were you tempted to ignore the experiment and conform with the way you are expected to behave on an elevator? If so, you now have a better understanding of Burgoon's Expectancy Violation Theory!

Communication SH RK™

Unit #3:

Interpersonal Communication

Interpersonal Communication Foundations

Interpersonal Communication Conflict

Key Terms to Know

Chapter 7—Interpersonal Communication Foundations

- Breadth
- Communication Climate
- Compromise
- Depth
- Interpersonal Communication
- Intimacy
- Johari Window
- Self-Disclosure
- Social Penetration Model

Chapter 8—Interpersonal Communication Conflict

- Accommodation
- Anger
- Avoiding
- Competition
- Compromise
- Conflict
- Collaboration

Chapter Seven

Interpersonal Communication Foundations

In this chapter:

Characteristics of Interpersonal Communication

Types of Interpersonal Relationships

Interpersonal Communication Patterns

Intimacy and Self-Disclosure

Models of Self-Disclosure

CHARACTERISTICS OF INTERPERSONAL COMMUNICATION

What makes communication interpersonal? Communication researchers have identified the act of two humans interacting as a **dyad**. Although this definition of dyad and interpersonal communication is covered in Chapter One's Foundation of Communication, we also wanted to include it here in more detail as it relates to relationships. Dyad is the term that is often utilized in research of human beings communicating in various communication contexts. Most commonly, the term used to describe **human behavior and interaction between two individuals is referred to as interpersonal communication**, "inter" (meaning between) and "personal" (meaning person to person).

We need others to interrelate with us. Although we have a multitude of personal relationships that we interact with on a daily basis, we will focus on the most significant personal relationships that we develop over our lifetime.

TYPES OF INTERPERSONAL RELATIONSHIPS

Family Relationships	What constitutes a family? As you investigate your own family circle, you see blood relatives (mother, father, siblings, grandparents), adopted family members, stepparents and siblings, honorary aunts/uncles, and others.
Friendships	It is important for all of us to have good friends, as they provide a sense of happiness, with the support and love that improves our health and self-esteem. When friends enter our lives, they provide varying levels of intimacy and interaction that meet our emotional needs.
Romantic Relationships	Developing and strengthening romantic relationships requires time, commitment, trust, and emotional expressiveness to ensure sustainability.

INTERPERSONAL COMMUNICATION PATTERNS

At the core of interpersonal relationships is effective communication. But how does communication integrate into our interpersonal relationships? We know that relationships form, develop, and cycle based on the dynamic of our expectations. One of the best models depicting the phases of communication in relationships was developed by scholar Mark Knapp and later integrated with research from Anita Vangelisti. Based on their model of communication interactions stages, we can better identify how relationships form and develop. The stages are broken down into ten stages. Five stages indicate elements of a relationship forming or coming together and the last five stages indicate elements of a relationship ending or falling apart. It is imperative to note that not all relationships progress through each stage in order, and given the dynamic element of relationships, aspects of communication are in constant flux. However, the model described below is to provide context on how communication interacts with your relationship partners. You may utilize these stages to monitor and provide stability in your relationship maintenance.

Mark Knapp and Anita Vangelisti's Stages of Relational Development

Five Steps Leading to Commitment

Bonding

Integrating

Intensifying

Experimenting

Initiating

Five Steps Leading to Termination

Differentiating

Circumscribing

Stagnating

Avoiding

Terminating

Notice in the Five Steps Leading to Termination, the arrows are separated because there is quite a bit more time, effort, turmoil, and energy spent in terminating a relationship than you might find in building one. Here is an explanation of the two different stages: the stages of coming together and the stages of coming apart.

The five steps leading to commitment are also noted as the **stages of coming together** and include initiating, experimenting, intensifying, integrating, and bonding.

- **Initiating:** In this stage, you have your first encounter with someone. Generally, it is basic, polite conversations that also help formulate first impressions.
- **Experimenting:** In this stage, individuals exchange information in an effort to share likes, interests, hobbies, and so forth. Generally, this basic exchange of small talk determines whether we will pursue future interaction.
- **Intensifying:** In this stage, intimacy and self-disclosure are developed. During this period of increased communication, individuals express their emotions and develop pet names and nicknames to create stronger connections with each other.
- **Integrating:** In this stage, individual identities and personalities converge. As the integration develops, the dynamic becomes more established to function as a unit, couple, or friendship.
- **Bonding:** In this stage, individuals engage in some type of public commitment. This could include a marriage proposal, union, or some other type of ritual that would unite the individuals who form a romantic bond. For those who are forming or strengthening a friendship or familial bond, this could be a public display of friendship such as walking in the park together each afternoon or meeting regularly for coffee or a meal.

The five steps leading to termination are also noted as the **stages of coming apart** and include differentiating, circumscribing, stagnating, avoiding, and termination.

- **Differentiating:** In this stage, the individuals revert from the unit dynamic and refocus on establishing separate identities.
- **Circumscribing:** In this stage, individuals decrease communication. This leads to a pattern of lack of interest in spending time together and willingness to engage in conversations, including conflict and disagreements.
- **Stagnating:** In this stage, individuals experience little to no growth in the relationship. In many cases, the relationship interactions are simply routine and going through the motions of behavioral patterns.
- **Avoiding:** In this stage, individuals clearly signal the desire to escape or distance themselves from the relationship. Generally, excuses are utilized to prevent any interactions.
- **Termination:** In this stage, individuals formally end the relationship. This exchange is conducted with both individuals expressing dissatisfaction in the relationship and the desire to remove themselves from the situation.

Consider how relationships progress from the perspective of Knapp and Vangelisti's Stages of Relationships. Using the diagram on the previous page, chart the following three relationships:

Relationship	Question	Analysis
Professional Relationship (Academic, Job-Related, Etc.)	How do the stages differ? How are the stages similar? What stages have the highest levels of self-disclosure? What stages have the lowest levels of self-disclosure? What stages experience conflict?	Do all relationships progress through each stage? Do all relationships terminate? Can all relationships be charted on this model?
Family Relationship	How do the stages differ? How are the stages similar? What stages have the highest levels of self-disclosure? What stages have the lowest levels of self-disclosure? What stages experience conflict?	Do all relationships progress through each stage? Do all relationships terminate? Can all relationships be charted on this model?
Personal Relationship (Romantic, Friendship, etc.)	How do the stages differ? How are the stages similar? What stages have the highest levels of self-disclosure? What stages have the lowest levels of self-disclosure? What stages experience conflict?	Do all relationships progress through each stage? Do all relationships terminate? Can all relationships be charted on this model?

INTIMACY AND SELF-DISCLOSURE

Part of developing strong and healthy relationships requires the sharing of intimate insights into who we are. Intimacy is a method in which we express ourselves to allow others to know us deeply.

How do we know how and when to share personal thoughts, secrets, dreams, and fears? A key ingredient in developing and strengthening interpersonal relationships is the use of appropriate self-disclosure.

Area	Definition
Intimacy	The state of knowing someone deeply. There are four forms in which we express ourselves to others. **Dimensions of Intimacy** • **Physical:** The use of affection to express intimacy • **Intellectual:** The use of similar belief systems to express intimacy • **Emotional:** The use of emotions to express intimacy • **Shared Activities:** The use of similar interests to express intimacy
Self-Disclosure	The process of deliberately revealing personal information to others that would not otherwise be known. A key ingredient in developing and strengthening interpersonal relationships is the use of appropriate self-disclosure. **Models of Self Disclosure** • **Social Penetration Model** by Irwin Altman and Dalmas Taylor • **Johari Window** by Joseph Luft and Harrington Ingham

MODELS OF SELF-DISCLOSURE

Social Penetration Model by Irwin Altman and Dalmas Taylor

The Social Penetration Model is a model of relationship bonding in which self-disclosure represents two interconnected components:

- **Depth:** a shift from non-revealing messages to more personal messages.
- **Breadth** which includes the range of topics.

When describing how this might look, Altman and Taylor used an onion to show the different layers of personality and even called it the "onion theory." Here is a diagram of how this might look as time passes and the layers of our personality begin to reveal the center or the core of a person.

#6: This illustrates the very core of our being and is the area where we honestly reveal the concept of ourselves and our self-worth.

#5: The arrow is pointing one level above the core—also, the center of the onion. This is the point where we reveal our deepest secrets and most intimate information regarding our deeply held fears and fantasies.

#4: This area illustrates our religious convictions.

#3: This arrow shows where we reveal our goals and aspirations for life.

#2: This area—almost to the surface—is where we share our preference for clothes, music, food, and other areas which are not completely private.

#1: This outside area illustrates information we provide to the world that is not private at all and includes our name, age, and gender.

Joseph Luft and Harrington Ingham's Johari Window

The Johari Window is a model for understanding how the connections between self-disclosure and feedback impact relationship development and growth. To understand this better, think of this as a large window with four separate window panes. The opening on the bottom right is the area which is **Unknown**. In this area, no information has been disclosed by either individual in the relationship. The bottom left is the area noted as **Hidden**. It is considered as hidden because the information is known to self but is not disclosed to others. The top left area is considered **Open** and is the area where information is known to self and to others. We saved the last pane because it could very well be the area that is most elusive. This is the **Blind** area and includes information which is disclosed to others, but not known to self. In other words, others can read this particular thing about you that you cannot see. Here is a diagram to help you visualize the model.

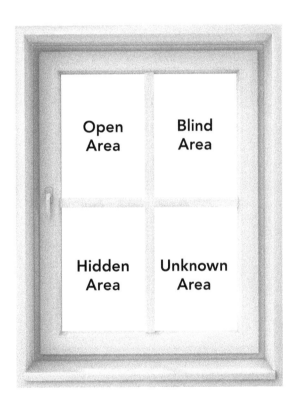

You won't fear a shark attack when you keep your eyes open and are prepared for whatever comes your way! Some refer to shark movements as a feeding frenzy. Truthfully, it is no frenzy at all, but a graceful ballet in which the sharks are fast and swim confidently toward their goal. You can do this too! Be a Communication Shark! Use this section to test your skills and understanding.

Interpersonal Communication Foundations

1. What is the standard definition for Interpersonal Relationship?

   _____

   _____

2. Provide the THREE types of interpersonal relationships discussed in the chapter.

   _____

   _____

3. What dimension of intimacy highlights the aspect of bonding over shared activities?

   _____

   _____

4. How is intimacy defined according to your textbook?

   _____

   _____

5. How do researchers Knapp and Vangelisti chart relationships? What are the five steps of a relationship coming together?

   _____

   _____

6. How do researchers Knapp and Vangelisti chart a relationship? What are the five steps of a relationship falling apart?

_____

_____

7. How is self-disclosure defined?

_____

_____

8. What are the FOUR windows incorporated in the Johari Window Model?

_____

_____

9. How does the Social Penetration Model of self-disclosure equate intimacy in relationships?

_____

_____

10. Who developed the Social Penetration Model?

_____

_____

Shark Bites

Analyzing Self-Disclosure

Label each of the following statements below. This exercise will reflect how comfortable you are with information you disclose to others.

L = ⬇ (lowest risk): I would disclose this information to anyone.

M = ↔ (moderate risk): I would disclose the information to those individuals I have established a friendship with and know fairly well.

H = ⬆ (highest risk): I would disclose this information to a few extremely close friends or family members that I trust.

X = ✖ I feel it would not be appropriate to disclose this information to anyone.

Information	L	M	H	X
Your favorite hobbies, how you spend your spare time.				
Musical styles you like and dislike.				
Your level of education and your grades in classes.				
Your personal political views.				
Personality quirks and pet peeves that bother you.				
Your personal accomplishments.				
Your religious views and beliefs.				
Unhappy times in your life.				
Happiest moments in your life.				
Decisions you have made and regretted.				
Your deepest, darkest secret.				
Your views on marriage.				
Unfulfilled dreams, goals, or aspirations.				
Someone in your life that you resent.				
Person in your life that you admire most.				
Your biggest fear.				
Your sexual relationships and partners.				
How much money you make.				

Shark Bites

Greater Breadth + Greater Depth = Greater Intimacy

For Activity #1, we have learned that self-disclosure has two components: breadth and depth. **Breadth** is the range of topics discussed and **Depth** is the shift from non-revealing messages to more personal messages (Altman and Taylor).

In the example shown below, Caleb and Kailey are two friends who have a relationship where self-disclosure is about topics like significant others, career goals, families, classes, roommates, and money. How deep is their relationship?

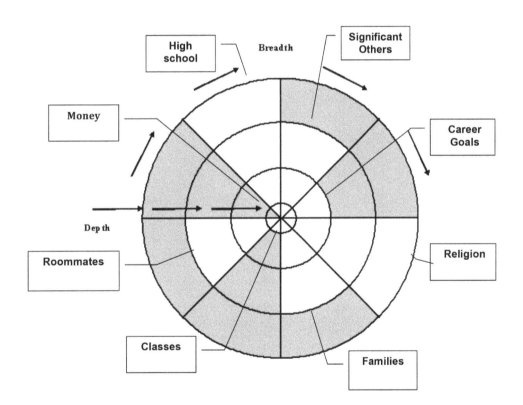

Shark Bites

Analyzing Your Relationship Using the Social Penetration Model

Activity #2 Directions: Think of a relationship in which you are involved. Think of different areas that you could talk about with your partner. Some possible areas are listed on the example on the previous page. Other possible topic areas are children, where you want to live, values, views on pets, views on sports, views on television, religion, and politics. How deep is your relationship? Analyze the relationship using the chart below by coloring in the appropriate area with color the depth of area for each topic. Also, indicate one topic for each of the eight areas.

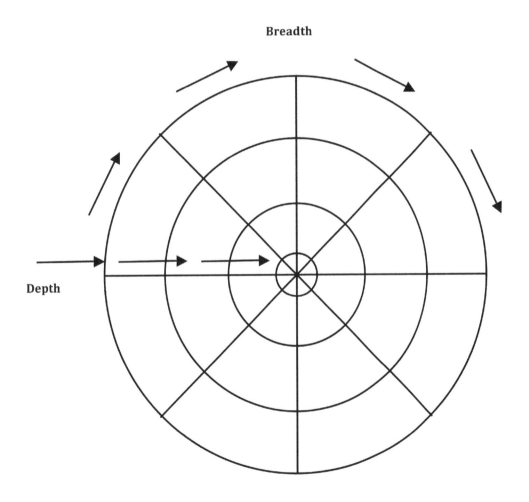

Chapter Eight

Interpersonal Communication Conflict

In this chapter:

Understanding Interpersonal Conflict

Approaches to Conflict Styles

Managing Interpersonal Conflicts

UNDERSTANDING INTERPERSONAL CONFLICT

Even the most effective communicators in healthy relationships face interpersonal conflict. Although it is not possible to eliminate conflict, there are strategies to manage it and anger effectively.

Interpersonal Conflict

The disagreement that occurs in relationships when differences are expressed.

- **Constructive:** Expressing disagreement in a way that respects others and promotes problem-solving.
- **Deconstructive:** Behaviors that create hostility or prevent problem-solving.

Understanding Anger

- An emotional response to unmet expectations that ranges from minor irritation to intense rage.
- Effective anger management requires you to know how to communicate your anger appropriately.

APPROACHES TO CONFLICT STYLES

According to research by Thomas-Kilmann, individuals process conflict in one of the five methods shown below:

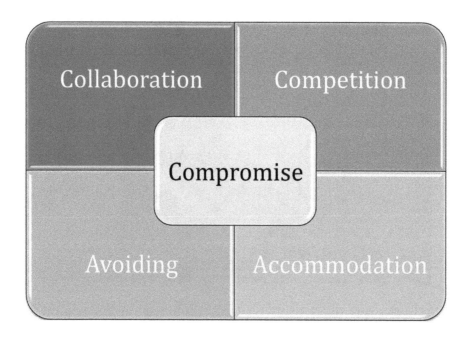

- **Collaboration:** Problems are solved in ways in which an optimum result is provided for everyone. Both sides get what they want.
- **Competition:** Authoritarian approach. I win, you lose.
- **Avoiding:** The non-confrontational approach. Prefers not dealing with conflict.
- **Accommodation:** Giving in to maintain relationships.
- **Compromise:** The middle ground approach. Give a little, get a little.

MANAGING INTERPERSONAL CONFLICTS

Conflict Resolution

Although there is no ideal or best way to resolve conflict, there are steps you may consider to ensure that you are managing and resolving conflict in an appropriate manner.

A = Assume that the other person wants to resolve the conflict
E = Express your feelings
I = Identify what you would like to happen
O = Outcomes you expect should be clear
U = Understanding on a mutual basis

You won't fear a shark attack when you keep your eyes open and are prepared for whatever comes your way! Some refer to shark movements as a feeding frenzy. Truthfully, it is no frenzy at all, but a graceful ballet in which the sharks are fast and swim confidently toward their goal. You can do this too! Be a Communication Shark! Use this section to test your skills and understanding.

Interpersonal Communication Conflict

1. What is the definition of conflict?

   _____

   _____

2. What approach to conflict highlights each individual "gives a little, to get a little"?

   _____

   _____

3. What approach to conflict is the most desirable?

   _____

   _____

4. How is anger defined?

   _____

   _____

5. Please provide the six steps in effective conflict resolution.

   _____

   _____

Shark Bites

Conflict Management Styles Activity

How do you deal with conflict? The five major styles of conflict management approaches (collaboration, competition, avoidance, accommodation, and compromising) discussed are based on elements including personality, environment, and our professional communication skills. While there is no "one size fits all" for conflict management, it is imperative to select the most effective method for managing conflict. Please consider the conflict scenarios below and describe how you would respond in these situations.

Scenario:
You have been in a relationship with a significant other, and they unexpectedly break up with you via text or social media.   **Conflict Style:**
You have been working at an organization for over a year, and your boss or supervisor passes over you for a promotion or raise.   **Conflict Style:**
You live with a roommate and agree to split the rent and bills 50/50. Your roommate is consistently late and never seems to have enough money to cover their portion.   **Conflict Style:**
You are partnered with a classmate for a debate presentation. You both have differing perspectives regarding controversial topics and find it challenging to work together.   **Conflict Style:**

You work very hard as a restaurant host and feel the other employees are not carrying their weight.

Conflict Style:

You work at a retail store and notice clothing items missing once a customer leaves the dressing room.

Conflict Style:

You are a college student, dependent on your parents paying college tuition. You have spent the money they provided you on an exotic vacation and now face asking your parents for additional funds.

Conflict Style:

You and a co-worker have been working on a planned sales pitch; however, on the day of the presentation, the co-worker calls in sick.

Conflict Style:

You are on a first date and things are not going as expected. You want to leave the date early.

Conflict Style:

You are a cashier and the customer complains that you provided them the incorrect amount of change.

Conflict Style:

To identify your most preferred style, review the conflict management style you selected the most often in scenarios. It is likely that style is the one you most commonly use when engaged in conflict. However, if you are working to increase your CommunicationShark skills, you will need to develop the ability to engage in all styles of conflict management, as you must be prepared to deal with conflict on a regular basis.

Communication SH🔺RK™

Unit #4:

Communication in Groups and Teams

Communication in Groups and Teams

Problem-Solving in Groups and Teams

Professional Communication

CommunicationSHARK.

Key Terms to Know

Chapter 9—Communication in Groups and Teams

- Authoritarian Leadership
- Bruce Tuckman Model
- Democratic Leadership
- Group
- Group Goals
- Hidden Agenda
- Laissez Faire Leadership
- Maintenance/Relationship
- Monroe's Motivated Sequence
- Norms
- Roles
- Self-Centered
- Social Loafer/Slacker
- Task
- Trait Theory of Leadership

Chapter 10—Problem-Solving in Groups and Teams

- Authority Rule
- Consensus
- Group Cohesion
- Groupthink
- Problem-Solving Process
- Voting

Chapter 11—Professional Communication

- Interview Questions
- Resume

Chapter Nine

Communication in Groups and Teams

In this chapter:

Group Communication

Characteristics of Groups and Teams

Group Dimensions and Development

Group Norms

Group Cohesion

Group Member Roles

Leadership in Groups and Teams

Effective Group Meetings

113

GROUP COMMUNICATION

We all interact in groups and teams, whether at work, school, church groups, or volunteer organizations. It is critical to understand the dynamics of working in groups and teams and the skills needed to successfully collaborate with others. The broad definition of a **Group** is the interaction of three or more interdependent people working together to achieve a common goal.

CHARACTERISTICS OF GROUPS AND TEAMS

Have you been placed into a team working on a group project for class or at work? Groups have different characteristics, serve different purposes, and encounter positive and negative experiences and outcomes. It is imperative for the following characteristics to be identified to ensure group success.

- What is the purpose for the group?
- What are the group's goals?
- What are the group members' individual goals?

Ensure that no hidden agendas are counteracting with the group's overall purpose or goal. Having open and honest discussions can help to counteract the disruptive power of hidden agendas.
Hidden agendas occur when a group member's private goals conflict with the group's common goal.
No matter the group goal, all groups share common characteristics. Understanding the patterns in effective group development is crucial as the group begins to develop.

GROUP DIMENSIONS AND DEVELOPMENT

According to researcher and group expert, Bruce Tuckman, there are specific patterns of interactions involved in a group or team's development.

Bruce Tuckman's Group Development Model

Forming	Getting acquainted and comfortable with group members
Storming	Competing for status and influence
Norming	Defined roles and expressing opinions
Performing	Working effectively and harmoniously

The **forming stage** occurs when group members are acquainted with each other and in the process of working in a group or team. There are several factors that influence this group development stage, such as personalities, skill set, and resources of each group member.

During the **storming stage** of group development, decisions pertaining to the group's purpose, norms, and rules are being determined. Conflict may ensue as members compete for status or influence in the group structure.

The **norming stage** of group development emerges as the expectations about each individual role becomes solidified. In addition, group norms and expectations have stabilized, ensuring group productivity.

In the **performing stage** of group development, members are working harmoniously toward the completion of the task or goal. All skills, resources, and talents of group members are being utilized to create positive synergy to succeed, accomplish, and perform to the group's ability.

The following diagram on Team Development is based on Bruce W. Tuckman's model of Group Development:

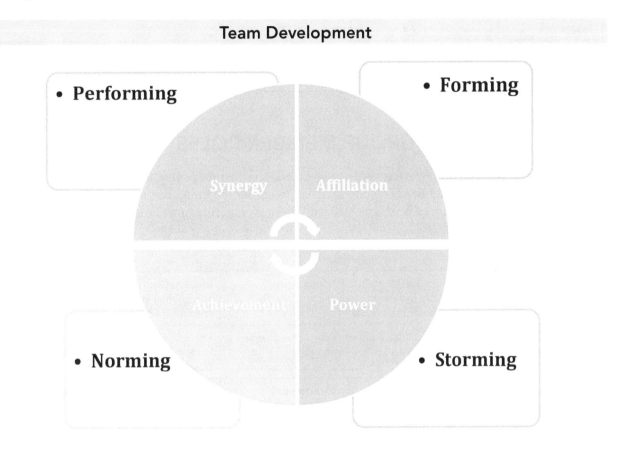

GROUP NORMS

Group Norms are guidelines or expectations that govern a group's behavior. They determine how members communicate and work together. The behavior can be identified as constructive or destructive. It is important to establish both implied and explicit norms to properly govern the group's interactions.

- **Constructive:** Group members conform to a norm while still working to promote the group goal.
- **Deconstructive:** Group members resist conformity without regard for the best interests of the group and its goal.

GROUP COHESION

Having established norms within the group or team, it is important to generate cohesion to solidify the group morale. Cohesion can positively increase morale within groups and teams when the appropriate level commitment, productivity, and satisfaction are balanced among members.

Group Cohesion is the commitment and mutual attraction that holds the members of a group together. The following table will help to define the process involved with group cohesion:

Expectations	Action involved with cohesion.
Group Identification	Use pronouns such as *we* and *our*.
Teamwork	Emphasize group rather than individual accomplishments.
Rewards	Use appropriate methods to reward individual effort within the group.
Respect	Treat everyone with respect by showing concern for personal needs.

GROUP MEMBER ROLES

Each group member has unique talents, skills, and experiences that they bring to a group or team. Based on that concept, roles and related behaviors are assigned to ensure the group can accomplish its task or goal. **Group roles** serve as a pattern of behaviors associated with an expected function of each group member.

Group Role	Definition	Descriptor
Task-Oriented Role	Behavior that positively affects a group's ability to manage a task and to achieve its common goal.	Initiator, Contributor, Information Seeker/Giver, Opinion Seeker/Giver, Clarifier, Organizer, Energizer, Secretary
Relationship-Oriented Role (Maintenance)	Behavior that positively affects how group members get along with and work harmoniously while pursuing a common goal.	Encourager, Supporter, Harmonizer, Compromiser, Tension Reliever, Gatekeeper, Observer, Follower, Evaluator
Self-Centered (Dysfunctional)	Behavior in which a member does not contribute effectively to the group's task or goal. Other terms used are social loafer or slacker.	Aggressor, Blocker, Dominator, Clown, Deserter, Confessor, Recognition Seeker, Avoider, Help Seeker

LEADERSHIP IN GROUPS AND TEAMS

Leadership is the ability to make decisions effectively in order to ensure group members will achieve a common goal. Understanding leadership is essential to ensure a group will successfully meet its task or goal. Most individuals recognize the importance of leadership; however, the absence of effective leaders in groups and teams often leads to disorganization and lack of strategy needed to complete tasks and goals.

What constitutes an effective leader? According to early research, there are characteristics that individuals are born with that give the perception of an effective leader. This concept is often referred to as the trait theory of leadership.

Trait Theory of Leadership

According to this theory, leaders are *born,* not made. This theory identifies specific characteristics of good leaders that include the following: personality, charisma, persuasion, intelligence, power, and energy.

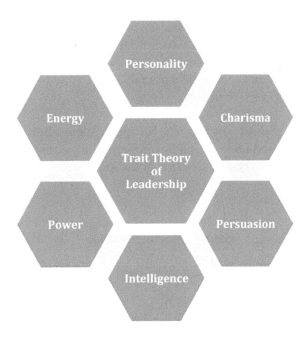

Given the varying perspectives on what skills or attributes make an effective leader, it is valuable to understand the situational components reflected in the most common styles of leadership.

Three Leadership Styles

Leadership Style	Descriptors
Authoritarian or Autocratic Leaders	Makes decisions with a "my way or the highway" perspective, no input from the group. Centralized authority but yields low participation from others because they TELL instead of asking or motivating.
Democratic Leaders	Makes decisions after ensuring opinions of all group members are considered. These are involved leaders and they get a high participation rating from employees and others because they ask for feedback before making decisions that affect the group.
Laissez-Faire Leaders	Embraces a "hands off" approach to leadership, allowing team members to function independently. This type leader does not seem to care what the group does and will stand back and instruct them to do whatever they think will work. The result is that there is no clear direction for anyone and progress is not made.

Each of the leadership styles described have pros and cons depending on the group dynamic. However, it is within the best interest of whoever is leading the group to be able to exercise the characteristics of all the leadership styles to be a well-rounded leader and to keep their team moving forward in a positive direction.

EFFECTIVE GROUP MEETINGS

When conducting group meetings, it is important for the leader to consider the following when planning meetings: Who, What, When, Where, Why?

- Who (What group members need to be present)?
- What (What is the purpose or agenda for the meeting)?
- When (When will the meeting take place)?
- Where (What location will the meeting take place)?
- Why (Why does the group need to meet)?

Effective Group Meetings don't just happen, but are possible with careful planning, preparing an agenda, conducting the meeting, and taking minutes for the meeting. It is a good idea to have a designated notetaker for each meeting in order to ensure accuracy of the group's discussion and activities.

Sample Meeting Agenda

Company Logo

Date:

Time:

Location:

1. Call to Order

2. Approval of Minutes and Agenda

3. Reports by Officers

4. Committee Reports

5. New Business

6. Announcements

7. Adjournment

Group Presentation

Group members often have to make group presentations. The task of presenting a Group Presentation is not always met with enthusiasm. That is because most of us have had the experience of working with a group and doing a majority of the group work on our own to make sure the project was completed on time and in good shape. We often think of group projects gone south when we think of group work in college. However, I can assure you that group work can also be a struggle in the corporate world. We wanted to cover Group Presentations in this book because you will be met with this task more often than you would like and it is a good idea to understand what is involved with a Group Presentation!

Everyone in a group is unique. That can be a bonus for your presentation, if you are able to use the strengths present within your group. As with any presentation, you should conduct an audience analysis, consider the purpose of the presentation and develop a topic that will enhance the knowledge of your audience members.

There are advantages for presenting a project as a Group Presentation. First, realize that you cannot possibly know everything. Working with a group will allow the opportunity to expand the knowledge base and will cause you to add to your own knowledge of the subject your group will be covering.

Avoid disagreements regarding the division of labor by verbally acknowledging the value brought to the group by your group members. This also builds a feeling of teamwork among group members and fosters collaboration for the project.

Brainstorming is always much more effective when you can include more brains! This will also cause more active discussions to erupt which in turn will spark more ideas for the topic. Since each group is unique and there are many diverse cultures and thoughts present in a group, this will allow the group to incorporate different speech styles during the presentation.

Finally, speakers who are a bit shy usually feel more confident when they realize they are not alone on the stage making a presentation, but surrounded by their peers who are working together for a positive result.

From *Speech Shark: A Public Speaking Guide,* Second Edition, by Penny Joyner Waddell, Ed. D. and Travice Baldwin Obas, M. Ed. © 2018 Kendall Hunt Publishing Company. Reprinted by permission.

Use this checklist when planning a Group Presentation:

Things to Consider	Explanation
Know Group Members	☐ Introduce yourself to the group. ☐ Exchange names and contact information. ☐ Discover strengths and weaknesses of group members. ☐ Determine a meeting schedule that works with everyone. ☐ Record information and distribute it to group members.
Discuss Group Expectations	☐ Ask questions. Answer questions. ☐ Divide tasks equally among group members. ☐ Be realistic with due dates and job responsibilities. ☐ Indicate group member responsibilities. ☐ Exercise accountability/responsibility duties. ☐ Establish consequences if a group member does not follow through.
Understand the Task	☐ Research the topic. ☐ Learn the time requirement for the presentation. ☐ Know what is expected. Do you need a visual aid? ☐ Do you need handouts? ☐ Create a timetable for responsibilities. ☐ What order will group members speak? ☐ Is there a Question/Answer segment during the presentation? ☐ Will you have a group moderator to introduce and conclude the speech? ☐ How will you be evaluated?
Respect Diversity	☐ Keep an open mind for other ideas. ☐ Encourage members to speak without reservation. ☐ Allow opportunities for members to interject opinions for the project.
Communicate Effectively	☐ Use effective listening skills. ☐ Speak clearly and make yourself heard. ☐ Ask for clarification, if you do not understand something. ☐ Use positive communication skills with group members.
Rehearsals	☐ Plan rehearsal dates. ☐ Rehearse together as a group. ☐ Assign a Tech Team member to manage the visual aids. ☐ Assign a Tech Team member to distribute handouts. ☐ Rehearse using visual aids for the presentation.

During the presentation, there is a protocol that should be followed. Here is the plan to follow for a Group Presentation:

1. **Moderator:** The moderator will open with an attention step, establish a need/relevance for the group presentation topic, establish speaker credibility for the group by introducing each speaker (first name and last name) and provides a clear thesis and list a brief description of each main point identifying the group member designated to cover. The moderator will then transition to the first speaker by again stating the speaker's first and last name along with the topic they will cover. *One thing to note: the moderator will be responsible to keep the presentation flowing. If at any time there is an awkward moment, the moderator has the responsibility of keeping the presentation advancing in a positive direction.*

2. **Speaker #1:** The first speaker will thank the moderator for the introduction and then will proceed to cover the main point. This will include an introduction, body, and conclusion of the point. Speaker #1 will then transition to the second speaker by stating the speaker's first and last name along with the topic the second speaker will cover.

3. **Speaker #2:** The second speaker will thank Speaker #1 for the introduction and then will proceed to cover the next main point. This will include an introduction, body, and conclusion of the point. Speaker #2 will then transition to the third speaker by stating the speaker's first and last name along with the topic the third speaker will cover.

4. **Speaker #3:** The third speaker will thank Speaker #2 for the introduction and then will proceed to cover the next main point. This will include an introduction, body, and conclusion of the point. Speaker #3 will then transition to the fourth speaker. If there is not a fourth speaker, then Speaker #3 will transition back to the Moderator using his or her first and last name.

5. **Moderator:** The Moderator will thank the last speaker and will proceed to summarize the three main points covered listing each Speaker's first and last name with the summary. Next, the Moderator will open the floor for a question and answer session. During the Q & A, the Moderator is responsible for keeping the conversation flowing, directing questions to different group members, and making sure that not one member monopolizes the conversation. If questions from the audience are all directed to one or two members, the Moderator can call for the audience that may have a question for the Speaker who has not been questioned. After a few questions and answers, the Moderator can then close the Q & A and thank the audience for their attention as they discussed the topic and participated in the Q & A session. Finally, the Moderator will again thank the group speakers, one at a time before closing the speech with a prepared Appeal to Action, which should be designed to keep the audience thinking about the group presentation topic.

NOTE: Research will be needed to support the individual points. The Moderator and each of the Group Speakers are responsible for conducting research to provide credible support of the points covered. Personal stories and personal experiences are also very helpful to support the points and to bring in a personal touch regarding the topic.

For a Group Presentation to be successful, the group needs to work together as a cohesive unit to make one presentation. They should choose a topic with the audience in mind, make a plan to achieve the purpose, decide on tasks and work divisions, create visual aids and handouts, set times for completion dates, individually work on identified tasks which includes research for the point to which the group member is assigned, evaluate progress, rehearse as a group and then of course, present the Group Presentation.

Group Presentations may not be the easiest presentations on the schedule, but they can be very effective because the group has different levels of knowledge about the topic and can also bring diverse thoughts and ideas to the table for discussion.

How Does the Moderator Handle the Question and Answer Sessions?

The way the Moderator handles the Q&A session will have a direct impact on the success of the group presentation. First, ask the audience members who want to ask a question to stand, identify themselves by first and last name, and then direct the question to a specific group member. The audience member should remain standing while the question is answered. Following the delivery of the answer, the audience member should thank the group member and then take their seat.

Group members should make sure the audience member has finished asking the question before they begin to answer the question. A good rule of thumb is to thank the audience member for the question and then repeat the question as mental preparation before answering. This step is important because it will mean that the group member will be answering the question that was asked. It also gives the speaker a moment to formulate the answer that will be given. After the question is answered, the speaker should say to the audience member, "I hope this has answered your question." The audience member can give a verbal or non-verbal response prior to sitting down so that the next question can be asked. Depending upon the time allotted for the Group Presentation, the Moderator can choose to take three to five questions or more.

The Question and Answer (Q & A) Session takes on the model of an impromptu speech. As the group member responds to unrehearsed questions and attempts to further add knowledge regarding the point, it is great to use the PREP model that is reserved for impromptu speeches and interview type situations. Here is how you PREP to prepare for any question!

P.R.E.P.

P = Point. Restate the question asked because that is the POINT. As you restate the question, it helps you to hear the question again and formulate the answer in your mind. Before you answer the question, be sure to follow the next step!

R = Relevance. Thank the person who asked the question for asking the question. Then, explain why the question is important because that is the RELEVANCE. After you cover the importance, then it is time to answer the question.

E = Example. Give a clear EXAMPLE as a follow-up to the answer of your question to make sure the audience has an understanding of the POINT. There is only one thing left to do, now!

P = Point. All good speeches will offer a summary and an impromptu speech requires the same. As you conclude, be sure to restate the question because that is the POINT and ask if you completely answered their question. If you get a head-nod or an affirmation, then you are good to go!

Group Presentations will use a different type of outline than other speeches because it involves information that will be covered by several people. We suggest using a One Point Outline for this type of presentation.

GROUP PRESENTATION BRAINSTORMING WORKSHEET

Speech Category: Group Presentation

Identify Group Members:

Moderator: _____

Group Member #1: _____

Group Member #2: _____

Group Member #3: _____

Speech Title: Give your speech a clever title _____

Specific Purpose: Write a full sentence to show the purpose of your speech.

_____

_____

Introduction—This will be covered by the Moderator: _____

Attention Step: Consider how you will get your audience's attention. Write all you plan to say using full sentences.

_____

_____

Establish Need/Relevance: Explain why this topic should interest the listener. Write all you plan to say using full sentences.

_____

_____

Establish Credibility: Explain why the group is credible to speak about this topic. Write all you plan to say using full sentences. Introduce each group member and establish their credentials.

_____

_____

Thesis (Preview) Statement: Write a full sentence that clearly states the three points you will cover:

_____

Point #1: Name of Group Member and The Point to be Covered: _____

_____

Point #2: Name of Group Member and The Point to be Covered: _____

_____

Point #3: Name of Group Member and The Point to be Covered: _____

_____

Body:

Transition Sentence: Write a full sentence to transition from the Introduction Step to the first main point.

_____

_____

    I. First Main Point (Covered by Name of Group Member):
       A. Sub-Point.
       B. Sub-Point.

Transition Sentence: Write a full sentence to transition from the first main point to the second.

_____

_____

II. **Second Main Point (Covered by Name of Group Member):**
  A. **Sub-Point.**
  B. **Sub-Point.**

Transition Sentence: Write a full sentence to transition from the second point to the third point.

_____

_____

III. **Third Main Point (Covered by Name of Group Member):**
  A. **Sub-Point.**
  B. **Sub-Point.**

Transition Sentence: Write a full sentence to transition from the third main point to the conclusion.

_____

_____

Conclusion—This will be covered by the Moderator.

Summary: Write in full sentence format a summary of your three main points. Identify the name of each Group Member covering each point.

_____

Point #1: _____

Point #2: _____

Point #3: _____

Moderator: Opens the floor for the Question and Answer Session.

Moderator: Concludes the speech with Appreciation and a Wrap-Up: _____

_____

(NOTE: Be sure to add a Works Cited Page as a page separate from the Outline. Include all sources used.)

Works Cited

(Note: If you use Visual Aids, please include a Visual Aid Explanation Page as a page separate from the Works Cited Page and separate from the Outline.)

Visual Aid Explanation Page

GROUP PRESENTATION ONE POINT OUTLINE TEMPLATE

Group Name 1

List All Group Members' Names Alphabetically
First Name/Last Name
Group Presentation
Day Month Year

Speech Category: Group Presentation
Title:
Purpose:

Introduction:
Attention Step:
Establish Need/Relevance:
Establish Speaker Credibility: Introduce each group member by first and last name.

Thesis: Today, I want to share three points about (Topic): (1) _____,

(2) _____, and (3) _____.

Body:

Transition/Link: First, I will start at the beginning by sharing a little about (Point #1).
    I. First Main Point—Presented by _____
       A. Sub-point
       B. Sub-point

Transition/Link: I've shared (Point #1) with you, now I'd like to tell you about (Point #2).
    II. Second Main Point—Presented by _____
       A. Sub-point
       B. Sub-point

Transition/Link: You've heard about (Point #1 and Point #2), now I'll cover (Point #3).
    III. Third Main Point—Presented by _____
       A. Sub-point
       B. Sub-point

Transition/Link: My purpose today was to (insert purpose and add a statement about the topic).
Conclusion:
Summary: Today, I shared with you three points—include each group member's name:

(1) Point #1_____, (2) Point #2 _____, and

(3) Point #3 _____.
Appeal to Action: As I conclude this speech, (End with a BANG).

(NOTE: Be sure to add a Works Cited Page as a page separate from the Outline. Include all sources used.)

Works Cited

(Note: If you use Visual Aids, please include a Visual Aid Explanation Page as a page separate from the Works Cited Page and separate from the Outline.)

Visual Aid Explanation Page

You won't fear a shark attack when you keep your eyes open and are prepared for whatever comes your way! Some refer to shark movements as a feeding frenzy. Truthfully, it is no frenzy at all, but a graceful ballet in which the sharks are fast and swim confidently toward their goal. You can do this too! Be a Communication Shark! Use this section to test your skills and understanding.

Communication in Groups and Teams

1. Who created the group development model?

    _____

    _____

2. Which stage of the group development highlight all individuals working effectively and in harmony?

    _____

    _____

3. What are group norms?

    _____

    _____

4. Please provide ONE example of a task-oriented role.

    _____

    _____

5. What term is given to an individual that does not contribute effectively to the group task or goal?

    _____

    _____

6. Which leadership style demonstrates a *hands off* approach to policy?

_____

_____

7. What are the basic characteristics of the authoritarian leadership style?

_____

_____

8. Which leadership style is generally preferred and has the most effective track record?

_____

_____

9. What is the importance of an agenda for an effective group meeting?

_____

_____

10. What is the definition of leadership?

_____

_____

Shark Bites

Group Commercial Activity

Objective of this activity:

- To meet and work well with a group of people
- To foster critical and original thinking skills
- To develop a greater understanding of your audience by creating a product which will meet their needs

Assignment

1. Develop a product (or use an existing product) you think would be beneficial for the audience in your class. *It must be realistic and not some pie in the sky magical pill that cures all.*

2. Prepare a commercial/infomercial-style presentation. It should be approximately five minutes long. Please use the Group Presentation Materials and Brainstorming Worksheet found in this chapter.

3. Present the commercial/infomercial using Monroe's Motivated Sequence (See Chapter Ten for more information about this strategy):

    a. **Attention**—Grab our attention;
    b. **Need**—Describe the need/problem they have, which your product can solve;
    c. **Satisfaction**—Reveal the product and tell us how it works;
    d. **Visualization**—Show us how our lives will be benefited if we use this product;
    e. **Action**—Tell us how we can get the product

4. Create a typed and double-spaced script in which you identify and discuss each step of the infomercial and how it fulfills the criteria for the Monroe's Motivated Sequence. *Remember, steps should be in the order listed above in Step 3.*

5. The infomercial should include a mock-up of the product as a visual aid. The product may be 3-D or may be a professional style graphic. Please include marketing/advertising such as a brand name and logo.

6. Think about infomercials you have seen on TV. You are encouraged to have fun with this assignment. Be creative. Use any presentation style (panel discussion, demonstrations, volunteers, PowerPoint, music, etc.). Demonstrate original thought, creativity, and effort into your presentation.

GROUP REFLECTION

Group Members:

_____   _____

_____   _____

_____   _____

Product Selling: _____

Roles of Each Group Member/Contribution to Group:

	Name	**Role**
Group Member #1	_____	_____
Group Member #2	_____	_____
Group Member #3	_____	_____
Group Member #4	_____	_____
Group Member #5	_____	_____
Group Member #6	_____	_____

Group Leader: _____

Leadership Style Used: _____

Decision Method Used: _____

Conflict Resolution Strategies: How was conflict resolved?

Provide one example of conflict in the group and how it was ultimately resolved.

Summary of Overall Experience:

Chapter Ten

Problem-Solving in Groups and Teams

In this chapter:

Problem-Solving in Groups and Teams

Stages of Group Problem-Solving Process

Groupthink

Decision-Making Strategies

PROBLEM-SOLVING IN GROUPS AND TEAMS

We make independent decisions regarding ourselves on a daily basis; however, there are decisions that benefit from the advantages of groups evaluating effective solutions from differing perspectives. As discussed in an earlier chapter, employers rank group and teamwork skills as a desirable trait when evaluating a potential employee. It is imperative to understand the dynamic of group decision-making and problem-solving to allow groups and teams to function and perform effectively.

- **Decision:** Making a judgment, reaching a conclusion, or simply making up your mind.
- **Problem-Solving:** A complex process in which groups evaluate decisions as they analyze a problem and develop a plan for solving the problem.

Monroe's Motivated Sequence

The best strategy for being persuasive without sounding preachy or gimmicky is to follow **Monroe's Motivated Sequence**. Perhaps you would like to know a little more about Monroe's Motivated Sequence, especially if you have never heard of this term before. According to Frymier and Shulman, authors of the article, "What's in It for Me?" published by the *Communication Education Journal*, one way to truly motivate someone to do something or to think differently about something is to show the benefits or "What's in it for me?" This allows the speaker the opportunity to make the content relevant to the listener and to increase their motivation toward a solution.

The person who developed the Motivated Sequence Theory was Alan H. Monroe, a professor at Purdue University and well known for his theory of persuasion. **Monroe's theory involves five steps:** begin with a strong attention step, describe a problem showing a need for change, introduce a realistic solution which includes having the listener help solve the problem, help the listener visualize the results of solving the problem, and finish by challenging the listener to solve the problem.

First, the speaker should describe the problem using examples that will get the attention of the audience and will cause the audience to agree that there is, indeed, a problem.

Second, credible research and/or experiential research should be used to support the problems listed. Explain the problem in detail and show how this problem affects listeners. It is important that the audience relate to problems described in order for them to be motivated to take part in the next step.

Third, the speaker should propose realistic solutions to solve the problem. The solutions should be something that every person in the audience can do to help solve the problem. If the solution is too difficult, the listener will not be motivated to help with the solution. It is imperative that the speaker present steps toward solving the problem and uses research to prove this solution is effective and doable. Using this strategy does

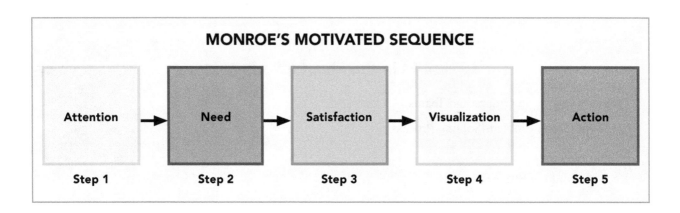

not sound preachy because you are not blaming the audience for the problem, but enlisting their help to solve the problem. It is not gimmicky because the solutions are realistic and attainable.

Fourth, the speaker should help the audience visualize the results of solving the problem, whether it is the benefits of successfully solving the problem or consequences if the problem is NOT solved. This strategy involves connecting with the audience so they can see the vision of solving the problem as something that actually can happen.

Fifth, the speaker will need to challenge the audience to become an integral part of the solution. The Appeal to Action portion of the Persuasion Speech is the moment where the speaker challenges the audience with such passion and enthusiasm that the audience members are motivated to begin work that very moment to solve the problem that has been described. If the speaker has indeed influenced the values, beliefs, attitudes, and behaviors of the audience members, they will feel compelled to help the speaker solve the problem and they will want to begin immediately!

STAGES OF GROUP PROBLEM-SOLVING

It is the responsibility of groups and teams to solve problems as effectively as possible. There are numerous variations of the problem-solving process. We've already shared Monroe's Motivated Sequence with you, but think you might also like to see an effective model developed by John Dewey in 1910. This structured model approach follows six steps in which a group can identify and objectively determine the best way to resolve a problem.

John Dewey called his theory a **Reflective Thinking Process** and it involves the following steps:

- Identify the Problem
- Analyze the Problem
- Brainstorm Solution(s)
- Evaluate Solutions
- Implement Solution
- Follow-up Solution

Here are more details about each of the steps in this process.

- **Identify the Problem:** Group members begin by identifying the issues or problems that the group faces. This crucial step ensures that everyone is clear and on the same page regarding the problem.
- **Analyze the Problem:** Group members answer questions related to the problem or issue. Questions such as who, what, when, where, and why must be answered. Any information pertaining to what has contributed to the issue are identified and analyzed.
- **Brainstorm Solution(s):** Group members engage in dialogue pertaining to potential solutions to resolve the problem or issue. This process is often referred to as brainstorming and is a creative exchange of ideas.

- **Evaluate Solutions:** Group members establish a list of criteria in an effort to evaluate potential solutions. Once potential solutions have been established, each solution is systematically analyzed against the criteria determined by the group.
- **Implement Solution:** Group members develop and implement a plan of action for the solution. Specific tasks, roles, and resources are defined and determined.
- **Follow-Up Solution:** This final step is crucial to ensure the proper assessment of the implementation of the solution. Determine if modifications or adjustments are needed.

GROUPTHINK

Groupthink suppresses the natural flow of information or disagreement and creates a barrier to effective decision-making and problem-solving. According to researcher Irving Janis, we refer to this phenomenon as **Groupthink**. Unfortunately, groupthink is the deterioration of group effectiveness that results when groups simply agree for the sake of agreeing, stemming from in-group pressure. Groupthink tends to occur when one or more of these symptoms or conditions exist:

- The group is highly cohesive
- Fear of disagreements, arguments
- Ineffective leadership or flaws in group structure
- Rush to decision or agreement
- Conformity pressure

In an effort to minimize the potential for groupthink, groups are encouraged to do the following:

- Equitably disperse responsibilities and tasks amongst group members
- Encourage and track input and contributions from each group member
- Consider having decisions reviewed by a neutral outside party

To avoid groupthink and to foster a more effective group, consider decision-making strategies which can help propel your group forward.

DECISION-MAKING STRATEGIES

What makes some group and teams' decisions effective or ineffective? Although there are many methods to come to a decision, groups must consider the BEST approach or strategy to arrive at a resolution.

Strategy	Definition
Voting	Majority vote. Some members win, but others lose.
Consensus	*All* group members help shape a decision that everyone agrees is acceptable.
Authority Rule	An individual, generally the leader, makes a final decision with or without recommendations from the group.

You won't fear a shark attack when you keep your eyes open and are prepared for whatever comes your way! Some refer to shark movements as a feeding frenzy. Truthfully, it is no frenzy at all, but a graceful ballet in which the sharks are fast and swim confidently toward their goal. You can do this too! Be a Communication Shark! Use this section to test your skills and understanding.

Problem-Solving in Groups and Teams

1. What is Monroe's Motivated Sequence?

   _____

   _____

2. What is the definition of decision-making?

   _____

   _____

3. Provide TWO examples of decision-making methods.

   _____

   _____

4. What are the SIX steps of the problem-solving process?

   _____

   _____

5. What is ONE example of a groupthink symptom?

   _____

   _____

Shark Bites

Who Should Survive Group Conflict Exercise

Activity: Read the following scenario and choose seven people who should be on the survival list.

The following people are in an atomic bomb shelter. An atomic bomb has just exploded. These fifteen people are the only humans left alive on Earth. It will take two weeks for external radiation to drop to a safe survival level. The food and supplies in the shelter can barely sustain seven people for two weeks. In brief, only seven people can minimally survive. It is the group task to decide which seven should survive.

Mr. Dane: 29, white, no religious affiliation, PhD in history, college professor, good health, married, one child (Bobby), active, and enjoys politics.

Mrs. Dane: 28, white, Jewish, MA in psychology, counselor in mental health clinic, good health, married, one child (Bobby), active, and enjoys boating.

Bobby Dane: white, 10 years old, Jewish, Special Education classes for four years, mental challenges, IQ 70, good health, enjoys playing video games.

Mrs. Lopez: 33, Spanish American, Roman Catholic, 9th grade education, cocktail waitress, former prostitute, good health, abandoned as a child, sexually abused by foster parent at age 12, ran away from home, in a reform school until 16, one child, 3 weeks old (Jean).

Jean Lopez: 3 weeks old, Spanish American, good health, nursing for food.

Mrs. Evans: 32, African American, Protestant, Bachelor and Masters in Elementary Education, teacher, divorced, 1 child, (Mary), good health, won award for outstanding teacher, enjoys working with children.

Mary Evans: 8, African American, Protestant, 3rd grade, good health, excellent student.

John Jacobs: 13, white, Protestant, 8th grade, honor student, very active, father is Baptist minister.

Mr. Newton: 25, African American, good health, claims to be an atheist, started last year in medical school, an active homosexual, seems bitter about racial problems, wears hippy clothes.

Mrs. Clark: 28, Protestant, African American, college graduate in electrical engineering, married, no children, good health, enjoys outdoor water sports, grew up in ghetto.

Sister Mary Kathleen: 27, Nun, college graduate—studied English, grew up in upper middle-class neighborhood, good health, father is wealthy businessman.

Mr. Blake: 51, White, Mormon, high school graduate, mechanic, "Mr. Fixit," married, four children, good health, enjoys outdoor sports and working in his shop.

Miss Harris: 21, Asian, college senior, nursing major, good health, enjoys reading, likes people.

Father Frenz: 37, White, Catholic, college and seminary, priest, active in civil rights, liberal views, former college athlete.

Dr. Gonzalez: 66, Mexican, Catholic, medical doctor, had two heart attacks in five years.

Source: http://www.oays.org/images/toolbox/5/who_should_survive.pdf

The Survival List:

1.

2.

3.

4.

5.

6.

7.

Chapter Eleven

Professional Communication

In this chapter:

Professional Communication

Resume Tips

Job Interview Skills

The Interview Process

PROFESSIONAL COMMUNICATION

As discussed in an earlier chapter, effective communication skills are imperative to success in the workplace. Professional relationships are characterized by interaction with others to accomplish a goal or perform a task in a workplace context. In effort to secure a professional workplace opportunity, it is crucial to understand the basics of creating a resume, potential job interview questions, and how to properly dress for an interview.

Professional Communication Behaviors

- Research the company or organization
- Assess your strengths and weaknesses
- Create a resume
- Practice answering possible interview questions

RESUME TIPS

A résumé is a brief summary of your skills, education, experience, and abilities. Its main task is to get you an interview; therefore, it is important to remember that a résumé must accomplish its main task quickly. Employers or personnel officers may look through hundreds of applications and résumés, and they may only take a minute or two to glance at yours. Start preparing your résumé in advance. The more preparation time you put into your résumé, the more likely it will get the attention you want from potential employers.

Gather Information

The usual headings for a résumé are Education, Experience, Honors, Skills, and Activities. Jot down the headings and under each heading start brainstorming and filling in the following content.

- **Education:** This usually means college. If you are just entering college, you may include high school information. List your degrees with the month/year obtained or expected. Include the names and locations of schools. Include a major and minor, along with a grade point average (GPA). You might want to include a brief summary or listing of any relevant coursework.
- **Experience:** This area can include part-time jobs, full-time jobs, internships, academic research projects, and volunteer work. List the month/years you worked, position title, name and location of employer or place, and responsibilities you had.
- **Honors:** List academic awards such as honors lists, scholarships, fellowships, professional awards or recognition, or community awards.
- **Skills:** List computer languages and software, research, laboratory, teaching or tutoring, communication, leadership, athletic, or other skills relevant for the position.
- **Activities:** List academic, professional, or community organizations in which you hold office or are currently a member. List professional and community activities, whether volunteer work or professional experience. Listing extracurricular activities and hobbies are optional.

Computer-Friendly Résumé Tips
Focus on nouns, not verbs.
Use a sans serif font size of 12 to 14 points.
Use light-colored paper—white is best—standard sized 8-1/2 inch x 11 inch paper that is printed on one side.
Avoid typographical, grammar, or spelling errors.
Keep resume to ONE page. Add a note at the bottom that says "References available upon request."
Avoid staples and folds. If you must fold, do not fold on a line of text.

JOB INTERVIEW SKILLS

Interviews

We often associate interviews as part of a job-search process and that is true; however, interviews can provide information to help further your knowledge about a subject. An **interview** is defined as the asking of specific questions with the intent to gather information from the person being interviewed. All interview types follow the same basic formula. Prepared questions are chosen depending upon the purpose. Questions are asked and answers are provided. Here are the different types of interviews:

- **Information gathering interviews** are often conducted with many people responding to a question asked.

- **Job interviews** are structured conversations with a goal to discover if a person is suitable for an open position within a company.

- **Problem-solving interviews** are designed to bring peace or solve grievances between two parties. A mediator is usually present in the event of a problem-solving interview.

- **Performance reviews** are considered interviews and are initiated by management authorities in a company to review the performance of employees.

There are three parts to every interview: opening, body, and closing.

The **opening** sets the stage for the type of interview and is usually a time where the interviewer creates a rapport with the interviewee to establish open communication lines in the hope of having a positive interaction between the two.

The **body** of the interview includes questions that are asked. There are different types of questions used for interviews. The most appropriate question to use during the interview is the **open question**. These are broad questions that cannot be answered with a simple "yes" or "no" answer. These questions open the interviewee to answer in-depth thereby adding knowledge for your topic.

Probing questions are good questions to use during an interview because these questions encourage the interviewee to elaborate about the topic.

Avoid asking **closed questions**, as this limits the responses you might receive and will also limit the amount of information you are able to gather about the topic. Closed questions are usually answered by a "yes" or "no."

The **closing** of the interview is an opportunity to summarize the interview and to close on a positive note. Each person, the interviewer and the interviewee, has a responsibility to the other.

Audio or video recording an interview is a good idea, especially when you will be writing and presenting a transcript of the interview. After the introductions and before beginning the interview, ask your interviewee if he/she would mind if you record the interview. You can decide if you want to audio or video record the session. Most electronic devices, whether it is your phone, tablet, or iPad, have the audio and video recording feature, making this an easier task. If the interviewee agrees to the interview, place your electronic device in full view of the interviewee and pointed toward the speaker so that it will pick up both of your voices. If by chance the interviewee does not allow the recording, then it will be your responsibility to repeat back the interviewee's answers to make sure that your note-taking skills are accurate and that you are able to fully understand the interviewee's response.

The purpose of this unit is to work through expectations so that your next interview will be successful. E-mail, telephone, and Skype interviews are sometimes appropriate; however, face-to-face interviews yield the most promising results.

There are advantages and disadvantages of both types of interviews:

Advantages:	Disadvantages:
E-mail, telephone, and Skype interviews take less time than a personal visit.	You cannot be sure who is replying to your e-mail or phone questions.
E-mail questions are efficient and provide a paper trail.	A breakdown in communication can happen with phone conversations.
E-mail questions allow the interviewee time to formulate a response.	Skype interactions rely on Internet connections and contact could be disrupted.
E-mail responses are useful if the interviewee lives in another time zone.	E-mail restricts your ability to question the response.
E-mail, telephone, and SKYPE are more convenient for both parties.	E-mail and telephone interviews cannot communicate non-verbal cues.

BEFORE the Interview
☐ Decide who you will interview.
☐ Prepare interview questions.
☐ Craft open-ended questions that cover your topic.
☐ Contact the interviewee.
☐ Request an appointment.
☐ Pack a recording device.
☐ Arrive ten minutes early.
☐ Dress professionally.
☐ Have note-taking materials.
☐ Introduce yourself to the receptionist.
☐ Wait to enter until you are invited into the office.

DURING the Interview
☐ Behave professionally.
☐ Shake hands with the interviewee.
☐ Smile and make eye contact.
☐ Wait to sit until you are invited by the interviewee.
☐ Ask permission to audio record the interview.
☐ Ask questions clearly and one at a time.
☐ Wait patiently for answers.
☐ If necessary, clarify the questions.
☐ After all questions, stand and extend your hand for a handshake.
☐ Thank the interviewee for his time.
☐ Invite him to hear your speech.
☐ Provide the day/time/location.
☐ Do not overstay.
☐ Thank the receptionist for her assistance.

AFTER the Interview
☐ Write a thank you note or e-mail as soon as you return from the interview.
☐ Include an invitation to hear the speech.
☐ Using the audio recording, write a transcript of the interview.
☐ Include the entire conversation in the transcript.
☐ Using the transcript, include the research in your outline and speech.
☐ Correctly cite the interview source verbally and in writing.

Tips for Having a Successful Interview

Imagine this scenario: You are about to go to your first interview with a company you really like and you are nervous. That is to be expected, and it is normal. Here are tips to help you overcome the jitters and allow you to walk into the interview relaxed and projecting self-confidence.

- Arrive about 10–15 minutes ahead of time.
- Read company materials while you wait.
- Introduce yourself in a courteous manner.
- Have a firm handshake.
- Use body language to show interest during the interview.
- Nod, smile, and give nonverbal feedback to the interviewer.
- Engage in dialogue. Don't put yourself in a question/answer mode. It is fine to let silence occur.
- Be engaging and enthusiastic.
- Listen carefully to all questions.
- Speak clearly and directly.
- Maintain eye contact.
- Relate academic courses to the job requirements.
- Relate experience to the job requirements.
- Take notes as you listen.
- Ask about the next step in the process.
- Thank the interviewer.
- Write a thank-you note to anyone you have spoken with.

Above all, don't forget to PREP! Review the P.R.E.P. Model found in Chapter 10 of this book

What to Wear to an Interview

Wear clothes that make you look like you will fit in with your prospective employer. Make a point to drive by your prospective employer's office prior to the interview and observe the type of clothing worn by other employees. This also helps you to get a good idea of how much time should be budgeted for the drive from your home to the interview site. When in doubt about what to wear, opt for a more conservative look.

Men

- Wear traditional business attire for the first interview. A dark suit pressed and ironed, collared dress shirt, and a tie is always a good choice. You can opt for a blue shirt, the friendliest color, which says, "I am approachable."
- Remove earrings or facial piercings before the interview.
- Avoid wearing fragrance (cologne or perfume).
- Have your hair clean and cut above neckline.
- Wear shoes that are polished and coordinate with your suit. Your socks should be dark and over the calf.
- Make sure you are clean-shaven.

Women

- Wear traditional business attire for the first interview. A conservative suit or dress is appropriate, avoiding skirts that are too short. A medium-length skirt is great (right above the knee).
- Wear a light blue shirt, the friendliest color, which says, "I am approachable."
- Avoid wearing jewelry and makeup that is showy or distracting. Makeup should be light and natural looking.
- Forget the excessively long fingernails. If you wear nail polish, make sure it's a subtle color and neatly done.
- Avoid wearing fragrance (colognes or perfumes).
- Have a professional hairstyle.
- Wear shoes that are polished and coordinate with your suit or dress. They should be closed-toe pumps with two-inch non-clunky heels.

THE INTERVIEW PROCESS

Once you have secured an interview, be prepared for the types of questions you should expect. Answer questions honestly and articulately. Think about your answers NOW, before the interview. Practice them. There are no magical answers, only honest, clearly articulated ones. Remember to PREP!

Examples of Basic Interview Questions

- Tell me something about yourself.
- Why are you looking for a new job? Why did you leave your old one?
- What are your goals? Where do you see yourself in five years?
- What is your biggest strength?
- What is your most predominant weakness?
- Do you like to work with others or do you like to work alone?
- Why should I hire you?

Examples of Tough Interview Questions

- How has your personal background influenced what you are today?
- How do you define success? How "successful" have you been?
- What mistakes have you made during your career?
- What is the most adverse situation with which you have had to deal with in your personal or professional life? How did you deal with it? What was the outcome?

Examples of Illegal Interview Questions

- Have you ever been arrested?
- Do you have any disabilities?
- When do you plan to have children?
- What is your marital status?
- Are there any religious holidays you will want to take off?
- Are any of your immediate relatives United States citizens?

Generally, the questions above are identified as discriminatory, both in federal and state hiring practices and should not be addressed in your formal interview. If asked these questions, politely state that you are uncomfortable answering questions that could unnecessarily create elements of job discrimination.

What to Do after the Interview

So, you are sitting in front of the interviewer and he or she just said, "Well, I suppose that is all the questions I have for you today." What do you do now?

1. You SHOULD NOT say, "That's it? That is IT? What do you mean THAT'S IT! I researched this company up and down and inside and out. Isn't there a quiz for extra credit?"

2. You SHOULD ask the interviewer questions you prepared to show that you are interested in the position and the company.

Good Questions to Ask:

1. What has been your experience with people who have done this kind of work before?
2. Have I provided you with the information you need?
3. Where are you in the process of filling the position?
4. What will happen next?
5. When should I plan to follow up?
6. When can I expect to hear back from you?

Communication Shark Tip:

Carry thank-you notes and stamps with you and as soon as you leave the interview, write a thank-you note for every person with whom you spoke. Drop the thank-you notes in the mail on the way home. At the very least, a thank-you note should be mailed or e-mailed no longer than twenty-four hours after the interview. This important step is often overlooked. It's one of the extras that might set you ahead of the other applicants.

You won't fear a shark attack when you keep your eyes open and are prepared for whatever comes your way! Some refer to shark movements as a feeding frenzy. Truthfully, it is no frenzy at all, but a graceful ballet in which the sharks are fast and swim confidently toward their goal. You can do this too! Be a Communication Shark! Use this section to test your skills and understanding.

Professional Communication

1. What is the recommended length for a resume?

   _____

   _____

2. Provide THREE headings that should be included in the resume.

   _____

   _____

3. What are TWO tips for ensuring a successful interview?

   _____

   _____

4. Please provide ONE example for a basic interview question.

   _____

   _____

5. What is ONE example of a tougher or more challenging interview question?

   _____

   _____

6. How should you address being asked an illegal interview question?

   _____

   _____

7. Provide ONE tip for women's interview attire.

   _____

   _____

8. What is the color that indicates that you are friendly or approachable?

   _____

   _____

9. What is ONE example of a good question to ask at the end of an interview?

   _____

   _____

10. What is the BEST thing to do following the interview?

    _____

    _____

Shark Bites

Mock Interview Activity

- Gather a group of two to four individuals.
- Each interview should only last between four to five minutes. (A timer will be set for five minutes.) The interview outline is below.
- Take one to two minutes after each interview to complete a Mock Interview Evaluation Form.

Mock Interview Outline

I.   Introduction: Does the interviewee offer a firm handshake and keep eye contact?

II. You will not have a resume for this session.

III. Ask each interviewee five to six questions to keep the interview short. You can use sample questions found below or create your own.

    A.   Choose Three Traditional Interview Questions.

- Tell about yourself.
- What are you major strengths/weaknesses?
- Why should I hire you over other candidates?
- What leadership roles have you had?
- Why are your grades low? Do they reflect your ability?
- What do you know about our organization?
- What qualifications do you have that make you feel you would be successful?
- What have you read recently?
- What school activities do you enjoy the most?
- What are your long-range/short-range goals? How do you plan to achieve them?
- What do you see yourself doing five years from now?
- Why did you choose the career for which you are preparing?
- What would be your ideal job?

    B.   Choose Three Behavioral Interview Questions.

- Describe the best/worst team of which you have been a member.
- Tell about a time when your course load was heaviest. How did you get all of your work done?
- Give a specific example of a time when you sold someone on an idea or concept.
- Tell about a time when you made a bad decision.
- Give an example of a time when you had to work under pressure. Be specific.
- Give an example of a major problem you have had and how you dealt with it.
- Give an example of a mistake you have made. How did you overcome it?

IV. Interviewee Questions: Ask if the interviewee has one question for you.

V.   Closing the Deal: Does the interviewee ask about the next step of the process and/or request a business card?

Shark Bites

Mock Interview Evaluation

Interviewer Name: _____

Interviewee Name: _____

Evaluation Key:

   NI: Needs Improvement

   G: Good

   E: Excellent

*Evaluate the interviewee's performance for each category (**Boldfaced**)

Category	NI	G	E	Additional Comments
Appearance: ☐ Appropriately dressed and well-groomed.				
Properly Greeted Interviewer: ☐ Greeted interviewer with a smile, a firm handshake, and direct eye contact.				
Effectively Responded to Questions: ☐ Responses were relevant to the question and specific examples were given.				

Shark Bites

Knowledgeable about the profession and organization: ☐ Responses and questions were directly related to the profession.				
Asked Pertinent Questions: ☐ Questions were well thought out and were relevant to the organization.				
Effectively Concluded the Interview: ☐ Interviewee inquired about the next step in application process and requested contact information.				
Overall Performance: ☐ Positive body language, direct eye contact, minimal use of filler words (example: um, uh).				
Based on an overall impression: ☐ You're hired! ☐ You may get the job ☐ You need more practice and prep				

Overall Comments:

Communication SH▲RK™

Unit #5:

Public Communication

Communication and Public Presentation

Presentation Types and Delivery

Planning and Organizing the Presentation

Presenting and Rehearsing the Presentation

Key Terms to Know

Chapter 12—Communication and Public Presentation

- Attention Step
- Communication
- Connectors
- Conversational Tone
- Decoding
- Encoding
- Establish Credibility
- Establish Relevance

- Feedback
- Imagery
- Noise
- Public Speaking
- Shark-o-licious Treat
- Startling Statement
- Thesis
- Transitions

Chapter 13—Presenting Types and Delivery

- Behaviors
- Central Idea Speech
- Ceremonial Speeches
- Conversational Quality
- Demonstration Speech
- Entertaining Speech
- Extemporaneous Speech
- Group Presentation
- Impromptu Speech
- Informative Speech
- Key Idea Speech
- Manuscript Speech

- Memorized Speech
- Moderator
- Motivational Speech
- Persuasion Speech
- Question and Answer Session
- Questions of Fact
- Questions of Policy
- Questions of Value
- Sales Presentation
- Social Occasion Speeches
- Special Occasion Speeches
- Work-Related Speeches

Chapter 14—Planning and Organizing the Presentation

- APA
- Bibliography
- Blogs
- Category
- Causal Order
- Chronological Order
- Citations
- CMS
- Connective
- Credibility
- CSE
- Delivery Cues
- Ethos
- GALILEO
- General Purpose
- Goodwill
- Internal Summary
- Internet
- Interview
- Key Words
- Logos
- Main Points
- MLA
- Narrow
- Open Question
- Opportunities
- Paraphrasing
- Pathos
- Plagiarism
- Point
- Preparation Outline
- Preview Points
- Probing Question
- Problem-Solution Order
- Public Domain
- Research
- Rhetorical Question
- Signpost
- Spatial Order
- Speaking Outline
- Specific Purpose
- Strategic Organization
- Strengths
- Supporting Materials
- SWOT Analysis
- Threats
- Topic
- Topical Order
- Transition
- Type
- Weaknesses
- Wikis

Chapter 15—Presenting and Rehearsing the Presentation

- Bar Graph
- Body Language Cues
- Breathing
- Chart
- Chronemics
- Color
- Dialects
- Eye Contact
- Facial Expressions
- Filler Words
- Font
- Gestures
- Graph
- Head Tilting and Head Nodding
- Larynx
- Line Graph
- Movement
- Non-Verbal Communication
- Oral Interpretation
- Pace
- Paralanguage
- Physical Appearance
- Pie Graph
- Pitch
- Poise
- Posture
- Presentation
- Rehearse
- Smiling
- Speech Anxiety
- Storytelling
- TED Talks
- Verbal Communication
- Volume

Chapter Twelve

Communication and Public Presentation

In this chapter:

Public Speaking Basics

Speaker and Audience Responsibilities

Communication Tips from Experts at Speech Shark

PUBLIC SPEAKING BASICS

Have you ever felt like a guppy in a shark tank?

One day, I approached a client who was scheduled to present his first informative speech and he looked terrified! He was sweating, had almost no color in his cheeks, and his hands were shaking. I sat with him in the corner of the room for a few minutes and tried to help calm his fears. Following my instincts, I told the client that I was confident he would do a great job! For weeks, I watched this same man present impromptu speeches and he clearly had no trouble communicating his ideas to others. Yet, here he was looking quite frazzled. After a few minutes of "pep talk," I asked him to take a deep breath and then tell me exactly how he felt. He looked directly at me and said

with a shiver, "Have you ever felt like a guppy in a shark tank?"

Truthfully, we can all say that we have felt like a guppy in a shark tank when faced with presenting a speech! We feel like ALL eyes are on us and that we are the tender morsel of the day. We believe the audience members are staring at every part of our bodies, evaluating every piece of clothing, shoes, even judging the fact that we brought note cards to the lectern. They are listening to every word and hearing every unplanned pause, every stutter or stumble, and are critically judging us and finding fault with the information we are trying to share. Yes, we know what it feels like to be the guppy in a shark tank!

You don't have to feel like a guppy any longer—YOU are the Shark! Using the information in this book, along with the SpeechShark app, you can maneuver your way through murky waters and move confidently and fearlessly toward your goal! So, grab your device, click over to your speech notes, and walk to the stage area prepared to knock your audience out of the water! Make your points clearly because you wrote the speech with the end purpose and your audience in mind! No longer are you a guppy, you are a SpeechShark!

Do You Need Help Finding Your Voice?

Have you ever been asked what you think about an issue? Were you able to answer immediately? Did you feel confident with your answer? Did you feel like your answer was delivered effectively? Since before the time of Aristotle, it was evident that speaking and sharing opinions and facts are important to our society.

We all have opinions and the right to voice those opinions. Becoming a competent speaker is a goal that most of us have, but many of us are not entirely sure how to find our own voice, to exercise the freedom of speech, and to use our voices to bring about societal change.

Quite often, you will be asked to participate in group presentations or to make solo presentations. The higher you proceed in a college education and the more you advance in your company or organization, the more often you are going to be challenged with the prospect of public speaking. Since this is going to be an ongoing reality in your life, why not take time now to find your voice and learn to speak professionally and eloquently?

What is the difference between communication and public speaking?

When going into the ocean or into a business meeting, many things can go wrong. *Sharks* can be the changing business climates, creative investment strategies, communication opportunities, or problem-solving strategies. You might ask yourself, "Why do we keep swimming in spite of calculated risks that we can't always navigate?"

My plan to avoid a shark attack is to not resemble the seal! Understand your strengths and weaknesses. Become informed. Learn the difference between communicating and speaking in public! Just as sharks maximize water safety, SpeechSharks maximize stage safety. Become an educated communicator, focus on your goals, and swim confidently toward your prize!

Communication is defined as a process in which ideas or information are transmitted, shared, or exchanged. In other words, you can communicate through various methods that are verbal and non-verbal: writing, speaking, art, music, movement, food, clothing, e-mails, videos, gifts, and the list goes on.

Public Speaking is a communication process in which speakers and listeners participate together. Public Speaking operates with the intention that speaking will be done in a public setting and with an audience. This type of speaking integrates theory and practice. While theory is important, speaking situations demand that content should be adapted to the speaking situation and to the audience for which the speech is intended. The speaker will share content, which can be received by the listener. In turn, the listener communicates to the speaker through verbal or non-verbal cues to indicate understanding or the lack thereof. In other words, communication is a *transactional* process.

With public speaking, there is participation between the sender (speaker) and the receiver (audience). This diagram shows how the communication process might look.

First, the speaker decides to send a message. Before sending the message, the speaker encodes the message and content to send. **Encoding** is a process by which a person derives meaning and understanding. It may involve finding a common understanding to develop a deeper understanding of the point or topic. Many speakers find that conducting research or speaking to someone with experience about the topic will help them develop a deeper understanding of the topic.

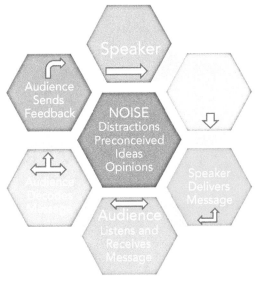

Once the speaker has a good understanding of the content, **the speaker delivers the message** to the audience. Each rhetorical situation is different; therefore, the speaker needs to consider many factors when deciding how to deliver the message. Finding common ground between the speaker and the audience, emphasizing the sharing of an idea with the audience, and determining an effective approach will help the speaker achieve the intended goal.

The audience receives the message, but the message may be distorted according to distractions in the surrounding area or by preconceived ideas and opinions of each audience member. As the audience receives the message, they decode what they have heard and understood before sending verbal and/or non-verbal feedback to the speaker. **Decoding** is a process by which we translate or interpret the content into meaning. The decoding process can be altered depending upon "noise" in the environment. **Noise** can be defined as distractions in the speaking environment, but also can include preconceived notions, opinions, and ideas. Sometimes **feedback** is verbal, but many times feedback is non-verbal. Feedback helps the speaker know if the content delivered has been effectively decoded and received. In order to have feedback, the receiver (audience) will need to listen.

Where Can You PRACTICE Your Public Speaking Skills?

Many people enjoy belonging to professional development organizations that encourage public speaking presentations and provide opportunities to improve leadership skills. Take public speaking courses through your local college's continuing education program. Find organizations in your area that provide a public forum to practice your skills. Options to consider are Toastmasters International, National Speaker's Association, National Communication Association, Church or Religious Organizations, College Clubs, Meet-ups, Civic Organizations, Community Functions, Sports Events, Political Organizations, Book Clubs, Craft Clubs, and Business Networking Events. Speak at every opportunity to improve your communication skills, and you will become a more effective listener, communicator, and leader!

The key to being a good speaker is to speak so that others can understand you and your message! Every time you speak, give your audience something wonderful to remember. Make it a pleasant experience and they will ask you to speak again. Speak again and you will get more experience. The more experience you have the better speaker you will be.

The key is . . .

SPEAKER AND AUDIENCE RESPONSIBILITIES

SPEAKER RESPONSIBILITIES

Speakers have a responsibility to the audience. It is your job to know who will be in your audience and to plan your speech for them! Just because it is your opportunity to deliver the speech does not mean that you can stand on your soap box and use the time with a captured audience to share just exactly what you think about anything and everything. No, you will need to provide content that the audience needs and it is your responsibility to present it in a way that is effective, clear, and to the point. Prove you are a competent speaker by the content that you provide and the manner in which you provide the content.

Speak to your audience using a conversational tone. Your speech should not sound canned or rehearsed. It should sound as if you are sitting with one person in your audience at your kitchen table and discussing the topic over a nice cup of hot tea! Audiences do not want to be talked at. They want a conversation between you and them. This is the type of interaction you want on a small scale between you and another person. This is also the type of interaction an audience desires with a speaker. Talking "with" someone, sharing information, feelings, convictions are so much more enjoyable than having someone talk "at" you! It is a more intimate transaction. Just remember, the same type of interpersonal communication skills that work on a one-on-one or in a small group setting will also work beautifully between a speaker and an audience.

Show the audience that you care about them with the content you provide. Mention their names or the town where you are speaking. Say something positive about their local sports team, mayor, or director of the business where you are speaking. This will help your audience to feel like you wanted to be there with them enough to know what is important to them. It will help you to get the audience in your corner and will also make your speech so much more effective! Consider yourself as a host or hostess at a gathering. Your job is to make your audience comfortable and to supply their every need. Serve them a "Shark-o-licious" speech!

SERVING UP A "SHARK-O-LICIOUS" TREAT?

My daughter brought home a bag of gummy treats yesterday that were shaped like sharks! Isn't that fun? Sharks are everywhere! These fun shark treats made me think about great speeches and how they have a lot in common with a great meal. Since you might be presenting a speech soon, I wanted to share this with you so that you can serve a "Shark-o-licious" treat to YOUR audience.

Every memorable meal begins with an appetizer and then moves to a second dish before leading to the main course which usually includes a protein dish, starch, and vegetable before concluding with a delicious dessert.

Memorable speeches should follow the same type of menu as I will explain in the following table:

Memorable Meal	Memorable Speech	Similarities
Appetizer	Attention Step	Just as you arrive at a meal hungry and ready to eat, your audience will arrive anxious to hear your speech. This is where you set the stage, get the audience's attention, and provide your audience with a "taste" of what is to come.
Soup	Establish Relevance for the Topic Establish Credibility to Speak About the Topic Preview of Main Points (Thesis)	The soup prepares your palate for the main course of a meal, but it is this step in the speech that prepares your audience for the topic. First, explain why it is important that the audience hear about the upcoming topic. Then, tell your audience why YOU are credible to speak to them about the topic. The next thing that you will do during this phase is to clearly state the three main points that you will cover. This prepares your audience and allows them to anticipate the "main course"!
Bread	Transitions	Bread during a meal is often used to cleanse the palate and is enjoyed between courses. For the speech, transitions, also called connectors, are essential as they transition the content from one thing to the next. A great speaker will use clear transitions to move from the Introduction Step to the Body of the speech, to each Main Point, and then finally into the Conclusion.

Main Course:
  Protein
  Starch
  Vegetable
	Body	The main course is the purpose of the meal and the body is the purpose of your speech! The body of the speech contains three main points that support the topic. Often the main points include research, stories, and examples that further define the topic.

Dessert	Conclusion	All great meals culminate with a sweet treat! The dessert that concludes the memorable meal is my favorite part of the meal because it leaves a sweet taste in my mouth! A great speech conclusion should leave your audience wanting more! Signal that you are concluding the speech, re-state the three main points, and then provide closing statements or an Appeal that will make your audience wish the speech could last just a little longer! Now, isn't that sweet?

It is time to start cooking, or should I say, writing the speech! How are you going to make sure your next speech is "Shark-o-licious"? Plan, Prepare, and Persevere! Keep these tips in mind and your next speech is sure to be a crowd pleaser with your audience having an appetite that will have them demanding an encore!

Plan

Even the simplest things need to be considered as you prepare for your presentation. And, yes, there are still more questions:

- What can you say or do to get your audience's attention from the very beginning?
- How can you get your audience to relate immediately to your topic?
- Why are YOU credible to talk to an audience about this topic?
- How can you conclude the speech so that your audience continues thinking about your speech topic even after your speech is over?

Answering these questions will help you prepare an Introduction Step that introduces the topic to your audience and will have them in the palm of your hand before you actually begin speaking about the topic. A strong Introduction Step (appetizer and soup) is important for an effective presentation, but this step cannot be written until AFTER you have planned the body (main course) of your speech (topic and three main points). This will also help you to prepare a Conclusion Step (desserts) that ends your speech with a BANG!

Prepare

The speaker has a responsibility to begin the speech with an Attention Step or Opener that will get their attention within the first few seconds of your presentation. Consider how you would feel if you were one of the audience members sitting and waiting to hear a great speech from YOU. Start strong with an engaging Attention Step. Here are some suggestions and why they work:

1. **Questions:** This works because a well-designed question is just begging to be answered. Be careful that your question leads directly to the topic you will be covering and remember that presentation is everything. A great question with a weak delivery will not make for a memorable Attention Step.

2. **Empathy:** This allows you to connect with your audience on a personal level. This starts the feeling of an intimate relationship between you and the audience in the first few seconds of your speech. Ask, "Have you ever thought about why. . .", "I'll never forget the moment when", or "Just like YOU, I was brought up to believe. . .".

3. **Announcement of a NEW Policy or Procedure:** While this might not always be met with full cooperation, it does get the attention of your audience and they will be very interested to see how this change will affect their own area or their lives.

4. **Secrets:** Everyone loves a secret! Start your speech by saying, "I want to let you in on a little secret—this is a secret that not even my husband knows. . ." Doing this provides you with the opportunity to promise something to your audience that they simply cannot refuse. They want to know the secret!

5. **Startling Statement:** Beginning your speech with a shocking statement that makes your audience feel like they may be making a huge mistake about something will certainly give them reason to sit up straight and listen to what you have to say!

6. **Warnings:** If you start your speech by saying, "There are three warning signs to look for when. . .", then your audience will want to hear you identify the three warning signs.

7. **Quotes:** This is always a good strategy, but can get a bit boring if every speaker that day begins with a quote. If you are going to use a quote, make sure that it is a quote that will make the audience want to sit up and take notice! Also, make sure you have the name of the person correct who is cited with the quote.

8. **Imagery:** You can start by saying, "Imagine, if you will. . ." People love imagery and they will enjoy an Attention Step that begins with imagery!

9. **Stories:** Everyone loves a good story. Start by saying, "Do you mind if I share a story with you? Last week when I was a XYZ, I heard about. . ." Now, they want to hear about it, too!

10. **Choices:** If I were to ask you to choose between this donut and an apple, which would you choose? Wait for the answer? Of course, you are hoping they will choose the apple, but you notice that more than half of your audience raised their hands saying they would choose the donut! Give them a choice! Then, allow that choice to help shape the direction of your speech topic.

Don't introduce yourself in the opening words of your speech. Save your introduction for the portion of your introduction step where you will establish your own credibility as a speaker for the topic. Here is an example:

Introduction to the Speech:

Attention Step:

Establish Need/Relevance for the Topic:

Establish Credibility: For the past twenty years, I have been a public speaking coach helping young people to prepare for interviews and competitions. Hello, my name is Dr. Penny Joyner Waddell and I am happy to be here with you today to discuss the importance of dressing for success when giving a speech presentation.

Thesis:

Persevere

Using the speech writing formula that we have presented in this book, we want you to begin thinking like a speech writer. You are on the right path—you are a SpeechShark swimming easily toward your target! Take a deep breath. It's almost time to meet your audience!

AUDIENCE RESPONSIBILITIES

Audiences have a responsibility, too! As the speaker enters the stage, please show appreciation for the speaker by giving your undivided attention and clapping until the speaker has taken his/her place on stage and is ready to begin the presentation! Your next task is to LISTEN to the speaker. Put away cell phones and electronic devices that would cause distractions and position your body to face the speaker. Using your nonverbal cues, show the speaker that she has your full attention and that you are anxious to hear her message. Smile at the speaker, nod your head in agreement, and show support with your face and body posture.

Prepare yourself to hear the speech. Listen carefully to identify the message delivered. Get plenty of rest and a good meal prior to the presentation. Just as the speaker has to prepare for you, it is your job to prepare yourself. Not enough sleep? You could be tempted to take a short nap during the presentation. YES, your speaker will know you are napping and that sends a negative non-verbal cue that you are bored and what the speaker is saying is of no consequence to you. If you are hungry, your stomach may growl or you could spend her speech thinking about what you might eat just as soon as the speech is over. Here are some tips to help you be a great audience member:

1. **Be an active listener** by showing appreciation for the speaker. Sending positive non-verbal cues such as smiling, head nods, leaning forward toward the speaker, and establishing eye contact, will show the speaker that you are glad to hear the speech. Just using the active listener posture will help you focus more on the speaker and become a better audience member.

2. **Resist distractions** and use your critical listening skills to focus in on the speaker and the message.

3. **Practice empathetic listening** and try to see the speaker's point of view, even if it differs from your own.

4. **Focus on verbal and non-verbal cues** being sent by the speaker. Are the speaker's verbal and non-verbal cues matching with the content of the speech?

5. **Take notes and create a presentation outline** during the speech. Informative listening is used during this time of the speech. Write down questions you may have so that you can ask them after the speech is over. Never interrupt the speaker to ask a question. Always save the questions to ask during a question and answer session or to pose privately to the speaker after she leaves the stage area.

COMMUNICATION TIPS FROM THE EXPERTS AT SPEECHSHARK

What is the worst thing that a person can do when trying to make a speech presentation?

If a speaker knows that a speaking engagement is approaching, the worst thing the speaker can do is to be so overly confident that he does not prepare for the event! Preparation includes knowing to whom you will be speaking and making sure you provide content that the audience needs. It also includes researching the topic to add support for your points and rehearsing the presentation several times.

How can you prevent that?

To prevent a failed presentation, the key is over-preparation. For example, if you are speaking to specific groups, learn the names of the directors and interject their names into the speech at an appropriate moment. Include projects or plans the group is making so they know you cared enough about the group to learn about them. Plan, prepare, and practice so your presentation will be perfect!

What are the characteristics of effective speakers?

- Effective speakers are great listeners. They listen to find out what is needed and then go the extra mile to research main points within the content and provide the audiences with credible information.
- Effective speakers are detail oriented and are planners. They LOVE using Speech Checklists! Once they have the content of the speech covered, they are effective in the delivery of the information.
- Effective speakers use energy to captivate their audiences so that enthusiasm and excitement for the topic is "caught" and not "bought"!
- Effective speakers learn to calm their nerves so they always appear confident and competent.

In a socially awkward situation like meeting someone for the first time, what is the best way to break the ice?

Let's face it, meeting someone for the first time can be very awkward. Understanding that there will be a short period of awkwardness before the relationship begins is a realistic way of approaching the situation. From a communicator's point of view, it is important to know your audience before speaking to them. What can you learn about this person before the meeting? What common ground might you have with this person? Do your homework before the meeting and the period of time between "Hello!" and "I'll look forward to seeing you again!" will be less awkward and more productive!

What sort of approach is best to avoid?

If you know your audience before the meeting, it will be easier to instigate conversation that is mutually satisfying. Stay away from topics and points that would cause a conflict. I am not saying that you should never speak about controversial matters, but that is a subject for another meeting once your relationship has progressed to the point where you can speak candidly about your thoughts.

"Do unto others as you would have them do unto you!" I know you have heard that a million times, but as you meet someone for the very first time, treat your new friend the way that you

would like to be treated. Be open to them and be a good listener. The awkwardness will soon pass and you will be the master of conversation before the meeting is over!

What can good communication skills do for someone?

Having good verbal and non-verbal communications skills are crucial to success in life! Effective communication skills will foster relationships, solve problems, promote teamwork, motivate and influence others, achieve goals, and the list goes on!

Non-verbal skills are just as important as verbal skills. Have you ever heard someone say, "What you do speaks so loudly that I can't hear what you are saying"? The truth is that people believe what they see before they believe what they hear. If you are going for a job interview, ask yourself the following questions:

- What will my potential employer see when I walk through the door?
- How are you dressed?
- What are you carrying with you?
- How is your poise and confidence?
- How is your handshake?
- Are you wearing a big smile?
- Are you demonstrating enthusiasm in your walk and the way that you carry yourself?

If all of these are positive, then you could very well get the job as long as your resume is as impressive as you are! If they are negative, then you will need to keep job searching, but please work on non-verbal skills before going to another interview.

I was speaking to a businessman the other day who shared with me that he likes to hire people who belong to Toastmasters International Clubs. He said that people who actively work on their images by improving their communication skills are also going to be conscious of improving the image of the business they represent. None of us are perfect communicators. Learning effective communication skills is not a destination, but a journey and something that we continue to improve as we move toward success!

Why do you think so many people fear public speaking?

It is no secret that most people fear public speaking more than they fear death. The truth is, everyone gets nervous when they need to speak in public. The good news is, no one has ever died from public speaking! Now, I know that the fear of public speaking is no laughing matter; however, if we realize we are perfectly normal and that everyone gets nervous, then we do not enter the stage feeling like we are the only nervous speaker in the world! We simply need to learn how to handle our own fears so that we can be effective speakers.

Usually people fear public speaking because they think everyone in the audience will be judging them—judging their appearance, voice, accent, body movements, content of speech, and the list goes on and on. Truthfully, people do not judge negatively and "take the speaker apart piece by piece." Instead, they want the speaker to be successful. After all, they are investing their time to hear this person speak and they don't want to waste their time. So, the audience is hoping for a knock-you-out-of-your-chair speech.

The question is not so much, "Why do so many people fear public speaking," but "How do I overcome my own fear of public speaking?" The answer to that is:

- Conduct an audience analysis prior to giving a speech.
- Choose a topic that is relevant for the audience.
- Conduct research to make sure you are covering points the audience wants to hear.

- Plan visual aids that support points.
- Craft a speech outline that includes an introduction, body, and conclusion. Let the first words you say grab your audience's attention. Establish why the audience needs to hear your speech. Establish why you are the person credible to speak to them. Clearly state the three points you will cover. Plan effective transitions between each main point. In the conclusion, clearly restate the three main points you covered. Finally, end with a BANG! Make sure your last words are something that will keep your audience thinking about your topic and about your speech.
- Rehearse, rehearse, rehearse! I say this three times because a speaker should rehearse speeches a minimum of three times before making the presentation.
- Positive self-talk will take you from "I can't do this" to "I can do this and I will do a great job!"
- Breathe! That's right, breathing exercises prior to the presentation can help you calm your heart rate and slow the flow of adrenaline in your body.
- Walk confidently to the stage realizing that you have earned the right to be the speaker of this particular event. Establish strong eye contact with your audience as you move toward the lectern, smile at them, and send non-verbal cues that send the message of your confidence and competence to speak!
- Do your best, but understand that you will never give a perfect speech. There will always be that one thing you forgot to say or there may be a time when you trip over your own words. Remind yourself that you are human—just like everyone in your audience—and do not beat yourself up over mistakes. Instead, dwell on all of the great things that you do!
- Be proud of yourself! Pat yourself on the back! Get ready for the next speech.

I am a SpeechShark! What is your super power?

You won't fear a shark attack when you keep your eyes open and are prepared for whatever comes your way! Some refer to shark movements as a feeding frenzy. Truthfully, it is no frenzy at all, but a graceful ballet in which the sharks are fast and swim confidently toward their goal. You can do this too! Be a Communication Shark! Use this section to test your skills and understanding.

Communication and Public Presentation

1. What is the definition of communication?

   _____

   _____

2. What is the definition of Public Speaking?

   _____

   _____

3. What are the six steps found in the communication process?

   _____

   _____

4. What happens through the encoding process?

   _____

   _____

5. Why should the speaker find common ground with the audience?

   _____

   _____

6. What happens during the decoding process?

_____

_____

7. What is noise?

_____

_____

8. Describe feedback.

_____

_____

9. What distractors can keep us from receiving communication signals sent our way?

_____

_____

10. When is your next speech? Are you prepared?

_____

_____

11. What is the speaker's responsibility to the audience?

_____

_____

12. What type of tone should be used when speaking to an audience?

_____

_____

13. When should the speaker introduce themselves?

_____

_____

14. What audience responsibilities should be expected?

_____

_____

Shark Bites

Consider how you might plan your next Shark-o-licious Speech using this table:

Memorable Meal	Memorable Speech	What are YOUR plans?
Appetizer	Attention Step	
Soup	Establish Relevance for the Topic Establish Credibility to Speak About the Topic Preview of Main Points (Thesis)	
Bread	Transitions	

Main Course:
  Protein
  Starch
  Vegetable
	Body
	
	Three Main Points
		1.
		
		2.
		
		3.

Dessert	Conclusion End with a BANG!	

How Do I Use the SpeechShark App?

Did you purchase the SpeechShark app? Excellent! If not, visit our Web site at www.SpeechShark.com to see a demonstration. The app is available for Android users in **GooglePlay** and for iOS users in the **Apple Store**. Using the app means you are on your way to creating effective and exciting speech presentations for your audience! Click on your SpeechShark app and let's get started!

Here are steps to follow:

15. Open the SpeechShark app.

16. Select "Home" to see options to create speeches, manage speeches, or select preferences.

17. If you want to create a NEW speech, select "Create Speeches."

18. A page will open that asks about the purpose of your speech. Read through each type of speech and choose the type that works best for your purpose. If you need more information about each type of speech, simply "LONG PRESS" the speech type to receive a brief tutorial regarding the speech. A "SHORT PRESS" of the speech type will take you directly to the next step in creating a speech.

19. Answer each prompting question using a complete sentence. Use correct grammar and spelling as this information will automatically begin building a speech outline.

20. Take your time and work through each step—one at a time—answering each prompting question, and when finished touch the "Continue" bar.

21. SpeechShark takes all of the guesswork out of crafting an effective speech, but it is up to you to answer the prompts, keep the purpose of your speech as your goal, and consider who will be listening to your speech. What does your audience need to know? What does your audience WANT to know? What can you do and say to connect with the audience and engage them?

22. As you have answered all of the questions, you will notice that SpeechShark will then deliver a full written outline that you can print, share, or e-mail. Additionally, you will see that SpeechShark will automatically generate three note cards that can be used for notes on your phone or tablet/iPad. This will make you a Card Shark because instead of standing in front of your audience with awkward 5x7 note cards, your notes are easily accessed using your electronic device and are available with a simple swipe.

23. Once the speech has been written, you can always retrieve it by going back to the "Home" file on the SpeechShark app and selecting "Manage Speeches." Every speech you craft will be stored there in a file with the "TITLE" that you give to the speech.

24. You, too, can be a **SpeechShark**!

Chapter Thirteen

Presentation Types and Delivery

In this chapter:

Types of Speeches

Delivery Methods

TYPES OF SPEECHES

There are three basic purposes or types of speeches: informative, entertaining, and motivational. Some speeches will address just one purpose or type, but there are many speeches that will include all three.

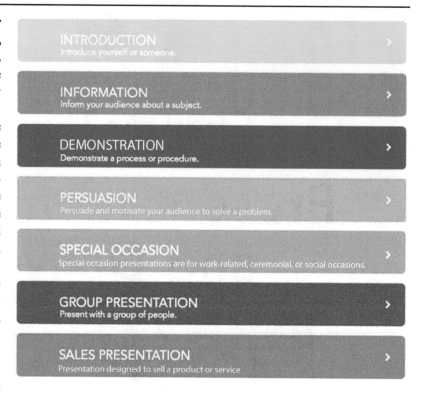

Informative speeches are designed for the speaker to provide interesting and useful information and to add knowledge to the listener's existing understanding of the topic. For this type of speech, the speaker takes on the role of an instructor and will teach, instruct, explain, report, and/or describe.

Entertaining speeches are enjoyable speeches. Some organizations list this type of speech as a humorous speech. Although not all speeches are categorized as entertaining speeches, it is possible for all speeches to contain entertaining aspects. Audiences enjoy speeches that are light-hearted, incorporate humor, and provide entertaining factors within the speech. Storytelling is considered one strategy for delivering an entertaining speech. Special Occasion Speeches usually include entertaining aspects. Due to the nature of this type of speech, speakers are able to build relationships, bond with the audience, and enhance networking possibilities.

Motivational speeches are designed to inspire the audience to act on information. Most often, Persuasion and Special Occasion Speeches will incorporate motivational strategies. Speakers who have the purpose of motivating the audience will need to consider incorporating information, research, and stories which will influence the audience's values, beliefs, attitudes, or behaviors. More information about this is covered in the Persuasion Speech section of this book.

Before you decide which type of speech to present, determine the purpose of the speech and ask yourself:

- What must I say to the audience to provide content they want to hear?
- Is your purpose to introduce yourself or someone else?
- Do you need to inform your audience about a specific topic?
- Will you need to demonstrate a process, product, or procedure?
- Do you want to persuade your audience to solve a problem?
- Is this a special occasion and will require a roast, toast, or presentation about the occasion? Is it a ceremony, work related, or a social event?
- Are you making a group presentation or trying to sell a project?
- Are you taking part in a fun PechaKucha event?
- Are you competing in a debate, oral interpretations, improvisation, or story telling competition?

Unsure about how to write a speech? The SpeechShark app was created just for you! Select the type of speech you need, answer the questions in full sentence format, and SpeechShark will do the rest of the work. For those who want to know more details about the types of speeches, here is a description and important facts about each type.

Introduction Speech

In your personal and business life, you will have plenty of opportunities to introduce yourself or others. Whether your introduction is planned or unplanned, understanding the tips below will help you complete the introduction with ease. Introduction Speeches are informative in nature because the purpose of the speech is to provide your audience with information about you or the person you are introducing.

Usually, Introduction Speeches are not very lengthy and last between two and three minutes. This isn't much time, so you will need to consider specific points to include, but without too much detail.

When introducing yourself, choose a theme and plan the introduction around the theme. If the setting is casual or informal, then you could introduce yourself with a theme about your hobbies, work, or family. Personal introductions on an informal scale will often include a handshake along with eye contact and a smile.

If the setting is business or formal, then you should introduce yourself by including information about your work, innovative ideas, experience in the field, and future goals. In both cases, consider the setting and provide information you think the audience would like to know. Avoid giving so much information that your introduction becomes tiresome! It should be light and positive.

One safe rule of thumb for an introduction speech is to follow a chronological or time-ordered sequence to introduce yourself or someone else. Begin your speech by briefly covering the **past**, then move to the **present**, and finally, share your hopes for the **future**.

If you are using the SpeechShark app to create this speech, then you can begin now to craft the speech. If you are not using the app, you may want to use the Introduction Speech Brainstorming Worksheet to get your thoughts together and prepare to write your presentation outline. Remember that all speech writers follow the **Standard Outline** procedure for creating a speech outline. We will only show you this type of outline in this book so that you will begin thinking like a professional speech writer!

SPEECH BRAINSTORMING WORKSHEET

Speech Category: Introduction Speech

Speech Title: Give your speech a clever title. _____

Specific Purpose: Write a full sentence to show what you plan to accomplish by introducing yourself or introducing someone else.

_____

_____

Introduction:

Attention Step: Consider how you will get your audience's attention. Write all you plan to say using full sentences.

_____

_____

Establish Need/Relevance: Explain why this introduction should interest the listener. Write all you plan to say using full sentences.

_____

_____

Establish Credibility: Explain why YOU are credible to introduce yourself or another person. Write all you plan to say using full sentences.

_____

_____

Thesis (Preview) Statement: Write a complete sentence and clearly state the three points you will cover:

_____

Point #1: Past _____

Point #2: Present _____

Point #3: Future _____

Body:

Transition Sentence: Write a full sentence to transition from the Introduction Step to the first main point.

_____

_____

    I. First Main Point—Past: (Share information about your past—stay with a theme.)
      A. First Sub-Point
        1. First Sub-Sub-Point (Not all points will require sub-sub-points.)
        2. Second Sub-Sub-Point
      B. Second Sub-Point
        1. First Sub-Sub-Point
        2. Second Sub-Sub-Point

Transition Sentence: Write a full sentence to transition from the past to the present.

_____

_____

    II. Second Main Point—Present: (Share information about your present—stay with the theme.)
      A. First Sub-Point
        1. First Sub-Sub-Point (Not all points will require sub-sub-points.)
        2. Second Sub-Sub-Point
      B. Second Sub-Point
        1. First Sub-Sub-Point
        2. Second Sub-Sub-Point

Transition Sentence: Write a full sentence to transition from the present to the future.

_____

_____

III. Third Main Point—Future: (Share information about your goals for the future—stay with the theme.)
    A. First Sub-Point
        1. First Sub-Sub-Point (Not all points will require sub-sub-points.)
        2. Second Sub-Sub-Point
    B. Second Sub-Point
        1. First Sub-Sub-Point
        2. Second Sub-Sub-Point

Transition Sentence: Write a full sentence to transition from the third main point to the conclusion.

_____

_____

Conclusion:

Summary: Write in full sentence format a summary of your three main points.

_____

Point #1: _____

Point #2: _____

Point #3: _____

Appeal to Action: Leave your audience thinking about your introduction. End with a **BANG!**

(NOTE: Be sure to add a Works Cited Page as a page separate from the Outline. Include all sources used.)

Works Cited

(Note: If you use Visual Aids, please include a Visual Aid Explanation Page as a page separate from the Works Cited Page and separate from the Outline.)

Visual Aid Explanation Page

INTRODUCTION SPEECH OUTLINE TEMPLATE

Last Name 1

First Name/Last Name
Introduction Speech
Day Month Year

Speech Category: Introduction Speech
Title:
Purpose:

Introduction:
Attention Step:
Establish Need/Relevance:
Establish Speaker Credibility:

Thesis: Today, I want to share three points about (Topic): (1) _____,

(2) _____, and (3) _____.

Body:

Transition/Link: First, I will start at the beginning by sharing a little about (Point #1).
    I. First Main Point
       A. Sub-point
       B. Sub-point

Transition/Link: I've shared (Point #1) with you, now I'd like to tell you about (Point #2).
    II. Second Main Point
       A. Sub-point
       B. Sub-point

Transition/Link: You've heard about (Point #1 and Point #2), now I'll cover (Point #3).
    III. Third Main Point
       A. Sub-point
       B. Sub-point

Transition/Link: My purpose today was to (insert purpose and add a statement about the topic).
Conclusion:

Summary: Today, I shared with you three points: (1) Point #1 _____, (2) Point #2 _____

_____, and (3) Point #3 _____.
Appeal to Action: As I conclude this speech, (End with a BANG).

(NOTE: Be sure to add a Works Cited Page as a page separate from the Outline. Include all sources used.)

Works Cited

(Note: If you use Visual Aids, please include a Visual Aid Explanation Page as a page separate from the Works Cited Page and separate from the Outline.)

Visual Aid Explanation Page

Informative Speech

What is an **Informative Speech**? It is an opportunity to share something of value with your audience. You may choose to provide information about a hobby, career, politics, religion, or something that is happening in your school, college, or community. The purpose of an informative speech is to share knowledge with your audience. Often, the audience may already have a good understanding of the topic, but you will then be able to expand their knowledge by providing credible research, data, and personal stories to support your main points.

Conducting research will allow the opportunity to provide a strong attention step and conclusion for the informative speech. You may choose to begin the speech with a great quote or startling statistics that will get your audience's attention and will also lead to the informative speech topic you will present. Research can also provide options for the conclusion to keep your audience thinking about the information you shared. Supplementing your informative speech with credible research and personal experiences will make the topic come alive for your audience and will help your audience to remain more attentive.

Once you know who will be in your audience, consider choosing a topic that will be interesting to those in your audience. Also, consider a topic that interests you. Remember, enthusiasm is contagious! If you are enthusiastic about your topic, then your audience will enjoy your speech so much more.

Don't be afraid to share a topic that may be personal in nature. Audiences truly enjoy hearing personal stories and your experience with the topic will help support the points in the speech. Let us see your personality and passion for the topic.

An **Informative Speech** is often called a **Key Idea Speech** or a **Central Idea Speech**. You will hear these titles interchangeably because you begin with one general topic idea, but find it necessary to narrow your topic down to one key or central idea. From that point, you will have a better chance of informing your audience about the topic you have chosen.

The best informative speeches have titles that lead to the information the speaker wishes to share. Most of these titles will begin with *"How to. . .", "Why You Should. . .", Did You Know. . .", "Tips for. . .", "The Pros and Cons of . . .", "Examples of. . .", and "The Problems With. . .".*

Here are some examples of informative speech titles:

Informative Speech Topics	
How to Make Brownies	How to Choose a Church That Is Right for Your Family
How to Start a College Club on Your Campus	Where to Go on Your Next Vacation
Why You Should NOT Text and Drive	The Problem with an HOA (Home Owners Association)
Why Homeowners Should Have an HO3 Insurance Policy	Examples of GMOs (Genetically Modified Organisms)
How to Hang Glide	Time Management Skills
Tips for a Winning Interview	How to Name Your Child
The Pros and Cons of Being a Stay-At-Home Mom	The Problem with Sugar

Visual aids are often used during informative speeches to help the audience visualize content being shared by the speaker. If you are not familiar with creating effective visual aids for a speech, please refer to Unit #4 of this textbook to learn more.

An important visual aid tip to remember for an informative speech is to keep it simple and show one slide per main idea. Too many slides and too much information will be distracting, but a visual aid that is effectively designed will help the audience to visualize the speaker's points. No murky waters here for Speech Sharks who know how to combine quality research, personal experience, and visual aids to paint a clear picture of the speech topic!

Whether you are informing your audience about people, places, careers, hobbies, objects, procedures, or events, you can be sure that the more time you spend crafting a speech FOR your audience, the more successful you will be communicating that information TO your audience. Use the Informative Speech Brainstorming Worksheet to help craft your next Informative Speech.

INFORMATIVE SPEECH BRAINSTORMING WORKSHEET

Speech Category: Informative Speech
Speech Title: Give your speech a clever title. _____
Specific Purpose: Write a full sentence to show the purpose of your speech.

_____

_____

Introduction:
Attention Step: Consider how you will get your audience's attention. Write all you plan to say using full sentences.

_____

_____

Establish Need/Relevance: Explain why this informative speech topic should interest the listener. Write all you plan to say using full sentences.

_____

_____

Establish Credibility: Explain why YOU are credible to speak about this topic. Write all you plan to say using full sentences.

_____

_____

Thesis (Preview) Statement: Write a full sentence clearly stating the three points you will cover:

_____

Point #1: _____

Point #2: _____

Point #3: _____

Body:

Transition Sentence: Write a full sentence to transition from the Introduction Step to the first main point.

_____

_____

  I. First Main Point:
    A. First Sub-Point
      1. First Sub-Sub-Point (Not all points will require sub-sub-points.)
      2. Second Sub-Sub-Point
    B. Second Sub-Point
      1. First Sub-Sub-Point
      2. Second Sub-Sub-Point

Transition Sentence: Write a full sentence to transition from the first main point to the second.

_____

_____

  II. Second Main Point:
    A. First Sub-Point
      1. First Sub-Sub-Point (Not all points will require sub-sub-points.)
      2. Second Sub-Sub-Point
    B. Second Sub-Point
      1. First Sub-Sub-Point
      2. Second Sub-Sub-Point

Transition Sentence: Write a full sentence to transition from the second point to the third point.

_____

_____

  III. Third Main Point
    A. First Sub-Point
      1. First Sub-Sub-Point (Not all points will require sub-sub-points.)
      2. Second Sub-Sub-Point
    B. Second Sub-Point
      1. First Sub-Sub-Point
      2. Second Sub-Sub-Point

Transition Sentence: Write a full sentence to transition from the third main point to the conclusion.

_____

_____

Conclusion:

Summary: Write in full sentence format a summary of your three main points.

_____

Point #1: _____

Point #2: _____

Point #3: _____

Appeal to Action: Leave your audience thinking about your speech. End with a **BANG!**

(NOTE: Be sure to add a Works Cited Page as a page separate from the Outline. Include all sources used.)

Works Cited

(Note: If you use Visual Aids, please include a Visual Aid Explanation Page as a page separate from the Works Cited Page and separate from the Outline.)

Visual Aid Explanation Page

INFORMATIVE SPEECH OUTLINE TEMPLATE

Last Name 1

First Name/Last Name
Informative Speech
Day Month Year

Speech Category: Informative Speech
Title:
Purpose:

Introduction:
Attention Step:
Establish Need/Relevance:
Establish Speaker Credibility:

Thesis: Today, I want to share three points about (Topic): (1) _____,

(2) _____, and (3) _____.

Body:

Transition/Link: First, I will start at the beginning by sharing a little about (Point #1).
    I. First Main Point
        A. Sub-point
        B. Sub-point

Transition/Link: I've shared (Point #1) with you, now I'd like to tell you about (Point #2).
    II. Second Main Point
        A. Sub-point
        B. Sub-point

Transition/Link: You've heard about (Point #1 and Point #2), now I'll cover (Point #3).
    III. Third Main Point
        A. Sub-point
        B. Sub-point

Transition/Link: My purpose today was to (insert purpose and add a statement about the topic).
Conclusion:

Summary: Today, I shared with you three points: (1) Point #1 _____, (2) Point #2 _____

_____, and (3) Point #3 _____.
Appeal to Action: As I conclude this speech, (End with a BANG).

(NOTE: Be sure to add a Works Cited Page as a page separate from the Outline. Include all sources used.)

Works Cited

(Note: If you use Visual Aids, please include a Visual Aid Explanation Page as a page separate from the Works Cited Page and separate from the Outline.)

Visual Aid Explanation Page

Demonstration Speech

Sometimes the audience needs to see a **Demonstration Speech** in order to fully comprehend the process or procedure needed to complete a task. Demonstration speeches are informative type speeches, but will include a demonstration to complete the purpose. Usually this speech is a bit longer than the Central Idea (Informative) Speech and involves audience participation. This type speech also includes an entertaining aspect. Perhaps that is why this type of speech is so popular! Audiences are able to retain and comprehend information better when they actively take part in the demonstration and can visualize how the process or procedure works. It is because of this fact that Demonstration Speeches often appeal to diverse audiences and to people with varying learning styles. To summarize, the audience will hear the information, see the demonstration, and participate in the demonstration to retain the information much longer.

As with any speech topic, the speaker will need to choose a topic tailor-made for the intended audience. This is a great speech to incorporate your creativity and bring an element of entertainment to the speaking arena. Make it informational and useful so that you can add value to your audience's knowledge of the topic. Topics may include crafts, sports, hobbies, food preparations, horticulture, home or automotive repairs, but can also include how to budget, create a will, or participate in stock trading. If you have more time, your topic could involve the process of flipping a house, starting a business, or designing a website. Again, the topic you choose needs to be a topic that will be interesting and useful for the audience that will hear your speech. Demonstration Speech titles almost always begin with, "How to. . .". The title lends itself to the purpose of the speech.

Here are examples of good Demonstration Speech titles:

Demonstration Speech Topics	
How to Arrange Flowers	How to Organize Your Closet
How to Bake a Cake	How to Pack for a Trip
How to Clean a House	How to Paint a Room
How to Tie a Bow Tie	How to Play Dominoes
How to Change a Diaper	How to Wrap a Gift
How to Use Twitter	How to Write a Resume
How to Make Egg Rolls	How to Fold a Flag
How to Make a Picture Frame	How to perform CPR

The best plan to follow for a Demonstration Speech is to: (1) describe the history of the process or procedure you will demonstrate, (2) list and describe the materials needed for the demonstration, and (3) demonstrate the process or procedure. This plan may seem simple, but it truly is the clearest way to present demonstration information in such a way that will make sense to the audience.

Handouts and visual aids are important for a successful Demonstration Speech. The visual aids can help with the actual demonstration and handouts are given to audience members following the demonstration as a reminder of the process or procedures followed.

Understanding the setting of where the speech will be given may help you choose the topic and visual aids. Where will you be giving the demonstration speech? Will it be inside or outside? Will it be in a traditional classroom setting or in a public hall?

Rehearsals for a Demonstration Speech are different from rehearsals needed for other types of speeches. The Demonstration Speech will incorporate more visual aids than an Informative Speech. You might have a PowerPoint or Prezi Slide Presentation to illustrate steps in the process or procedure, but a table display is almost always used for a Demonstration Speech. The speaker stands behind the table and uses the props on the table display to demonstrate the process or procedure while speaking. It is for this reason that rehearsals should always include the actions that will be taken during the speech. Rehearse using the PowerPoint or Prezi Slide Presentation, but also using the props on the table display. Rehearse completing the steps needed to demonstrate the process or procedure. You'll notice that your speech time will actually last longer when you are giving the speech using the props to demonstrate than when you rehearse the speech without the props. This speech will involve using a Tech Team to help set up and break down the demonstration stage. Rehearse with your Tech Team so they know exactly what you want them to do and when you want them to do it.

DEMONSTRATION SPEECH BRAINSTORMING WORKSHEET

Speech Category: Demonstration Speech
Speech Title: Give your speech a clever title. _____
Specific Purpose: Write a full sentence to show the purpose of your speech.

_____

_____

Introduction:

Attention Step: Consider how you will get your audience's attention. Write all you plan to say using full sentences.

_____

_____

Establish Need/Relevance: Explain why this demonstration speech topic should interest the listener. Write all you plan to say using full sentences.

_____

_____

Establish Credibility: Explain why YOU are credible to demonstrate this topic. Write all you plan to say using full sentences.

_____

_____

Thesis (Preview) Statement: Write a complete sentence and clearly state the three points you will cover:

_____

Point #1: The history of _____

Point #2: Materials needed for the demonstration: _____

Point #3: Demonstration of _____

Body:

Transition Sentence: Write a full sentence to transition from the Introduction Step to the first main point.

_____

_____

    I. First Main Point:
      A. First Sub-Point
        1. First Sub-Sub-Point (Not all points will require sub-sub-points.)
        2. Second Sub-Sub-Point
      B. Second Sub-Point
        1. First Sub-Sub-Point
        2. Second Sub-Sub-Point

Transition Sentence: Write a full sentence to transition from the first main point to the second.

_____

_____

    II. Materials needed
      A. First Sub-Point
        1. First Sub-Sub-Point (Not all points will require sub-sub-points.)
        2. Second Sub-Sub-Point
      B. Second Sub-Point
        1. First Sub-Sub-Point
        2. Second Sub-Sub-Point

Transition Sentence: Write a full sentence to transition from the second point to the third point.

_____

_____

    III. Demonstration
      A. First Sub-Point
        1. First Sub-Sub-Point (Not all points will require sub-sub-points.)
        2. Second Sub-Sub-Point
      B. Second Sub-Point
        1. First Sub-Sub-Point
        2. Second Sub-Sub-Point

Transition Sentence: Write a full sentence to transition from the third main point to the conclusion.

_____

_____

Conclusion:

Summary: Write a full sentence summary of your three main points.

_____

Point #1: The History of (Product or Process) _____

Point #2: Materials needed: _____

Point #3: The Demonstration _____

Appeal to Action: Leave your audience thinking about your demonstration. End with a **BANG!**

(NOTE: Be sure to add a Works Cited Page as a page separate from the Outline. Include all sources used.)

Works Cited

(Note: If you use Visual Aids, please include a Visual Aid Explanation Page as a page separate from the Works Cited Page and separate from the Outline.)

Visual Aid Explanation Page

DEMONSTRATION SPEECH OUTLINE TEMPLATE

Last Name 1

First Name/Last Name
Demonstration Speech
Day Month Year

Speech Category: Demonstration Speech
Title:
Purpose:

Introduction:
Attention Step:
Establish Need/Relevance:
Establish Speaker Credibility:

Thesis: Today, I want to share three points about (Topic): (1) _____,

(2) _____, and (3) _____.

Body:

Transition/Link: First, I will start at the beginning by sharing a little about (Point #1).
    I. First Main Point
        A. Sub-point
        B. Sub-point

Transition/Link: I've shared (Point #1) with you, now I'd like to tell you about (Point #2).
    II. Second Main Point
        A. Sub-point
        B. Sub-point

Transition/Link: You've heard about (Point #1 and Point #2), now I'll cover (Point #3).
    III. Third Main Point
        A. Sub-point
        B. Sub-point

Transition/Link: My purpose today was to (insert purpose and add a statement about the topic).
Conclusion:

Summary: Today, I shared with you three points: (1) Point #1 _____, (2) Point #2 _____

_____, and (3) Point #3 _____.
Appeal to Action: As I conclude this speech, (End with a BANG).

(NOTE: Be sure to add a Works Cited Page as a page separate from the Outline. Include all sources used.)

Works Cited

(Note: If you use Visual Aids, please include a Visual Aid Explanation Page as a page separate from the Works Cited Page and separate from the Outline.)

Visual Aid Explanation Page

Persuasion Speech

We use persuasion strategies all day long as we inspire or motivate others to do something. It begins in the morning when you are persuading your child to get dressed for school, it continues as you go to work and try persuading your co-workers to embrace a new policy or procedure at the office. Then at night when you go home, you are still using your persuasion strategies to motivate your family to get outside for a little exercise after supper. Just face it, we will use this type of skill more often than any other. Not only are you attempting to persuade others to think of something in a different way, but they will also be attempting to persuade you to think another way.

Did you sit with friends or family members after the last presidential election and try to persuade them to think like you? Were they trying to change your mind about the way you think about politics? These types of interactions happen quite often. Sometimes we actually stop to consider another way of thinking. What strategy motivates you to think of things in a different way? What strategy motivates you to action?

The key word here is—motivate! That is because as we attempt to persuade someone to consider the view we present, we are actually motivating or influencing their values, beliefs, attitudes, or behaviors. Let's look at an explanation for each one of these areas.

Area to Influence (Motivate):	Explanation
Values	Do you think something is right or wrong? Do you consider something is good or bad?
Beliefs	Do you perceive the topic to be true or false?
Attitudes	Do you look at the topic in a favorable or unfavorable light? What is your attitude toward the topic?
Behaviors	Behaviors are a combination of your personal values, beliefs, and attitudes. We behave a certain way when we are reacting to these different areas.

The best strategy for being persuasive without sounding preachy or gimmicky is to follow **Monroe's Motivated Sequence**. Perhaps you would like to know a little more about Monroe's Motivated Sequence, especially if you have never heard of this term before. According to Frymier and Shulman, authors of the article, "What's in It for Me?" published by the *Communication Education Journal*, one way to truly motivate someone to do something or to think differently about something is to show the benefits or "What's in it for me?" This allows the speaker the opportunity to make the content relevant to the listener and to increase their motivation toward a solution.

The person who developed the Motivated Sequence Theory was Alan H. Monroe, a professor at Purdue University and well known for his theory of persuasion. **Monroe's theory involves five steps:** begin with a strong attention step, describe a problem showing a need for change, introduce a realistic solution which includes having the listener help solve the problem, help the listener visualize the results of solving the problem, and finish by challenging the listener to solve the problem.

First, the speaker should describe the problem using examples that will get the attention of the audience and will cause the audience to agree that there is, indeed, a problem.

Second, credible research and/or experiential research should be used to support the problems listed. Explain the problem in detail and show how this problem affects listeners. It is important that the audience relate to problems described in order for them to be motivated to take part in the next step.

Third, the speaker should propose realistic solutions to solve the problem. The solutions should be something that every person in the audience can do to help solve the problem. If the solution is too difficult, the listener will not be motivated to help with the solution. It is imperative that the speaker present steps toward solving the problem and uses research to prove this solution is effective and doable. Using this strategy does not sound preachy because you are not blaming the audience for the problem, but enlisting their help to solve the problem. It is not gimmicky because the solutions are realistic and attainable.

Fourth, the speaker should help the audience visualize the results of solving the problem, whether it is the benefits of successfully solving the problem or consequences if the problem is NOT solved. This strategy involves connecting with the audience so they can see the vision of solving the problem as something that actually can happen.

Fifth, the speaker will need to challenge the audience to become an integral part of the solution. The Appeal to Action portion of the Persuasion Speech is the moment where the speaker challenges the audience with such passion and enthusiasm that the audience members are motivated to begin work that very moment to solve the problem that has been described. If the speaker has indeed influenced the values, beliefs, attitudes, and behaviors of the audience members, they will feel compelled to help the speaker solve the problem and they will want to begin immediately!

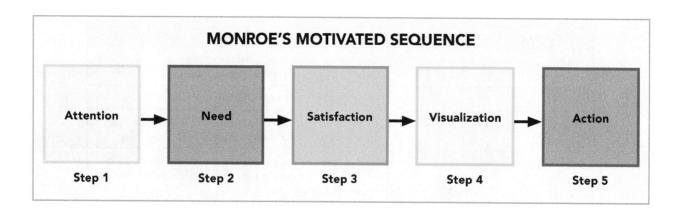

When choosing a topic for a persuasion speech, avoid choosing topics that are too controversial. Topics that are overly controversial can alienate your audience and you might find yourself in an unpleasant and hostile situation. In the few short minutes you have been given to present a Persuasion Speech, you will never be able to persuade an audience to completely change their way of thinking. Remember, people spend years deciding how they feel about things, whether it is religion, politics,

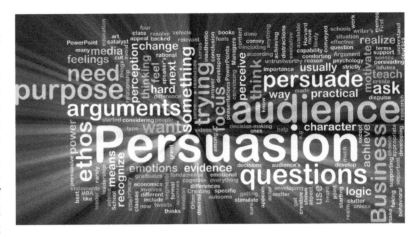

personal rights, or simply things they like and dislike. Since people have very strong feelings about things, your topic will automatically be met with support or with opposition. Most speakers do not choose to cover a topic that would make most of the audience members angry. Even if your topic is not overly popular, you can motivate your audience to think about your topic in a different way. That is why following Monroe's Motivated Sequence is the best way to influence and motivate audience members to action!

What is a **Persuasion Speech**? This is a type of speech in which the speaker provides useful information and supporting research that will motivate the listener to action. When crafting a persuasion speech, the speaker will need to answer questions of fact, value, and policy. Let's take a moment to look at all three of these areas.

Questions of Fact: During the problem statement, it is important to answer questions of fact by using credible research for support. Choose one side or the other as your topic. This is not a good time to "sit on the fence." If your speech is titled, "Don't Text and Drive," then you will want to motivate your audience to never text and drive—ever! If you say it is allowed to text while you are at a traffic light, then you are defeating your point. Your audience needs to know you are 100% committed to the topic you are covering; otherwise, you will destroy your credibility as a speaker for the topic and will not be able to motivate the audience to help solve the problem you describe.

Questions of Value: The problem statement will also need to cover questions of value. For most of us, this involves whether something is moral or immoral, whether it is just or unjust, whether it is good or bad. Choose the moral argument to cover and then offer appeals that will tug at the hearts of your audience members. A good strategy for this is to use arguments that will strengthen the audience's attitudes or beliefs toward the topic.

Questions of Policy: The questions of policy are answered during the portion in the speech where you offer a realistic solution to solve the problem. Solutions often involve changing laws or enforcing existing laws or revising procedures that are not working effectively. The speaker should focus on offering solutions that are something that any person in the audience can do. Audience members will not be able to change a law and many of them are also not in the position to enforce an existing law. Many of us are not in the position to revise procedures that are no longer working. So, what can we do to solve a problem? We can talk to those in our circle of friends and family about the problem. We can volunteer to help in areas that will impact the problem. We can contact or write the mayor, Governor of our state, County Commissioner, or State Representative. We can let those people know that we want to see a solution to the problem, a change to laws, or the enforcing of existing laws. THAT is something we can do and this will answer questions of policy.

PERSUASION SPEECH BRAINSTORMING WORKSHEET

Speech Category: Persuasion Speech
Speech Title: Give your speech a clever title. _____
Specific Purpose: Write a full sentence to show the purpose of your speech.

_____

_____

Introduction:
Attention Step: Consider how you will get your audience's attention. Write all you plan to say using full sentences.

_____

_____

Establish Need/Relevance: Explain why this persuasion speech topic should interest the listener. Write all you plan to say using full sentences.

_____

_____

Establish Credibility: Explain why YOU are credible to speak about this topic. Write all you plan to say using full sentences.

_____

_____

Thesis (Preview) Statement: Write a full sentence and clearly state the three points you will cover:

_____

Point #1: Description of the Problem: _____

Point #2: Proposed Solution to the Problem: _____

Point #3: Visualization of the Results of Solving the Problem or the Consequences if the Problem Is NOT

Solved: _____

Body:

Transition Sentence: Write a full sentence to transition from the Introduction Step to the first main point.

_____

_____

    I. **The Problem:**
       A. **Discuss the problem you are covering.**
          1. **Support the problem with research.**
          2. **Support the problem with a personal example.**
       B. **Why is there a need for change?**
          1. **Who or what is negatively affected by this problem?**
          2. **Use logical and emotional Appeals.**
Transition Sentence: Write a full sentence to transition from the first main point to the second.

    II. **Solution to the Problem:**
       A. **Offer a realistic, detailed solution which solves the problem.**
          1. **Explain how the audience can help to solve the problem.**
          2. **Provide personal examples and research to support your solution.**
       B. **Answer questions of policy.**
          1. **The solution affects values, beliefs, attitudes, and behaviors.**
          2. **Use logical and emotional appeals.**
          3. **Support points with credible research.**
Transition Sentence: Write a full sentence to transition from the second point to the third point.

    III. **Visualization of Results**
       A. **Benefits of Solving the Problem**
          1. **Does it answer questions of value?**
          2. **Use descriptions to help audience members visualize benefits.**
       B. **Consequences if the Problem is Not Solved**
          1. **Use imagery to show the consequences of not solving the problem.**
          2. **Use personal examples and vivid descriptions.**
Transition Sentence: Write a full sentence to transition from the third main point to the conclusion.

Conclusion:

Summary: Write a full sentence to summarize your three main points.

_____

Point #1: The Problem _____

Point #2: The Solution to the Problem _____

Point #3: Visualization of Results _____

Appeal to Action: Leave your audience challenged to help solve the problem. End with a **BANG!**

(NOTE: Be sure to add a Works Cited Page as a page separate from the Outline. Include all sources used.)

Works Cited

(Note: If you use Visual Aids, please include a Visual Aid Explanation Page as a page separate from the Works Cited Page and separate from the Outline.)

Visual Aid Explanation Page

PERSUASION SPEECH OUTLINE TEMPLATE

First Name/Last Name
Persuasion Speech
Day Month Year

Speech Category: Persuasion Speech
Title:
Purpose:

Introduction:
Attention Step:
Establish Need/Relevance:
Establish Speaker Credibility:

Thesis: Today, I want to share three points about (Topic): (1) The Problem with _____,

(2) Possible ways to solve the problem _____, and (3) a Visualization of the world if

this problem is solved _____.

Body:

Transition/Link: First, I will start at the beginning by sharing a little about (Point #1).
  I. First Main Point—Problem
    A. Sub-point
    B. Sub-point

Transition/Link: I've shared (Point #1) with you, now I'd like to tell you about (Point #2).
  II. Second Main Point—Solutions
    A. Sub-point
    B. Sub-point

Transition/Link: You've heard about (Point #1 and Point #2), now I'll cover (Point #3).
  III. Third Main Point—Results
    A. Sub-point
    B. Sub-point

Transition/Link: My purpose today was to (insert purpose and add a statement about the topic).
Conclusion:

Summary: Today, I shared with you three points: (1) Point #1 _____,

(2) Point #2 _____, and (3) Point #3 _____.

Appeal to Action: As I conclude this speech, (End with a BANG).

(NOTE: Be sure to add a Works Cited Page as a page separate from the Outline. Include all sources used.)

Works Cited

(Note: If you use Visual Aids, please include a Visual Aid Explanation Page as a page separate from the Works Cited Page and separate from the Outline.)

Special Occasion Speech

EVERYBODY LOVES A PARTY!

See how happy they are? This group of students just finished toasting each other and you can tell how much fun they had! There is always an abundance of laughter and mouths frozen into happy smiles as friends come together to celebrate! This is why we have Special Occasion Speeches. Although there are many reasons and occasions for Special Occasion Speeches, not all of them are the happy celebration that you see above. Some are more formal and subdued. Others are informal and spontaneous. Whether formal or informal, it is always a great opportunity to share your expertise at presenting a Special Occasion Speech as long as you understand the occasion and make a presentation your audience will remember fondly!

Most Special Occasion Speeches are not very lengthy. They are usually short and to the point, so they need to pack a punch! The words used during this type of speech need to be carefully chosen and precisely delivered to achieve the results that you want. Tribute speeches are delivered with dignity, grace, and sincerity. Ceremonial speeches will involve pomp and circumstance. Roasts and toasts can be delivered with humor. All Special Occasion Speeches will take on the personality of the occasion. With this in mind, it is important that you understand the different types of Special Occasion Speeches so you can choose the right one for your special occasion.

The three basic types are (1) work-related speeches, (2) ceremonial speeches, and (3) social occasion speeches. Most of these speeches will last three to seven minutes. A Keynote Address, Eulogy, Commencement, or Commemoration could last between twenty to forty minutes. As with any speech, you should always check with the host who invites you to speak and ask for the time frame the host requires. A good rule to remember is that you should always end your speech before the final time that you are given. A three- to seven-minute speech should last five minutes. A twenty- to forty-minute speech should last no longer than thirty-five minutes.

Work-Related Speeches

- **Keynote Address:** Consider yourself a good speaker if you have been chosen to deliver the Keynote Address of a meeting or conference. This honor is usually reserved for established speakers with an impressive résumé. The first order of business is to establish a connection or bond with the audience and then welcome them to the event. Make sure that you thoroughly research the event, audience members, and organization sponsoring the event so that your speech will reflect the values, attitudes, beliefs, and behaviors of audience members. Choose a topic that will set the tone for the meeting or conference. Realizing the participants at this meeting or conference are already quite knowledgeable about the purpose for the gathering, your topic will need to be on-point to add to their existing knowledge and create value for each participant.

- **Announcement:** Regardless of the organization, you can bet there will be announcements delivered at each meeting. If asked to make the announcement, plan to deliver a brief explanation and address the announcement in a speech that is short and to the point. Having notes for this speech is a good idea so you do not leave out pertinent information which might lead to the need for a second announcement.

- **Public Relation:** This type of speech is made to inform the audience about aspects that are designed to improve a problem. It may deal with attendance, insurance changes, policy, procedure adjustments, or changes in protocol. This speaker will need to establish goodwill and a positive atmosphere prior to delivering the required information. It is important to set a stage that will encourage the audience to accept the information you are sharing. Public Relation Speeches are not always met with approval; therefore, it is important that you have the audience in your corner before giving the information needed.

- **Report:** The purpose of presenting a report is to communicate information to the audience. This information will not be entertaining and usually involves numbers, charts, and data as a vehicle for the information. Audience members will appreciate a visual aid to see a visual report in the form of charts or graphs as you provide the information. Keep your visual aids simple, but include all necessary material for a complete report. This report is short, to the point, and detail oriented.

- **Nomination:** Corporations and Clubs that follow Roberts' Rules of Order will allow formal nominations to nominate people for positions or to make a motion to consider a change or alteration of a policy or procedure. This is usually not considered a formal speech, but will need to be treated as such as the person making the nomination will need to offer verbiage that is concise, clear, and complete.

Ceremonial Speeches

- **Installation:** Installations usually take place during a ceremony, but are also delivered in workplace situations. The purpose of this type speech is to install a person into a particular office or position. Once installed, the person who is installed will usually offer a few, well-chosen words of thanks to those who might have made the decision for the installation. This speech usually lasts two to three minutes.

- **Presenting an Award:** The actual presentation of an award is an extremely short speech. This involves referring to the occasion, acknowledging the contributions of the recipient, and then presenting the award with dignity and grace. This is a solemn presentation and care must be made to correctly name the award and to pronounce the recipient's name correctly.

- **Accepting an Award:** Often, the recipients of the awards will not know ahead of time that they are receiving an award. In this impromptu type situation, it is important that the recipient understand the gravity of the honor and accept the award in such a manner that the presenter of the award feels they made a good choice. The recipient should show sincere appreciation for receiving the award, delivering the acceptance speech with dignity and grace and should acknowledge the organization presenting the award. If advance notice is given, the recipient could add personal stories that led to the award and could thank individuals who contributed to the presentation of the award.

- **Dedication:** Dedication ceremonies happen at the birth of new babies, and for the opening of new buildings, parks, or monuments. This type speech is short and to the point. The person or object being dedicated is the focal point of the speech and allows those gathering to honor the occasion. The person chosen to present the Dedication Speech is usually someone quite close to the child being dedicated or to the organization or person who initiated the building, park, or monument. The speaker will need to establish a connection with the audience in the beginning before completing the formal dedication service.

- **Eulogy:** A Eulogy is a ceremony delivered with the purpose of honoring or paying tribute to the deceased. Some people say they are *paying respects* to the person. Culture dictates how this speech presentation will be handled. The length of this speech will vary according to the culture of those attending and the circumstances to which the group has gathered. Often the speaker who has this task will recount personal experiences and stories of times spent with the person being honored.

- **Commemorative:** This type of ceremony is appropriate when a group wishes to celebrate a person or event and is most often delivered as a tribute speech. The speaker will need to emphasize people or history involved with the subject being commemorated. Accurate data and stories are necessary to present the information with dignity and honor. The speaker will need to correctly pronounce the person's name or the subject of the commemoration.

- **Commencement:** Everyone enjoys attending the graduation of a loved one, but no one enjoys a Commencement Speech that is long and boring! Therefore, it is important that the speech focuses on the actual event and those who are graduating, offers words of encouragement and motivational stories for the graduates, and keeps the speech short and to the point. It is a good idea to include research data and facts of positive employment trends that will give hope and encouragement to the graduates and their families.

I would like to propose a toast to all the SpeechSharks in our world!
To those of you who said you would never give a speech
and to those of you who are great at sharing your thoughts and feelings with others,
*I invite ALL of you to raise your glasses high as I wish you **oceans of success**.*
May you be as stealthy and goal driven as a shark
and may all of your speeches be delivered with ease and finesse.
Cheers!

Social Occasion Speeches

- **Toast:** While not everyone at your event may drink alcohol, a Toast is a wish that can be shared with everyone. Always make sure the glasses are filled prior to making the Toast. Raise your glass to eye level as you present the Toast. Plan your Toast ahead of time making sure to put a great deal of thought into the sentiment so that it truly means something to the person you are honoring. Memorize the Toast (it isn't cool to read notes at a Toast). Acknowledge those present in the room and those who are not there to share the moment. Show emotion and passion for the moment. Keep the Toast short, light, and meaningful. As you  finish, raise the glass above your head as a symbol of extending the wish.

- **Welcome:** This is another speech that could easily move over to the Work-Related speeches; however, it is also appropriate to list it with the Social Occasion Speeches. The Welcome Speech is presented at the beginning of a social event. This should be used as a point to welcome those who are attending the event and should be short, light, and to the point. This also may be the time to introduce the agenda for the day and to introduce the next speaker or event on the agenda.

- **Farewell:** There are two different ways to offer a Farewell Speech. It can be presented by someone who is leaving or it can be presented by a person who is remaining and chooses this opportunity to honor the person who is leaving. It can be work-related or socially-related. Again, this is a speech that is offered in less than two minutes and offers regards with kindness, grace, and dignity. The Farewell can also be delivered as a Toast. There are lots of options here, but it is always important that it is brief and that every word is carefully chosen to say the things that need to be said.

- **Retirement:** There are distinct similarities with the Farewell and the Retirement Speech, in that the speech can be presented by the person who is retiring or by a person from the organization who would like to honor the person who is retiring. This should be a short presentation that highlights the accomplishments of the person retiring and delivered with kindness, grace, and dignity.

- **Roast:** Full disclaimer about this type of speech . . . we saved this one for last because it truly is one of our favorites. Also, this type speech is BEST when combined with a Toast at the end of the Roast. This type of speech has become quite popular recently and creates a stand-alone event where people attend just to hear and participate in the Roast. Usually this type of gathering begins as a dinner and ends with the Roast as the after-dinner entertainment. A traditional Roast will involve several speakers and might focus on just one person or can focus on many people. Each speaker will take three to five minutes to Roast the guest of honor and the purpose is to have lots of laughter. Research is not always necessary for this type of speech, but if research is used, please make sure that you correctly cite the source in the outline and include a Works Cited page to show the complete citation. My speech class always ends the semester with a Roast followed by a Toast. During the assignment, the students are asked to Roast the people who are in their class. Often, they will Roast the three or four people in their Speech Groups providing one funny item about each person; however, they can also choose to Roast one person in the class and include three areas of humorous events about that one person. We tell the students that they have a full semester to gather material for the Roast that is held the last day of class. The result is three hours of non-stop laughter and an opportunity for the classmates to bid farewell to each other. They all conclude their speech by ending with a well-designed Toast to the person or persons that they just roasted.

Each Special Occasion Speech should be planned according to the occasion where the speech will be presented. Since the Roast and Toast is our favorite Special Occasion Speech, we will provide an example to help as you plan your next Roast and Toast! Use the Brainstorming Worksheet as you plan for your own Special Occasion Speech!

SPECIAL OCCASION SPEECH BRAINSTORMING WORKSHEET

Speech Category: Special Occasion Speech

Identify whether your speech will be Work-Related, Ceremonial, or Social: _____

Identify which category you will cover: _____

Speech Title: Give your speech a clever title: _____

Specific Purpose: Write a full sentence to show the purpose of your speech.

_____

_____

Introduction:

Attention Step: Consider how you will get your audience's attention. Write all you plan to say using full sentences.

_____

_____

Establish Need/Relevance: Explain why this topic should interest the listener. Write all you plan to say using full sentences.

_____

_____

Establish Credibility: Explain why YOU are credible to speak about this topic. Write all you plan to say using full sentences.

_____

_____

Thesis (Preview) Statement: Write a full sentence and clearly state the three points you will cover:

_____

Point #1: _____

Point #2: _____

Point #3: _____

Body:

Transition Sentence: Write a full sentence to transition from the Introduction Step to the first main point.

_____

_____

    I. First Main Point:
        A. Sub-Point.
        B. Sub-Point.
Transition Sentence: Write a full sentence to transition from the first main point to the second.

_____

_____

    II. Second Main Point
        A. Sub-Point.
        B. Sub-Point.
Transition Sentence: Write a full sentence to transition from the second point to the third point.

_____

_____

    III. Second Main Point
        A. Sub-Point.
        B. Sub-Point.
Transition Sentence: Write a full sentence to transition from the third main point to the conclusion.

_____

_____

Conclusion:

Summary: Write a full sentence to summarize your three main points.

_____

Point #1: _____

Point #2: _____

Point #3: _____

Toast: Plan a Toast to leave with your audience as you conclude the speech. Toasts can be original or you may use one that has been passed down for years and years. If you use a Toast that has a copyright, be sure to cite the source and include a Works Cited page.

(NOTE: Be sure to add a Works Cited Page as a page separate from the Outline. Include all sources used.)

Works Cited

(Note: If you use Visual Aids, please include a Visual Aid Explanation Page as a page separate from the Works Cited Page and separate from the Outline.)

Visual Aid Explanation Page

SPECIAL OCCASION SPEECH OUTLINE TEMPLATE

Last Name 1

First Name/Last Name
Special Occasion Speech
Day Month Year

Speech Category: Special Occasion Speech
Title:
Purpose:

Introduction:
Attention Step:
Establish Need/Relevance:
Establish Speaker Credibility:

Thesis: Today, I want to share three points about (Topic): (1) _____,

(2) _____, and (3) _____.

Body:
Transition/Link: First, I will start at the beginning by sharing a little about (Point #1).
    I. First Main Point
        A. Sub-point
        B. Sub-point

Transition/Link: I've shared (Point #1) with you, now I'd like to tell you about (Point #2).
    II. Second Main Point
        A. Sub-point
        B. Sub-point

Transition/Link: You've heard about (Point #1 and Point #2), now I'll cover (Point #3).
    III. Third Main Point
        A. Sub-point
        B. Sub-point

Transition/Link: My purpose today was to (insert purpose and add a statement about the topic).
Conclusion:

Summary: Today, I shared with you three points: (1) Point #1 _____,

(2) Point #2 _____, and (3) Point #3 _____.

Appeal to Action: As I conclude this speech, (End with a BANG).

(NOTE: Be sure to add a Works Cited Page as a page separate from the Outline. Include all sources used.)

Works Cited

(Note: If you use Visual Aids, please include a Visual Aid Explanation Page as a page separate from the Works Cited Page and separate from the Outline.)

Visual Aid Explanation Page

Sales Presentation

Sales Presentations follow much of the same strategies as Persuasion Speeches; therefore, we suggest that you review the Persuasion Speech section in this book. Pay close attention to the section about motivation. The purpose of your sales pitch is to motivate the audience to purchase an item or service that you are selling! To do this you will need to motivate and influence **values, beliefs, attitudes, or behaviors**.

Consumers today are quite different from consumers in the past and the sales force has changed from strictly face-to-face interactions to include Internet, telephone, videos, photographs, and social media. If you truly want to be a great salesperson, you will soon realize the importance of walking a fine line to create a balance between being persuasive, but not too pushy. This takes planning and practice. Once you can establish a solid strategy that works for your personality, then you will begin to close more deals.

Here are proven strategies to help you find success in sales:

1. **Identify the decision maker:** Whether you are making a sales pitch to a company or to a couple, you must first know the person that will ultimately make the decision to buy. Once you identify the decision maker, you can customize your sales presentation to the person. This is where it is important to use good listening skills. Listen carefully to understand the needs of the individual or the corporation so that you can provide what the customer needs.

2. **Care for the best interest of the customer:** Instead of working hard to sell the one product your boss is pushing, try to provide the product or service that your customer truly needs. Let the customer know that you care about their business and that your first priority is to help them solve the problem they are having by providing the product or service they need. The "deal" should not be more important to you than their satisfaction with the product or service. This is the way to foster repeat customers.

3. **Identify the deadline:** Again, you need to be a good listener. When do they need this product or service? Does your organization have a special price deal that is or will be available for the product or service they need? Can you help them make the right choice at the right time to save money or time?

4. **Overcome obstacles:** This is the time to focus on the problem which is motivating customers to make this purchase. Do they need to purchase the car you are selling by a certain date to meet a deadline? Is this a seasonal purchase? What potential objections might slow down the decision-making process? What questions or concerns may the customer have? If you can think ahead to prepare for problems or obstacles that could slow down or stop the sale, then you will have time to find a solution and close the sale!

5. **Know your competitors:** Depending upon the product or service you will be selling, you should understand that competition can be tough! Why is your product superior, less expensive, or more effective than the competition? If you want to make the sale, you need to conduct research on any competitors that might waltz in and take your business. Take time to prepare your sales presentation, conduct research to learn about any and all markets that may stand in your way, and make sure that you are providing something that your competitor will not, such as customer service and care for your

customer. It has been proven time and again that customers return to the same salesperson if they feel like the salesperson has their best interest at heart.

6. **Create a positive reputation:** Say what you mean and mean what you say! If you tell your customer you will do something, make sure you do it. Even if it is a simple phone call to provide additional information. Make sure your conversations stay on the product or service that the customer wants. Customers don't want to hear about your problems, your bad cold, or your car that will not start. The customer is there because they are in the market for a product or service that your organization may be able to provide. They are not there to visit. Keep conversations professional and to the point. Create a reputation of caring for your customers, having their best interest at heart, and making the sales transaction a fast and enjoyable experience.

7. **Close the Sale:** Do you remember the Kenny Rogers song with the lyrics, "You've got to know when to hold 'em, know when to fold 'em, know when to walk away, know when to run!"? I wouldn't advise singing this song out loud around your customers, but it is good advice. If you are an effective listener, then you will know your customer's deadline for purchasing the product or service you represent and you should know when to make the pitch, when to back off and let the customer consider what you have shared, and then know when to provide a sense of urgency to purchase the product or service. Many salespeople are not successful because they simply do not know how to close the sale. A good salesperson will tell you that closing the sale is a matter of knowing when to encourage the customer to make the decision. The customer has a problem to solve. You can solve the problem with the product or service your organization provides. It is your job to convince the customer that the money charged is a deal and the time to purchase is now.

   Here are some good phrases to use as a closer:

- If our company can provide a solution to your problem, would you make this purchase?
- When would you like to get started?
- Is there anything I can do to help you with this decision?
- It looks like we have two options for what you need. Would you prefer to choose A or B?
- It is against our policy to push an item on a customer that they really do not need; however, it appears that this (product or service) has exactly what you are looking for and the price is competitive with all others on the market. Are you ready to complete the paperwork?
- During our first meeting, you mentioned that you needed this product or service by July 1st. If you make this decision by Friday of this week, we will be able to meet your deadline and help solve your problem. Does this date sound like something to which you can commit?
- Are you ready to get started? I'll be happy to start the paperwork.
- We have a special price on this product or service that will begin next Monday. Do you want me to save that price for you?

Closing strategies are important, but there are no magic words or phrases that will work every time. That is why you must begin by listening to your potential customer and help the customer identify needs, wants, budget, and deadline to purchase the product or service.

Be a SpeechShark and not a sales shark! There are differences. No one enjoys a slicked-up salesperson whose only concern is the commission they will put in their own pocket. When it is time to make a purchase, customers want an honest salesperson who has their best interest in mind and will help them search to find the right product for the right price and available at the right time. Now, that is a sales strategy that will win every time. And, you will enjoy the benefits of having repeat customers!

Use the Sales Presentation Brainstorming Worksheet to help create your best sales pitch:

SALES PRESENTATION BRAINSTORMING WORKSHEET

Speech Category: Sales Presentation

Speech Title: Give your speech a clever title _____

Specific Purpose: Write a full sentence to show the purpose of your presentation—what are you trying to sell?

_____

_____

Introduction:

Attention Step: Consider how you will get your customer's attention. Write all you plan to say using full sentences.

_____

_____

Establish Need/Relevance: Explain why this product or service should interest the customer. Write all you plan to say using full sentences.

_____

_____

Establish Credibility: Explain why YOU are credible to sell this product or service. Write all you plan to say using full sentences.

_____

_____

Thesis (Preview) Statement: Write a complete sentence that clearly states the three points you will cover:

_____

Point #1: Describe the problem with the product or service the customer has now:

_____

Point #2: Identify the new product or service that will solve the customer's problem:

_____

Point #3: Visualization of the results of solving the problem or the consequences if the problem is NOT solved:

_____

Body:

Transition Sentence: Write a full sentence to transition from the Introduction Step to the first main point.

_____

_____

    I. The Problem:
        A. Discuss the problem they are having.
            1. Support the problem with research.
            2. Support the problem with examples.
        B. Explore the need for purchasing the new product or service.
            1. Identify who or what is negatively affected by this problem.
            2. Use logical and emotional Appeals.

Transition Sentence: Write a full sentence to transition from the first main point to the second.

_____

_____

II. Solution to the Problem—the product or service you plan to sell:
  A. Offer a realistic, detailed explanation of the product or service as a solution to the problem.
     1. Explain how the customer can help to solve the problem.
     2. Provide examples and research to support your solution.
  B. Does your solution solve the problem?
     1. Does your solution affect values, beliefs, attitudes, and behaviors?
     2. Use logical and emotional Appeals.

Transition Sentence: Write a full sentence to transition from the second point to the third point.

_____

_____

III. Visualization of Results
  A. Describe the benefits of using the new product or service.
     1. Does it answer questions of value?
     2. Use descriptions to help audience members visualize benefits.
  B. Consequences if the product or service is not purchased
     1. Use imagery to show the consequences of not purchasing the product or service.
     2. Use examples and descriptions.

Transition Sentence: Write a full sentence to transition from the third main point to the conclusion.

_____

_____

Conclusion:

Summary: Write in full sentence format a summary of your three main points.

Point #1: The Problem _____

Point #2: The Solution to the Problem _____

Point #3: Visualization of Results _____

Appeal to Action: Leave your customer challenged to purchase the product or service and CLOSE THE SALE!

(NOTE: Be sure to add a Works Cited Page as a page separate from the Outline. Include all sources used.)

Works Cited

(Note: If you use Visual Aids, please include a Visual Aid Explanation Page as a page separate from the Works Cited Page and separate from the Outline.)

Visual Aid Explanation Page

SALES PRESENTATION OUTLINE TEMPLATE

Last Name 1

First Name/Last Name
Group Presentation
Day Month Year

Speech Category: Sales Presentation
Title:
Purpose:

Introduction:
Attention Step:
Establish Need/Relevance:
Establish Credibility:

Thesis: Today, As you consider making this purpose, first consider these points: (1) _____,

(2) _____, and (3) _____.

Body:

Transition/Link: First, let's begin with (Point #1).
    I. First Main Point—The Problem with the existing product or service.
        A. Sub-point—examples/research
        B. Sub-point—examples/research

Transition/Link: I've shared (Point #1) with you, now I'd like to tell you about (point #2).
    II. Second Main Point—Identify the new product or service that will solve the customer's problem.
        A. Sub-point—values, beliefs, attitudes, behaviors
        B. Sub-point—logical and emotional appeals

Transition/Link: You've heard about (Point #1 and Point #2), now I'll cover (Point #3).
    III. Third Main Point—Visualization of results
        A. Sub-point—benefits of using the new product or services
        B. Sub-point—consequences of not using the new product or services

Transition/Link: My purpose today is to give you information about (Topic).
Conclusion:
Summary: Today, I shared with you three important points about (Topic):

(1) Point #1_____, (2) Point #2 _____, and

(3) Point #3 _____.

Closing the Sale: End with a strong appeal/closing statement.

(NOTE: Be sure to add a Works Cited Page as a page separate from the Outline. Include all sources used.)

Works Cited

(Note: If you use Visual Aids, please include a Visual Aid Explanation Page as a page separate from the Works Cited Page and separate from the Outline.)

Visual Aid Explanation Page

METHODS OF DELIVERY

Effective delivery does not just happen. You have to plan for it. Delivery is the ability to convey your ideas clearly without distracting the audience. The most effective delivery combines elements of formal oratory skills along with the best attributes of conversational quality—directness, spontaneity, animation, vocal and facial expressiveness, and a sense of lively communication.

To attain effective speech delivery, it is important to relate methods of delivery concepts and skill. You can become a skilled speaker by following a set of guidelines and PRACTICE! You've heard it said, "Practice makes perfect!" Although there is no such thing as a perfect speech, discussed in this chapter are basic delivery guidelines to get you started in the right direction.

When planning your speech, concentrate on such basics as speaking intelligibly, avoiding distracting mannerisms, and establishing eye contact with the audience. Once you get these elements under control and begin to feel fairly comfortable in front of an audience, you can work on polishing your delivery to enhance the impact of your ideas.

Methods (Modes) of Delivery

There are four basic methods of delivering a presentation: (1) reading from a manuscript, (2) reciting from memory, (3) speaking impromptu, and (4) speaking extemporaneously.

MANUSCRIPT

Certain speeches must be delivered word for word, according to a meticulously prepared manuscript. One example would include the State of the Union address delivered by the president. In this situation, absolute accuracy is essential. Every word of the speech will be analyzed by the press and leaders from other nations. In the case of the president, a misused phrase could lead to an international incident.

Although it looks easy, delivering a speech from manuscript requires great skill. Some people do it well, they sound vibrant and conversational, while those lacking in skill come across as boring and artificial. They falter over words, pause in the wrong places, read too quickly or too slowly, speak in a monotone voice, or march through the speech without even glancing at their audience. In this instance, they come across as reading to their listeners, rather than talking to them.

If you are in a situation where you must speak from a manuscript, practice out loud to make sure the speech sounds conversational. Work on establishing eye contact with your listeners. Be certain the final manuscript is legible at a glance. Above all, reach out to your audience with the same directness and sincerity that you would if you were speaking extemporaneously.

MEMORIZED

Actors are known for the practice of presenting the longest and most complex content and dialogue entirely from memory. It is no longer necessary to memorize shorter speeches—toasts, congratulatory remarks, acceptance speeches, introductions, and so on.

If you are giving a speech of this kind and want to memorize it, by all means do so. However, be sure to memorize it so thoroughly that you will be able to concentrate on communicating with the audience, not on trying to remember the words. Speakers who gaze at the ceiling or stare out the window trying to recall what they have memorized are no better off than those who read from a manuscript.

IMPROMPTU

An impromptu speech is delivered with little or no immediate preparation. Few people choose to speak impromptu, but sometimes it cannot be avoided. In fact, many of the speeches you give in life will be impromptu. You might be called on suddenly to "say a few words" or provide feedback during a class discussion.

When such situations arise, don't panic. No one expects you to deliver a perfect speech on the spur of the moment. If you are in a meeting or discussion, pay close attention to what the other speakers say. Take notes of major points with which you agree or disagree. In the process, you will automatically begin to formulate what you will say when it is your turn to speak.

When speaking impromptu, present your speech in these simple steps: First, begin with some type of attention grabber. Second, state the point(s) you wish to make. Third, support your point with appropriate material. Fourth, summarize/conclude your point. This simple method will help you organize your thoughts quickly and clearly.

If time allows, construct a quick outline of your remarks on a piece of paper before you rise to speak. This will help you remember what you want to say and will keep you from getting off topic.

If the situation calls for you to speak from a podium, walk to it calmly, take a deep breath or two (not a visible gasp), establish eye contact with your audience, and begin speaking. No matter how nervous you are inside, do your best to look calm and assured on the outside.

Once you begin speaking, maintain eye contact with the audience. Help the audience keep track of your ideas with signals such as "My first point is . . . ; second, we can see that . . . ; in conclusion, I would like to say . . . " By stating your points clearly and concisely, you will appear organized and confident.

As with other kinds of public speaking, the best way to become a better impromptu speaker is to practice. You can do this on your own. Simply choose a topic on which you are already well informed and give a one- or two-minute impromptu talk on some aspect of that topic. Any topic will do, no matter how serious or frivolous it may be. For practice, you don't need an audience—you can speak to an empty room. You could even record the speech and review it to assess how you sound. The purpose is to gain experience in pulling your ideas together quickly and stating them succinctly.

EXTEMPORANEOUS

An extemporaneous speech is carefully prepared and practiced in advance. In presenting the speech, the extemporaneous speaker uses only a brief set of notes or a speaking outline to jog the memory. The exact wording is chosen at the moment of delivery.

This format is particularly effective for first-time presenters and college students. Once you have your outline (or notes) and know what topics you are going to cover and in which order, you can begin to practice the speech. Each time you rehearse, the wording will be slightly different. As you practice the speech over and over, the best way to present each part will emerge and stick in your mind.

The extemporaneous method has several advantages. It gives more precise control over thought and language than does impromptu speaking, it offers greater spontaneity and directness than does speaking from memory or from a full manuscript, and it is adaptable to a wide range of situations. It also encourages the conversational quality audiences look for in speech delivery.

"Conversational quality" means that no matter how many times a speech has been rehearsed, it still sounds spontaneous. When you speak extemporaneously—and have prepared properly—you have full control over your ideas, yet you are not tied to a manuscript. You are free to establish strong eye contact, to gesture naturally, and concentrate on talking with the audience.

You won't fear a shark attack when you keep your eyes open and are prepared for whatever comes your way! Some refer to shark movements as a feeding frenzy. Truthfully, it is no frenzy at all, but a graceful ballet in which the sharks are fast and swim confidently toward their goal. You can do this too! Be a Communication Shark! Use this section to test your skills and understanding.

Presentation Types and Delivery

1. What are the three basic purposes/types of speeches?

2. What are Informative Speeches?

3. What are Entertaining Speeches?

4. What are Motivational Speeches?

5. What is a good organizational strategy for introducing yourself?

6. What is an Informative Speech often called?

7. What three points should be covered in a Demonstration Speech?

_____

_____

8. Who developed the Motivated Sequence Theory?

_____

9. List the types of Social Occasion Speeches:

_____

_____

10. What strategy works best for a Sales Presentation?

_____

_____

11. List seven strategies important for making the sale:

_____

_____

12. What is the most important concept to consider when achieving effective speech delivery?

_____

_____

13. What are the critical elements of effective speech delivery?

_____

_____

14. What are the four methods/modes of speech delivery?

_____

_____

15. What type speech is used when the speech must be presented word for word?

_____

_____

Shark Bites

BRAINSTORMING A TOPIC

Let's work on a Clustering and Webbing strategy to help you brainstorm your next speech. Start with the speech topic. What three points will you cover? How will you begin the speech? How will you close the speech? Brainstorm the speech organization by filling in each bubble or use your new SpeechShark app to do this for you!

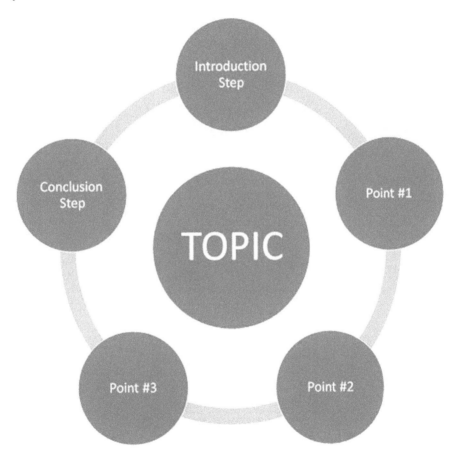

Shark Bites

An excellent way to improve your delivery skills is to read out loud selections from works that require emphasis and feeling. You could select one of your favorite poems or plays that falls into this category.

1. Practice reading the selection out loud. As you read, utilize your voice to make the selection come alive. Vary your volume, rate, and pitch. Find the appropriate places for pauses. Underline the key words or phrases you think should be stressed. Modulate your tone of voice and use inflections for emphasis and meaning. Following these strategies will go a long way toward capturing and keeping the interest of your listeners. If possible, practice reading the selection and record it. Listen to the playback. If you are not satisfied with what you hear, practice the selection and record it again.

2. Listen to a presentation. You could also watch a speaker via TED Talk, or other channels to complete the assignment. Prepare a brief report on the speaker's delivery.

First, analyze the speaker's volume, pitch, rate, pauses, vocal variety, pronunciation, and articulation. Then evaluate the speaker's personal appearance, bodily action, gestures, and eye contact. Explain how the speaker's delivery added to or detracted from what the speaker said. Finally, note at least two techniques of delivery used by the speaker that you might want to try in your next speech.

Chapter Fourteen

Planning and Organizing the Presentation

In this chapter:

Conducting and Audience Analysis

Defining the Purpose

Choosing a Topic

Conducting Research

Understanding Speech Outlines

Constructing the Outline

CONDUCTING AN AUDIENCE ANALYSIS

WILL YOU SINK OR SWIM?

Preparation is the key to success! It is the difference between success and failure and will make the difference in whether you will sink or swim! Never forget that the buck stops with YOU! When facing the task of making a speech presentation, it is your job to plan, prepare, and present the speech. These simple steps to SUCCESS will help you to swim with the sharks!

Even with a great tool, like the SpeechShark app, you still have to make time to work through the plan. The first thing that a speaker should do before planning a speech is to conduct an audience analysis and gain an understanding about the speaking environment.

Once you understand **WHO** is in your audience and **WHERE** you will be speaking, you will be able to make a better decision regarding **WHAT** content to include in the speech.

The following worksheet offers several key questions that you need to ask yourself as you begin the planning process. Take time to answer each of these questions every time you plan for a speech. The questions will lead you to the topic and main points that you should cover.

Conduct an Audience Analysis and Understand the Speaking Environment

Questions to Consider:	Answers to Help Plan:
What is the purpose of the speech?	
When will the speech be presented? (Date/Time of Day)	
Do you have a time limit for the speech?	
Is this speech being directed to a particular type of audience? (Example: Senior Citizens, High School Glee Club, Community Volunteers, etc.)	
What is the occasion for this speech?	
Is there a stage?	
Will you have a lectern for notes?	
Will you need visual aids?	
Will you require a Tech Team for sound, lights, setup, breakdown?	
Will you need a microphone?	
Will someone introduce you or will you introduce yourself?	
How many people will attend the speech?	
How many women will attend?	
How many men will attend?	
Is there a large gender gap?	
What is the average age of audience members?	
Is there a large age gap?	
What is the cultural background of the audience?	
Is there a large cultural gap?	
Are there political and religious differences to consider? If so, explain.	
What is the educational status of the audience?	
Are there restrictions which might limit your topic?	
Will the audience enjoy your topic?	
Will the audience be receptive to you as the speaker?	
What does your audience expect from you?	
What kind of information should you share with your audience?	
What type of clothing should you wear for this audience? Are there certain types of clothing and/or jewelry items that would distract your audience?	
Is this audience formal or casual?	
Are there other factors to consider?	

Once you answer these questions, you have entered the planning stage. All that you have to do at this point is to take a deep breath and dive in. There will be no sinking here—you will swim and you will swim with ease!

All of these steps may seem time-consuming, but if you want to SWIM and not sink, these are details that cannot be overlooked or ignored.

Here is a diagram to help you understand the planning process better:

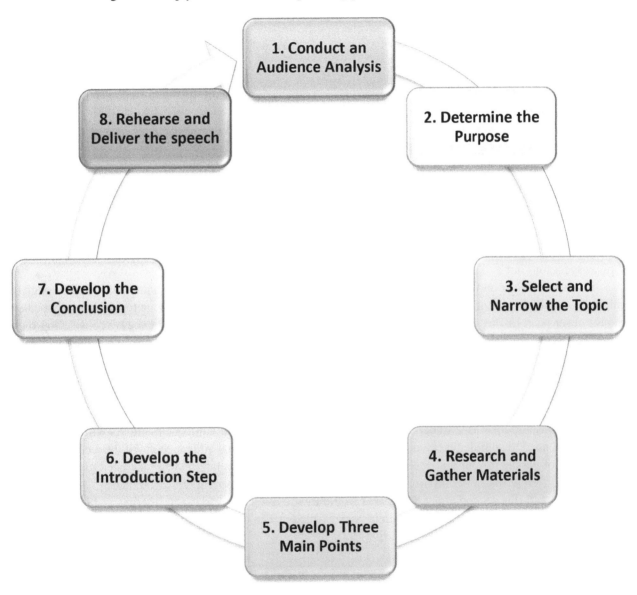

RESPECT DIVERSITY

Since all of us are unique in our own way, it is important that your presentation should be designed to respect everyone in your audience. Most likely, there will be diversity in religious and political beliefs, cultures, genders, age, educational levels, and a multitude of other pre-conceived notions held by each audience member. The larger your audience, the more diversity plays into the way you plan a speech.

Make no assumptions about the beliefs of your audience members and remain ethical by keeping this in mind as you plan presentations. Ethical issues should be considered as you speak and as you listen to the speeches of others. Establish positive ethos by being the kind of person the audience thinks you are based upon what you say and how you project yourself as a speaker.

You've heard the terms ethos, pathos, and logos. These are defined as follows:

Ethos is an appeal to ethics. This is answered as you establish credibility in the introduction section of your speech.

Pathos is an appeal to emotion. This happens as you appeal to the audience's passions or emotions and as you create an emotional response through story telling or argument.

Logos is an appeal to logic. We do this as we reason with our audience and provide logical uses of examples and research to support points we are making in the speech.

The combination of all three (ethos, pathos, and logos) are incorporated as we show respect to our diverse audience members. Know your audience so that you are sure to accomplish these appeals and exhibit respect. Avoid stereotyping and consider situations which might surface. As a speaker, seek to maintain the highest standards of ethics because you are responsible for the content you share with others. As you do this, you will show respect for your audience and they in turn will respect you.

Be aware of the non-verbal cues that are being sent your way during the speech and be flexible enough to change your plan if you notice that audience members are uncomfortable with your topic. A good speaker should never push his/her own agenda on the audience. Show respect for your audience by considering their views and incorporate them into your speech. This will show your audience that you are striving to meet them where they are.

Every person in your audience will have different perspectives, backgrounds, and experiences. We each see, hear, and respond to the world in our own way. It is because of this that we need to learn ways to embrace differences that we have and find common ground to connect with each person in our audience. Your primary responsibility as a speaker is to understand that differences between your audience members will exist. Therefore, you will need to consider every aspect in planning the speech so that your speech will be well received by the majority of people in your audience. In other words, for speaking situations you may need to adapt to others who are different than you and overcome barriers which tend to spotlight our differences.

Before I end this section about diversity, I would like to ask you to go to the Internet and in your search engine bar, type in: TED Talks: Chimamanda Ngozi Adichie: *The Danger of a Single Story.* For your convenience, I will post the URL Address and a link:

https://www.ted.com/talks/chimamanda_adichie_the_danger _of_a_single_story

You've all heard of TED Talks and I'm sure you have spent time watching great speeches through this venue. All of the topics offered in TED Talks are fascinating to me, but this one struck a different chord because of the honesty shared. In less than twenty minutes, this amazing young woman tells a story of the dangers of knowing only one story and not seeing the whole picture.

As I watched this speech, I realized just how guilty **all** of us are. For the most part, we understand our own cultures and we think we understand the cultures of others, but often we do not. It is our own assumptions and perceptions that dictate our innermost thoughts about others from different cultures. Whether we are talking about a culture of gender, age, race, ethnicities, locations, political or religious beliefs, or any number of other categories that we seem to box ourselves and others into, we need to be aware that we may only view that culture as a single story. And, that is wrong. To reach a diverse audience population means that we must look further than the box or category that we perceive as the only story to realize there are always more stories to uncover and more perceptions to understand. Please watch this video and let me know if it also helps you to think in a broader term when planning for your diverse audience members!

What are the most common mistakes beginning speakers make?

The speaker may be confident, have a beautiful voice, and great delivery skills; however, the speech will fall flat if the speech does not contain usable and credible content that will add value to the audience's current knowledge of the topic. Know what your audience needs to know, but also know their current level of understanding about your topic. Choose a topic in which you are the expert and then add to the audience's knowledge base.

How can we avoid these mistakes?

Three simple steps can help avoid mistakes: Plan, Prepare, and Persevere! Plan what you want to say by keeping the audience in mind and understanding the purpose of your speech. Prepare by conducting credible research and including examples that will paint a picture for your audience. Persevere by rehearsing several times until you know your content is being delivered in a manner that is clear, concise, and to the point. The common denominator here is to make sure you conduct an audience analysis. Know your audience and make your plans with them in mind. If you do this, you will be successful!

DEFINING THE PURPOSE

Strategic planning is needed for speeches. Once you understand who will be in your audience, your next step is to define the purpose of the speech. Size up the situation and use this information to make choices to help you reach your goal. Strategic planning includes knowing when to speak, what topics to cover, how to phrase your points, how to explain, how to demonstrate a process or procedure, how to defend a point or motivate your audience to solve a problem, how to organize the message and relate the message to the audience. Making choices are important for strategic planning!

Your speech will have two purposes: a general purpose and a specific purpose. The **general purpose** is the type speech you will present. Are you speaking to inform, entertain, motivate, or perhaps all three? This is your general purpose. The **specific purpose** is more detailed. As you determine the purpose for a speech presentation, you are actually creating a plan to achieve a particular goal. Determining the purpose helps the speaker know what information to share in the body of the speech, how to introduce the topic, and how to conclude the speech.

Here is an example of how this might look on your speech outline:

General Purpose: Inform
Specific Purpose: The purpose of this speech is to inform my audience about the dangers of texting while driving.

General Purpose: Motivate
Specific Purpose: The purpose of this speech is to motivate my audience to give blood at the Red Cross Blood Drive at City Hall next week.

General Purpose: Entertain
Specific Purpose: The purpose of this speech is to entertain my audience as I Roast and Toast our volunteers at the annual end of the year celebration.

GOALS

Having a clear understanding of the purpose of your speech presentation will help you to achieve your speaking goals, develop strategies for a successful presentation, and stay within the time frame that has been offered.

Some use the SWOT strategy to define speaking goals: **S**trengths, **W**eaknesses, **O**pportunities, and **T**hreats. Work through each area analyzing the area and recording your responses. Consider each area as they pertain to the specific speech type that you will be presenting. Each speech is different. Each audience is different. With this in mind, you will want to revisit the SWOT strategy each time you plan a speech.

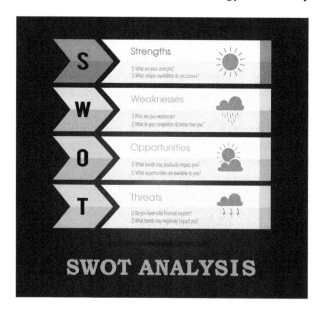

This table will help you understand the goal to achieve a general and specific purpose for each type of speech. Plan to use these suggestions for your general and specific purpose.

Type of Speech	General Purpose	Specific Purpose
Introduction Speech	Inform	The purpose of an Introduction Speech is to introduce yourself or someone else to the audience.
Informative Speech	Inform	The purpose of an Informative Speech is to inform the audience about a topic.
Demonstration Speech	Inform and Entertain	The purpose of a Demonstration Speech is to demonstrate a process or a product.
Persuasion Speech	Motivate	The purpose of a Persuasion Speech is to motivate the audience to solve a problem.
Special Occasion Speech	Inform and/or Entertain	The purpose of a Special Occasion Speech is to inform or entertain an audience through work-related, social, and ceremonial occasions.
Group Presentation	Inform, Entertain, Motivate	The purpose of a group presentation is to present a topic as a group effort with each member taking equal responsibility to inform, entertain, or motivate the audience according to the topic.
Sales Presentation	Motivate	The purpose of the sales presentation is to motivate a buyer to purchase a product or service.

STRATEGIES

Develop a timeline for creating and presenting the speech. Start with the date for the speech and work backward from there. Allow time to conduct the audience analysis, determine the purpose, and select the topic. Critical thinking skills are used during this stage as you plan the topic with the audience and purpose in mind. Once your topic has been selected, narrow the topic and begin conducting research to develop and support your points. Add personal stories and experiences along with research to appear more credible to your audience. Create the presentation outline by starting with the three main points of the body, build the introduction step, and finally, draft the conclusion. Once the outline has been completed, it is time to create a visual aid and handout to support the speech and make presentation notes. The final part of the task is to Rehearse, Rehearse, Rehearse to prepare for a successful presentation. Don't forget to pack supplies for your speech and meet with your Tech Team to make sure all is ready for your presentation! This is the easiest part, Sharks! This is where you are confident because you have taken the time to plan and prepare!

TIME

When asked to speak, make sure you meet with the organizer of the event and find out exactly how much time the organizer needs for you to speak. Plan your speech according to the time frame allotted. Many times, your speech will not be the only point of interest for the event. The organizer will appreciate knowing that you will stay on time because that will mean that her event will also end on time.

Time each rehearsal and take an average of each rehearsal time to get a good idea of the length of time for your speech. If you find that you are going "over time" you will need to cut some of your sub-points. If you find that you are going "under time" you will need to add sub-points. Now, you are almost ready! These details will not "just happen" and it is up to you to make sure that they do happen and at the time that you choose.

The SpeechShark app has a handy timer built in. Simply choose the amount of time you will need to complete your speech and the app will remind you when you need to move from one point to the next. Just another way that you can swim with ease through murky waters!

CHOOSING A TOPIC

SEARCHING FOR A TOPIC?

Now that you have conducted an audience analysis and determined the purpose of your upcoming presentation, you can begin to think of a topic that will interest your audience and a topic for which you have experience and prior knowledge! This can be an overwhelming task and you might feel like you are a shark circling the waters for just the right target. Truthfully, that is not too far from reality.

When asked to speak for a particular event, you may not have the luxury of choosing a topic because it may be assigned to you; however, you still have the freedom to plan, develop, and add your own personal touch to the topic. For this type situation, it is a good idea to meet with the organizer of the event and ask about their expectations. Some speakers have been known to make phone calls to random audience members to ask what topic they would like to hear and to pinpoint information that is relevant for their personal or professional situations.

If you are still having trouble settling on the topic for your presentation, look through books or magazines for inspiration. Meet with friends and colleagues to brainstorm possible topic choices. Listen to news stations or read news articles to pick up on trending topics. Dive into the Internet and search "Speech Topics" to see what you find. There are billions of topics. Choose the one that is right for your audience and the one that is right for you! Once you have your topic, you will be able to choose three main points, sub-points in the form of research, personal stories, and examples, and create your message to make it memorable for your audience!

NARROWING THE TOPIC

Narrowing the topic is one part of the process involved with choosing a topic. In a short five- to ten-minute speech, you will not be able to cover everything there is to say about the topic. With this in mind, it becomes necessary to narrow the topic to a manageable size.

Here is an example: You LOVE sports, so you are thinking about giving a speech about sports. But, sports is a huge topic and can't be covered in less than ten minutes. Choose one type of sport. Do you want to talk about baseball, basketball, tennis, soccer, racquetball, swimming, skydiving, biking, golf, running, boating, parasailing, skydiving, zip lining, or—Oh My Goodness! Do you see the problem with this? There are so many sports and I love them, ALL! How do I choose? Well, it is obvious you can't speak about all of them in less than ten minutes.

Settle on one **type** of sport and then from that category, narrow the large topic down to a smaller manageable **category**. You are still not finished. Break that down again into a **point** about that sport that is interesting. Almost done . . . Narrow that point into three clear **points**! Aha, now you are swimming and thinking like a SpeechShark!

Here is a way to narrow a topic:

TOPIC
- Topic - **SPORTS**

TYPE
- Narrow this broad topic to a type of sport that is interesting for the audience and for you.
- **Tennis**

Category
- Narrow the topic of tennis to one category.
- **Professional Tennis**

Point
- Narrow the category to a more specific point
- **Types of Tennis Courts**

Points
- Narrow the point into three support points
- **(1) Clay , (2) Hard, (3) Grass**

Does this help you understand the process? Often people try to make speeches without really thinking about the points they will cover. It's time to get to the point. Think of specific and clear points that will add information to your audience's existing knowledge.

Why not give this a try with your own topic for the next speech? Write your answers here:

Topic

- Topic

Type

- Narrow the broad topic to a type

Category

- Narrow the type to a category

Point

- Narrow the category to a point

Points

- Narrow this into three points
- 1.
- 2.
- 3.

Topic Suggestions to Get You Thinking

Informative Speech Topics:	
Bargain Shopping	Learning Disabilities
Body Piercings	Learning How to Knit
Carpooling Tips	Meditation
Cloning	Privacy Rights
College Requirements	Recycling
Coping with Online Courses	Rescuing Pets
Dressing for Success	Smoking Policies
Facebook Security	Television Viewing Habits
Finding Balance	To Tweet or Not to Tweet?
Going Green	Volunteering in Homeless Shelters
Home-schooling	Wikis are Wonderful
Healthcare Options	Working from Home
Kid-Friendly Activities	Would you like to go Skydiving?
Labor Unions	Zip-Lining in Costa Rica
Learning a Foreign Language	Zoo Animals at Risk

Demonstration Speech Topics – Notice They All Begin with "How to . . ."	
How to Arrange Flowers	How to Light a Fire
How to Ask for a Date	How to Make Ice Cream
How to Bake a Cake	How to Make a Mojito
How to Belly Dance	How to Pack a Suitcase
How to Change a Tire	How to Plan a Party
How to Clean Shoes	How to Rearrange Your Closet
How to Fold a Flag	How to Sew on a Button
How to Grate Carrots	How to Sing a Lullaby
How to Hang Christmas Lights	How to Tune a Guitar
How to Juggle Three Balls	How to Write a Speech

Persuasion Speech Topics – Notice the Topics All Begin with an Action Word	
Adopt a Grandparent	Go Back to School
Avoid Artificial Sweeteners	Grow a Vegetable Garden
Apply for Scholarships	Invest in Your Future
Ban Beauty Pageants	Join a Club
Be a Mentor	Join a Community Theater
Become a Vegetarian	Learn to Cook
Buy Organic	Learn to Play
Care for Your Elders	Lose Weight
Donate Blood	Lower the Drinking Age
Don't Text and Drive	Make a "Bucket" List
Dress for Success	Practice Safe Sex
Eat Healthy	Prayer in Schools
Exercise	Register to Vote
Keep Prayer in Schools	Save Money
Search Your Family History	Support the Arts
Make a Bucket List	Teach Children to Save Money
Freedom of Speech	Train Your Dog

Group Presentation Topics:
Choosing a College (Report on different aspects: history, courses, sports, campus life, cost)
Creating a Bucket List (travel, adventure, learning a new skill, volunteering)
Health Benefits of Exercising (heart, lungs, muscles, mental)
Making Money (time involved, benefits, getting started, mentor/mentee)
Movies to Remember (categories, story lines, themes, genres)
Plan a Meal (include recipes: appetizers, soup, salad, main course, desserts, beverages)
Plan a Trip (who, when, where, how)
Report on a Country (culture, foods, government, sports, traditions)
Sales Presentation (product, demonstration, costs, benefits)
Volunteer Opportunities (time, money, benefits, getting started)

If you are using the SpeechShark app (www.SpeechShark.com), there is a section early in the development stage where you will be prompted to share the topic of your speech. Before you begin that process, make sure you know the answer!

Whether you have been given a topic or if you can choose a topic, you will want to answer important questions to create a strategic plan.

Here is a guide to help choose the topic for your next speech.

Write Your Topic Choice Here: _____ Answer These Questions:	YES	NO
Does your topic satisfy the general purpose for the presentation?		
Is your topic narrow enough to be completed within your allotted time?		
Will your audience relate to the topic?		
Will this topic be meaningful to the audience?		
Can you add information about the topic that your audience may not already know?		
Is this topic appropriate for your audience? Consult your audience analysis again and examine the topic as it will appeal to diverse audiences.		
Is the topic you have chosen controversial?		
Will your audience be receptive to a controversial topic?		
Are you passionate about this topic?		
Are you excited about sharing this topic with others? Remember, enthusiasm is contagious. If you are excited and enthusiastic about the topic, there is a good chance that your audience will "catch" your enthusiasm.		
Can you choose three points to develop for this topic? List the three points here: 1. 2. 3.		
Do you need to conduct research to support your topic?		
What type of research do you need?		
Do you have personal stories and experience about this topic to share?		
Can you provide simple examples of your main points that are clear and easily understood?		
Will you need to supply your audience with a handout after the speech?		
Will you need to create a PowerPoint or Prezi Presentation as a visual aid?		
Will you have a Tech Team to handle your visual aids?		
Can you think of a creative way to introduce this topic to your audience?		
Is the setting for the speech conducive to this topic?		

CONDUCTING RESEARCH

Now that you have chosen a topic for your speech, it is time to develop your understanding of the topic by conducting research. During the research process, speakers will often refine three main points or use research they have gathered to craft sub-points. Information found during research can be used as the attention step, the conclusion, or as support for main points within your speech.

Research can come in the form of data, statistics, opinions, or ideas, but can also be as simple as someone's experience or a story that supports your topic. It is up to you to decide what type of research will be most effective for your particular topic. Speakers also use videos, music, art, photography, and other mediums to support points or create visual aids to support the speech topic. In all cases, if it does not belong to you, it is necessary to cite the source.

Research is defined as the process for finding support materials and credible information. This information will be added to your already vast knowledge of the topic you have chosen to cover. One mistake people often make is to use a base search engine on the Internet to find support material. While this is a simple way to conduct research, it does not always promise credible results.

Read the research guidelines and methods in this chapter to learn the best way to use online resources to support your topic. Credible research will help you appear more credible as a speaker. On the other hand, weak research choices can undermine your speaker credibility and may create confusion, especially if sources are not vetted and reviewed.

As you begin to conduct research, please follow these simple checkpoints:

- ✔ Use research that is current: preferably less than five years old.
- ✔ Use research that is credible. Avoid using Wikis, blogs, advertisements, or Web pages.
- ✔ Use research that will support the topic and your view of the topic.
- ✔ Use research that will clarify the topic.
- ✔ Use research that will expand your knowledge of the topic.
- ✔ Use research that has been written or published by recognizable credible sources.

In years past, the only way that someone could conduct research was to visit a brick-and-mortar library and spend hours looking through books and reference materials. Once the desired article or data was found, the research would need to be photocopied or typed into a document. Thankfully, finding credible research now is simply a click away as most of us conduct research using the Internet. If you do choose to visit a library to conduct research, you will be pleasantly surprised by the amount of online materials available through the library and also by the helpfulness of local librarians to help narrow down sources to find the most useful and productive sources for your topic.

Whether you conduct research online or at the library, you may find it helpful to create a speech materials file to store articles which may prove helpful as you plan your speech. Online articles can be e-mailed to yourself and digital files can be created to store quotes, data, brainstorming ideas, anecdotes, or stories to support your topic. This will be helpful as you sift through possible sources searching for the two or three best sources to serve your needs.

Plagiarism

We can't talk about research without including tips to avoid plagiarism. The interesting thing about plagiarism is that it can occur verbally as well as in writing, so make sure you cite everything you use that is not your own. **Plagiarism** is the act of using someone else's ideas or work as if they are your own. In essence, this is stealing and in the educational and professional arena, plagiarism is an act which may lead to immediate dismissal. Copyright laws are in place to protect authors of written works.

The best way to avoid plagiarism charges is to verbally or in writing cite everything that belongs to someone else. Turnitin.com is a Web site that checks for plagiarism. Many colleges and universities use this site regularly to check students' work for plagiarism. In the corporate world, a plagiarism charge can harm your reputation and career. Just to be safe, always verbally and in writing cite the source of research and give proper credit. Citation guidelines are noted toward the end of this chapter.

Guidelines

How do you know if a source of research is credible? Blogs on the Internet can appear to be quite credible. They can be written and posted by someone with a Ph.D., but even that will not determine if the source is credible. Often blogs or Wikis will provide interesting or amusing information, but that also does not determine if the source is credible. Interesting or amusing does not equal credible. With this in mind, I always warn the speech students that I coach to never use a blog, Wiki, or advertisement link—no matter how legitimate it may sound. The point is to evaluate the research and make decisions regarding whether or not the source is credible and offers information you can use to support your speech.

Use credible research owned, reviewed, and monitored by reputable organizations, government sources, newspapers, journals, books, and magazine sources. Stay away from blogs, Wikis, and advertisements which might link to credible sources, but are not credible in their own rights.

Use the following checklist to determine if the source is credible:

☐ Would my audience recognize the source?

☐ Does the source list an author?

☐ Does the author have credentials to verify his/her credibility?

☐ Does the source list copyright information?

☐ Was this source published within the past five years?

☐ Is the content clear and helpful? Is the content accurate and unbiased?

☐ Does the content offer opposing viewpoints?

☐ Does the content support my topic?

Research Methods

Gathering materials online has never been easier than it is right now. Through the Internet, online research has become the primary source for gathering information for college students and professionals. The Internet can be an incredible source for locating great information, but it is also a source for spreading misinformation! Take care to choose sources of research from credible sources and confirm that the information you share with your audiences is something that will clarify the topic and not confuse your audience.

The **Internet** is one of the most popular go-to sources for people who want to conduct research for any topic in the world. Online search engines like Google, Bing, Yahoo, and Google Scholar have become quite popular. Do not rely solely upon Google; however, if you search Google Scholar, it is possible to find credible research for your speech. Print materials from periodicals, newspapers, encyclopedias, dictionaries, journals, and books are also available through the Internet in digital formats.

Many states offer credible online search engines for a small fee. A student in any of the state of Georgia high schools, technical colleges, community colleges, and university systems are able to use the well-known virtual library called GALILEO (Georgia, Library of Learning Online). Everything in GALILEO is credible. Students are able to search, save, e-mail sources, and get citation help through this easy to navigate system. Many of the sites found in GALILEO offer audio versions of articles, as well as translations into many other languages. Other states have programs similar to GALILEO to help with student research.

Through various search engines, we are able to use key words in a search window to limit the search and to make the research process simpler. The downside is that search engines usually provide a broad expanse of materials, all of which are not credible or relevant for the topic you have chosen. Directories, on the other hand, allow people to link with key words or matches regarding the topic and are manned by a librarian who chooses the prospective sites based upon the quality of that site.

Here are other options:

- **Government and survey sites** such as the Gallup Polls offer reliable information that can be used as support materials.
- **Libraries** often have resources that cannot be found online; therefore, you may want to visit your local library as you conduct research for your speech.
- **Magazines and journals** are the most common forms of research and are readily available in hard copy and online.
- **Television and radio programs** provide transcripts of trending stories that can be used as support for speeches.
- **Newspapers**, available in hard copy and online, offer current and trending information about topics of interest.
- **Books** are an excellent source of information, but readers should understand that it takes months for books to be published and the information contained in a book may not be the very latest information released to the public. Be sure to check the copyright date before using a book.
- **Interviews** are a perfect way to get stories and personal experience about your topic. Just make sure your interviewee is a credible source for your topic.

When using **key words** to initiate a search, take care to spell the key words correctly, use nouns and avoid using more than six words per search. If your search is not successful, try using different key words. As you type in key words into the search box, you will notice that other popular searches will pop up. Sometimes following the pop-up trails will lead to sources that are useful, but other times they will not.

Research is a way to find the answers you need to support points and explore facts that will make you appear more credible to your audience.

Just remember that conducting research is a process. It's like fishing. You have to bait a lot of hooks before you catch the prize fish. With research, you have to review a lot of sources before you find the right data, anecdote, or information to support the point you want to make!

WRITTEN CITATIONS OF RESEARCH

Let's talk about citation of sources, since this is a big responsibility for the speaker! First, you should know that there are different ways to cite research. The most frequently used citation styles are APA, MLA, CSE, and CMS. With each style, you will notice a specific set of rules and guidelines established to indicate the author, title, publishing source, date of publication, and page numbers of the source.

Additionally, you will notice there are different ways to cite each type of source, whether it is a book, e-book, dissertations, Web sites, radio or television episodes, videos or film clips, magazines, journals, or newspaper articles, music, art, or pictures.

How do you know which style to use and what makes each style unique? Each style is formulated for a particular discipline. If you are not tasked with using one specific guideline, then please follow the notations below to make sure you are using the style most suited for the topic you are covering. We have also included the links to their Web sites so that you can go directly to the source to see clear instructions regarding how to cite the source of research in your outline or document.

Here is a breakdown of styles, a notation of when they should be used, and the link to their Web sites:

APA is known as the American Psychological Association style of citing research. Disciplines that cover psychology, sociology, social work, criminology, education, business, and economics may use the APA style of citing research. For APA Guidelines, please visit their website at http://www.apastyle.org/.

MLA is known as the Modern Language Association style of citing research. Documents using research for literature and language will use this style of citing research. Since you are learning about public speaking and crafting speeches to inform, persuade, and entertain, you will need to cite your sources of research using the MLA Guidelines for source citations. We'll provide examples of MLA citations in this book. For MLA Guidelines, please visit their website at https://www.mla.org/MLA-Style.

CSE citations follow the guidelines established by the Council of Science Editors and are used primarily when the writer or speaker is citing research in the applied sciences areas. These will include biology, chemistry, physics, astronomy, and earth science. For CSE Guidelines, please visit their website at https://www.councilscienceeditors.org/publications/scientific-style-and-format/.

CMS is known as the Chicago Manual of Style. These guidelines are used to cite research that involve the arts and humanities. For CMS Guidelines, please visit their website at http://www.chicagomanualofstyle.org/home.html.

VERBAL CITATIONS OF RESEARCH

Whether in writing or verbally, any source of research used must be cited. To avoid plagiarism charges during your speech, cite every source you use. In recent news, we learned of a case where one prominent politician plagiarized the words and ideas of another. The words used were so identical that the news reporters and commentators had a field day reporting how this one person blatantly used the very same words as the other. It was quite embarrassing for the politician, who then made a formal statement apologizing for the error. Make sure that you do not find yourself in the same situation.

When you are speaking to an audience and you want to support your point with a credible source of research, it is important to give a verbal indication that you are using someone else's work, ideas, or opinions. The best way to do this is to lead into the research and then indicate whether you are offering a direct quote of the research or paraphrasing the information. Audience members cannot see when the research begins or ends as they do when reading your written document and having the benefit of a parenthetical citation. For this reason, it is the speaker's responsibility to clearly detail the research verbally.

Transition into the research using a signal word which offers a cue for your audience that you are going to cite a source. Vary the signal words you use as the transition and use words that move nicely into the information you are sharing. Here is a short list of signal words that you might use: said, claims, asserts, denies, disputes, expresses, generalizes, implies, lists, maintains, offers, states, suggests, responds, replies, reveals, acknowledges, advises, or believes. Here is an example of how you might use these words:

> **Example of a verbal citation of a direct quote:** In his 2013 New York Times Bestseller book titled *Cooked*, Michael Pollan said this about bread, and I quote, "One way to think about bread—and there are so many . . . is simply this: as an ingenious technology for improving the flavor, digestibility, and nutritional value of grass." End quote.

This process will involve indicating the author's name, the title of the article or the title of the book, and the publication date—not necessarily in that order. If it is a direct quote, you will add the words, ". . . and I quote." Following the direct quote, you will end with the words, ". . . end quote."

PARAPHRASING

If paraphrasing, you will indicate the author's name, the title of the article or the title of the book and the publication date, just as you would for a direct quote. Then you will announce that you are paraphrasing the content. This allows your listener to know where your research begins and where it ends. The listener will know which words belong to the author of the source and which words belong to you. This can be a bit tricky, but with a little practice, you will find that inserting this information as you use a source of research will also help you to appear more credible for your audience. It is easier to paraphrase thoughts, opinions, or ideas, such as the following:

> **Example of a verbal citation of a paraphrased quote:** I would like to paraphrase a unique perception held by Michael Pollan in his 2013 New York Times Bestseller book titled *Cooked*. As the author was talking about bread, he explained how a great recipe can produce something extremely delicious, even though it is nothing more than grass.

Notice in the paraphrase example, the speaker still needed to transition to the research material, supply the author's name, the title of the book, and then paraphrase the idea of the information read in the book.

Some research can NOT be paraphrased. This would include information that includes numbers, dates, proper names, and places. For example, you cannot paraphrase the number 12,643,279. That number is too precise to be paraphrased. For the same reason, you cannot paraphrase June 30, 1935. To paraphrase these, you will need to generalize the information. You can do that by saying "over twelve million" or for the date you could say toward the middle of 1935. The same is true for a person's name or the name of a place. For example, you cannot paraphrase Savannah, Georgia. What do you think you would say, if you needed to paraphrase a person's name? How you would paraphrase the name of a city and state? When do you think paraphrasing would be appropriate?

CITING PRESENTATION AIDS

Citations also need to be included in your visual aids. The only time you will not need to cite visual aids will be if the visual aid belongs to you or if it is considered **public domain**. Merriam-Webster's Online Dictionary defines public domain as "the realm embracing property rights that belong to the community at large, are unprotected by copyright or patent, and are subject to appropriation by anyone" *("Public Domain").* Here is an example of a PowerPoint slide with a picture that belongs to me and therefore does not need to be cited:

Here is an example of using a picture that does not belong to me and is <u>not</u> public domain. In this case, I included a full citation on the PowerPoint slide where the picture is shown. It is not good to have a Works Cited slide at the end of your PowerPoint Presentation because the audience will not know which citation goes with which picture. Cite the picture in the footer area of the slide where the picture is shown.

Woman Traveler is Planning a Tour. 2018 © https://www.shutterstock.com/
Accessed 1 June 2018.

ADDING PERSONAL STORIES

Storytelling, personal stories, anecdotes, even hypothetical examples are ways to add interest to your speeches. While it is good to have credible sources to support points, don't forget to always add the human element by including stories. Whether they are your own personal stories or stories from some of your friends or family, including this into your speech will make your topics so much more interesting for the audience.

This is a good time to use material discovered while conducting a personal interview with an interviewee who has experience with your topic. Asking questions and receiving personal stories and information from the interviewee will provide strong material to support points during your speech. Don't forget to also verbally cite the sources for your stories!

Example of a verbal citation of an interview: Last week I was able to interview Mr. Thaddeus Nifong, who is a public speaking instructor and advises a college Toastmasters International Club. During the personal interview, I asked Mr. Nifong what is one of the biggest challenges of advising a college club? Mr. Nifong revealed, and I quote, "The biggest challenge of advising a college Toastmasters International Club is to continually recruit officers and members. College members are going to graduate, transfer to other colleges, and sometimes life just gets in the way. It is because of this that our club officers and members are continuously recruiting and spreading the word about this great club on our campus! With that said, yes, there are challenges, but the rewards far outweigh the challenges when you can become involved as a college club advisor." End quote.

As you can see, when verbally citing a personal interview, it is important to use a transition to lead into the quote, include the interviewee's name, tell your audience why you chose to interview this person based upon his experience, and set the stage for the response. Here is another way to think about it:

1. Transition to citation
2. State the interviewee's full name
3. State the interviewee's credentials
4. Share the question asked
5. Share the response

If you are including a direct quote, preface the quote with . . . "and I quote" before sharing the quote. Following the quote, it is important to conclude with . . . "End quote." In doing this, the audience will clearly differentiate between the words said by the interviewee and your own words. When paraphrasing content within the interview, include all of the information shown above, but indicate that you are paraphrasing instead of using a direct quote.

UNDERSTANDING SPEECH OUTLINES

ORGANIZATION IS IMPORTANT

There are many studies that show the importance of organization in effective speechmaking. Your audience will expect a cohesive and coherent presentation, so you the presenter must be sure the audience will be able to follow the progression of ideas in your presentation from start to finish. This requires that speeches be organized strategically. They should be put together in particular ways to achieve particular results with particular audiences.

Speech organization is important for other reasons as well. It is closely connected to critical thinking. When you work to organize your speeches, you gain practice in the general skill of establishing clear relationships among your ideas. In addition, using a clear, specific method of speech organization can boost your confidence as a speaker and improve your ability to deliver a message fluently.

STRATEGIC ORDER OF MAIN POINTS

Once you establish your main points, you need to decide the order in which you will present them. The most effective order depends on three things—your topic, your purpose, and your audience. Below are the five basic patterns of organization used most often by public speakers.

> **Chronological Order:** Speeches arranged chronologically follow a time pattern. They follow a series of events in the sequence in which they happened. Chronological order is also used in speeches explaining a process or demonstrating how to do something.
>
> **Topical Order:** Topical order results when you divide the speech topic into subtopics, each of which becomes a main point in the speech.
>
> **Spatial Order:** Speeches arranged in spatial order follow a directional pattern or geographical location. That is, the main points proceed from top to bottom, left to right, east to west, or some other route.
>
> **Casual Order:** Speeches arranged in causal order organize main points so as to show a cause-effect relationship. When you put your speech in causal order, you have two main points—one dealing with the causes of an event, the other dealing with its effects. Depending on your topic, you can deal first with the effects and then with the causes.
>
> **Problem-Solution Order:** Speeches arranged in problem-solution order are divided into two main parts. The first shows the establishment of a problem. The second presents a workable solution to the problem.

KEYS FOR MAIN POINTS

1. Keep main points separate
2. Use the same pattern of wording for main points
3. Balance the amount of time devoted to main points

Because your main points are so important, you want to be sure you allow sufficient time to develop each main point. This is not to say that all main points must receive exactly equal emphasis, but only that they should be roughly balanced. The amount of time spent on each main point depends on the amount and complexity of supporting materials for each point.

As you can see, clear organization is vital to speechmaking. Audience members demand coherence. They get only one chance to grasp the presenter's ideas, and they have little patience for presenters who ramble aimlessly from one idea to another. A well-organized speech will enhance your credibility and make it easier for the audience to understand your message.

The process of planning the body of a speech begins when you determine the main points. You should choose them carefully, phrase them precisely, and organize them strategically. Because audience members cannot keep track of a multitude of main points, most speeches should contain no more than two to five.

Supporting materials are the backup ideas for your main points. When organizing supporting materials, make sure they are directly relevant to the main points they are supposed to support.

Organize main points in various ways, depending on your topic, purpose, and audience. Chronological order follows a time pattern, whereas spatial order follows a directional pattern. In causal order, main points are organized according to their cause-effect relationship. Topical order results when you divide your main topic into subtopics. Problem-solution order breaks the body of the speech into two main parts—the first showing a problem, the second giving a solution.

Research studies confirm that clear organization is vital to effective public speaking. Your audience must be able to follow the progression of ideas in a speech from beginning to end.

Outlines are essential to effective speeches. It allows you to see the full scope and content of your speech. By outlining, you can determine if each part of the speech is fully developed, whether you have adequate supporting materials for your main points, and if the main points are properly balanced.

You will likely utilize two kinds of outlines for your speeches—one very detailed, for the planning stage (Preparation Outline) and one very brief, for the delivery of the speech (Presentation or Speaking Outline).

TYPES OF OUTLINES

The **preparation outline** is just what its name implies—an outline that helps you prepare the speech. Writing a preparation outline means putting your speech together—deciding what you will say in the introduction, how you will organize the main points and supporting materials in the body, and what you will say in the conclusion.

GUIDELINES FOR THE PREPARATION OUTLINE

A relatively uniform system for preparation outlines is explained below; however, you should check with your instructor to see what format you are to follow.

State Purpose of Your Speech

The purpose statement should be a separate unit that comes before the outline itself. Including the purpose makes it easier to assess how well you have constructed the speech to accomplish your purpose.

Label the Introduction, Body, and Conclusion

If you label the parts of your speech, be sure that you have an introduction and conclusion and have accomplished the essential components of each. Generally, the names of the speech parts are placed in the middle of the page or in the far left margin.

Use a Consistent Pattern of Symbolization and Indentation

In the most common system of outlining, main points are identified by Roman numerals and are indented equally so as to be aligned down the page. **Sub-points** (components of the main points) are identified by capital letters and are also indented equally so as to be aligned with each other. Here is an example of how your main point should look:

I. Main point

   A. Sub-point

   B. Sub-point

      1. Sub-sub-point

      2. Sub-sub-point

As outlines are essential to speechmaking, develop an outline to help ensure that the structure of your speech is clear and coherent. Once you have organized the body of your speech, identify the main points. The most important ideas (main points) are farthest to the left. Less important ideas (sub-points, sub-sub-points, and so on) are progressively farther to the right. This pattern reveals the structure of your entire speech.

Use sub-points and sub-sub-points, as necessary, to support the main points. Stating your main points and sub-points in full sentences will ensure that you develop your ideas fully.

Label Transitions

One way to make sure you have strong transitions is to include them in the preparation outline. Usually they are not incorporated into the system of symbolization and indentation but are labeled separately and inserted in the outline where they will appear in the speech.

Attach a Bibliography or Works Cited Page

Include with the outline a bibliography or Works Cited page depending upon the citation guideline you follow that shows all books, magazines, newspapers, and Web sources you consulted, as well as any interviews or independent research you conducted.

The two major bibliographic formats are those developed by the Modern Language Association (MLA) and the American Psychological Association (APA). Both are widely used by communication scholars; ask your instructor which he or she prefers.

Preparation Outline Checklist:

- Have I stated the purpose statement?
- Have I labeled the introduction, body, and conclusion?
- Are my main points and sub-points written in full sentences?
- Have I labeled transition sentences?
- Does my outline follow a consistent pattern of symbolization and indentation?
- Does my bibliography identify all the sources I consulted in preparing the outline?
- Does the bibliography follow the format required by my instructor?

The **Speaking Outline (also called a Presentation Outline)** is a condensed version of your preparation outline. The goal of your speaking outline is to help you remember what you want to say. It should only contain key words or phrases to jog your memory, as well as essential content you don't want to forget. But it should also include material not in your preparation outline, such as cues to sharpen your delivery. See the basic guidelines below.

GUIDELINES FOR THE SPEAKING OUTLINE

- Your speaking outline should use the same framework as your preparation outline.

- Make the outline legible.

- Your speaking outline must be instantly readable at a distance.

- As you work on your outline, organize it into three main points, each with two supporting points. Compose an outline that organizes the points in this manner. Some presenters opt to place speaking notes on index cards. It is best to select either 3 × 5 size or 4 × 6 size.

- Keep the outline brief. If your notes are too detailed, you will have difficulty maintaining eye contact with your audience. A detailed outline will tempt you to look at it far too often.

Keep your speaking outline as brief as possible. Most presenters use too many notes. You do not need all of them to remember the speech, and will find that too many notes can actually interfere with the presentation. Limit information to key words or phrases to help you remember major points and connectives. The best rule is that your notes should be the minimum you need to jog your memory and keep you on track.

Creating Useful Notes for Delivering the Speech

An effective speaking outline reminds you not only of what you want to say but also of how you want to say it. It is imperative to include in your speaking outline delivery cues—directions for delivering the speech. One way to do this is by highlighting key ideas that you want to be sure to emphasize. Then, when you reach them in the outline, you will be reminded to stress them. Another way is to jot down on the outline explicit cues such as "pause," "repeat," "slow down," "louder," "breathe," etc.

Outlines are essential to effective speeches. By outlining, you make sure that your thoughts flow from one to another, and that the structure of your speech is coherent. You will probably use two kinds of outlines for your speeches—the detailed preparation outline and the brief speaking outline.

In the preparation outline, you state your purpose, label the introduction, body, and conclusion, and designate transitions and connectives. You should identify main points and sub-points by a consistent pattern of symbolization and indentation.

The speaking outline should contain key words or phrases to jog your memory. Be sure your speaking outline is legible and includes cues for delivering the speech.

CONSTRUCTING THE OUTLINE

The first step in constructing an outline is to master the three basic parts of a speech—introduction, body, and conclusion—and the strategic role of each. We will focus on the body of the speech, in addition to the introduction and the conclusion.

There are good reasons for talking first about the body of the speech. The body is generally the longest and most important part. Also, you will prepare the body first. It is easier to create an effective introduction after you know exactly what you will say in the body. The process of organizing the body of a speech begins when you determine the main points.

MAIN POINTS (BODY)

The main points are the central features of your speech. You should select them carefully, phrase them precisely, and arrange them strategically.

How do you select your main points? Sometimes they will be evident from your specific purpose statement. Your main points may not be so easy to determine. Often, they will emerge as you conduct research and evaluate content to include in your presentation.

NUMBER OF MAIN POINTS

You will not have time during your speeches to develop more than four to five main points, and most speeches will contain only two or three. Regardless of how long a speech might last, if you have too many main points, the audience will have a difficult time keeping track of them in your presentation.

The Introduction

First impressions are important. A poor first impression may alienate the audience, so the presenter getting off on the correct foot is vital.

In most speech situations, the introduction has four objectives: (1) gain the attention and interest of your audience, (2) reveal the topic of your speech, (3) establish your credibility and goodwill, and (4) preview the body of the speech.

GAIN ATTENTION AND INTEREST

A presenter can lose an audience if they do not utilize the introduction to gain attention and interest. Gaining the initial attention of your audience is usually easy; however, keeping the attention of your audience once you start talking is more difficult. Discussed below are the most common methods utilized in presentations. Whether you choose to incorporate them individually or in combination, they will assist with engaging the audience in your speech.

Startle the audience: One way to arouse interest quickly is to startle your audience with an intriguing statement. This technique is highly effective and easy to implement. Be sure the startling introduction relates directly to the content of your presentation.

Arouse curiosity of the audience: People are curious. One way to draw them into your speech is with a series of statements that progressively engage their curiosity about the content of the speech. By building suspense about a subject, the presenter pulls the audience into the speech.

Question the audience: Asking a rhetorical question is another way to get your audience thinking about your presentation. Sometimes a single question will do. The audience will answer mentally, not out loud.

In other circumstances, you may want to pose a series of questions. When utilizing this technique, be sure to pause for just a moment after each question. This will give the question time to sink in. The audience could respond with a verbal response, or with a show of hands.

Begin with a quotation: Another way to arouse the interest of your audience is to start with an attention-getting quotation. You don't need to use a famous quotation. Generally, quotations are relatively short. Opening your speech with a lengthy quotation can bore your audience.

Tell a story: We all enjoy hearing stories, particularly if they are dramatic and have us on the edge of our seats. You can also use stories based on your personal experience. In some cases, this will expose your vulnerability, however it is worth it. Be sure to use vivid language to tell the audience members a story that they may or may not have experienced.

Relate topic to the audience: People pay attention to things that impact them directly. If you can relate the topic to your audience, they are much more likely to be interested in it.

State importance of your topic: This technique can be utilized when discussing social and political issues such as poverty, endangered species, and domestic violence, but it is appropriate for other topics as well. Whenever you discuss a topic whose importance may not be clear to the audience, you should think about ways to demonstrate its significance in the introduction.

Speech Introduction Checklist:

- Have I gained the attention and interest of my audience by using one or more of the methods discussed in this chapter?

- How do I relate the speech topic to my audience?

- How do I establish my credibility to speak on this topic?

- Have I defined any key terms that will be necessary for the audience to understand my speech?

- Have I provided a preview of the main points to be covered in the body of the speech?

- Is my introduction limited to ten to twenty percent of my entire speech?

- Have I practiced the delivery of my introduction so I can present it fluently, confidently, and with strong eye contact?

As you work on your presentations, work to craft an introduction that will capture the attention of your audience. It should arouse the interest of the audience and allow them to become emotionally invested in the speech.

The effectiveness of any introduction, particularly with a personal one, will rely on the presenter's delivery as well as on the content. The methods discussed are the ones used most often by speakers to gain attention and interest. Other methods include referring to the occasion, inviting the audience to participate, using a video or audio clip, visual aids, and beginning with humor. For the presentation, choose the method that is most suitable for the topic, the audience, and the occasion.

REVEAL THE TOPIC and ESTABLISH RELEVANCE FOR THE TOPIC

In the process of gaining attention, be sure to state clearly the topic of your speech. This is a basic point—so basic that it may hardly seem worth mentioning.

ESTABLISH CREDIBILITY

Besides getting attention and revealing the topic, you will need to establish your credibility in your introduction. Credibility is a matter of being qualified to speak on a certain topic, or being perceived as qualified by your audience.

Your credibility does not simply need to be based on firsthand knowledge and experience. It can come from research, from professionals, from interviews, from friends, etc. Whatever the source of your expertise, be sure to let the audience know.

CLEARLY STATE THREE MAIN POINTS (THESIS)

After you have gotten the attention of your audience, established relevance for the topic, established your credibility as a speaker for the topic, be sure to clearly detail the three or four main points that you will be covering during the speech. This needs to be crystal clear so the audience knows the direction you are taking and will be able to follow along.

TIPS FOR THE INTRODUCTION

Keep the introduction relatively brief. Under normal circumstances it should not constitute more than ten to twenty percent of your speech. Be creative in devising your introduction. Experiment with two or three different openings and choose the one that seems most likely to get the audience interested in your speech.

Don't worry about the exact wording of your introduction until you have finished preparing the body of the speech. After you have determined your main points, it will be much easier to make final decisions about how to begin the speech.

Work out your introduction in detail. You can write it out word for word, or outline it. Whichever method you use, practice the introduction over and over until you can deliver it smoothly from a minimum of notes and with strong eye contact.

When you present the speech, don't start talking too soon. Establish eye contact with the audience, smile, and then begin the presentation.

The Conclusion

Your closing remarks are your final impressions and will probably linger in your audience's minds. Be sure to craft your conclusion with as much care as your introduction.

No matter what kind of speech you are giving, the conclusion has two major functions:

1. To let the audience know you are ending the speech.
2. To reinforce the audience's understanding of main points.

SIGNAL END OF THE SPEECH

It may seem obvious that you should let your audience know you are going to stop soon. However, you have heard presentations in which the presenter concludes so abruptly that you are caught off guard. Too sudden an ending will leave the audience confused.

How do you let an audience know your speech is ending? One way is through what you say: "In conclusion," "To wrap things up," "Let me end by saying,"—these are all brief cues that you are getting ready to stop. Successful presenters craft their conclusions to leave a strong impression. The final words fade like the spotlight, bringing the speech to a definitive close.

Summarize Your Speech

Restating the main points is the easiest way to end a speech. The summary clearly restates all main points one last time. Once you have summarized your speech, leave the audience with a closing statement that will keep them thinking about your speech long after the speech is over.

Here are some examples of effective closing statements:

End with a quotation: A quotation is one of the most common and effective devices to conclude a speech. The closing quotation is particularly effective if it can perfectly capture your presentation's overall purpose.

Make a dramatic statement: Rather than using a quotation, you may want to devise your own dramatic statement to rivet your audience with a dramatic concluding statement.

Refer to the introduction: An excellent way to conclude your presentation is to refer to ideas in the introduction.

Summarizing the speech, ending with a quotation, making a dramatic statement, referring to the introduction—all these techniques can be used separately. But you have probably noticed that presenters often combine techniques. One other concluding technique is making a **direct appeal to your audience for action**. The techniques covered are appropriate for all types of presentations.

Conclude with a bang. Be creative in devising a conclusion that will capture the hearts and minds of your audience. Work on several possible endings and select the one that seems likely to have the greatest impact. **Try to be succinct.** The conclusion generally accounts for five to ten percent of your overall presentation.

Don't leave anything in your conclusion to chance. Work it out in detail, and give yourself plenty of time to practice delivering it. You may choose to write out the conclusion word for word. Make your last impression as forceful and as favorable as you can.

Speech Conclusion Checklist

- Did I signal that my speech is coming to an end?

- Have I summarized the main points of my speech?

- Is the conclusion limited to five to ten percent of my entire speech?

- Have I worked out the language of my conclusion in detail?

- Have I practiced the delivery of my conclusion so I can present it fluently, confidently, and with strong eye contact?

First impressions are important. So are final impressions. This is why speeches need strong introductions and conclusions. In most speaking situations, you need to accomplish four objectives with your introduction—get the attention and interest of the audience, reveal the topic of your speech, establish your credibility, and preview the body of the speech. Gaining attention and interest can be done in several ways. You can show the importance of your topic, especially as it relates to your audience. You can startle or question your audience or arouse their curiosity. You can begin with a quotation or a story.

Be sure to state the topic of your speech clearly in your introduction so the audience knows where the speech is going. Establishing credibility means that you tell the audience why you are qualified to speak on the topic. Previewing the body of the speech helps the audience listen effectively and provides a smooth lead-in to the body of the speech.

The first objective of a speech conclusion is to let the audience know you are ending. The second objective of a conclusion is to reinforce your main purpose. You can accomplish this by summarizing the speech, ending with a quotation, making a dramatic statement, or referring to the introduction.

CONNECTIVES

Many presenters, when speaking to an audience, often will rely on "filler words" unconsciously during the presentation. Example words like "alright" or "like" or "uhm" are utilized each time the presenter moves from one thought to the next. After awhile, the audience will begin keeping count. By the end of the presentation, most audience members are too busy waiting for the next filler word, rather than paying attention to the presenter's message. In most cases, presenters are unaware of the overuse of verbal fillers, and those simply pop out when they are unsure of what to say next in the presentation.

When a plethora of verbal fillers are utilized in a presentation, generally what is lacking are strong connectives—words or phrases that join one thought to another. Without connectives, a speech is disjointed and uncoordinated.

We all have stock phrases that we use to fill the space between thoughts. In casual conversation, they are not as much of an issue. However, in speechmaking they distract the audience by calling attention to themselves.

Three types of speech connectives are transitions, internal summaries, and signposts.

Transitions are words or phrases that indicate when a presenter has just completed one thought and is moving on to another. Here is an example: "Now that we have discussed this, let me discuss . . ." This phrase reminds the audience members of the thought just completed, as well as reveal the thought about to be developed.

INTERNAL SUMMARIES

Internal summaries let the audience members know what is coming up next or remind the audience of what they have just heard. Such summaries are an excellent way to clarify and reinforce main points. By combining them with transitions, you can also lead your audience smoothly into your next main point.

SIGNPOSTS

Signposts are very brief statements that indicate exactly where you are in the presentation. You can use signposts to indicate where you are in the speech, or focus attention on key ideas. You can do this with a simple phrase, as in the following example(s):

3. Be sure to keep this in mind . . .
4. This is crucial to understanding the rest of the speech . . .
5. Above all, you need to know . . .

Depending on the needs of your speech, you may want to use two, three, or even all four kinds of connectives in combination. The important thing is to be aware of their functions. Properly applied, connectives can make your presentation more unified and coherent.

Connectives help tie a speech together. They are words or phrases that join one thought to another and indicate the relationship between them. The four major types of speech connectives are transitions, internal previews, internal summaries, and signposts. Using them effectively will make your speeches more unified and coherent.

The new SpeechShark app available in the Apple Store for iOS users and in GooglePlay for Android users makes short work out of writing speech outlines. Just answer the questions and this amazing app does the work for you! Check it out at www.SpeechShark.com.

You won't fear a shark attack when you keep your eyes open and are prepared for whatever comes your way! Some refer to shark movements as a feeding frenzy. Truthfully, it is no frenzy at all, but a graceful ballet in which the sharks are fast and swim confidently toward their goal. You can do this too! Be a Communication Shark! Use this section to test your skills and understanding.

Planning and Organizing the Presentation

1. Why should a speaker conduct an audience analysis?_____

   _____

   _____

2. What are the eight steps for planning a speech? _____

   _____

   _____

3. What are the most common mistakes beginning speakers make? _____

   _____

   _____

4. What are three simple steps to help avoid speaking mistakes?_____

   _____

   _____

5. What should you consider first when planning a speech? _____

   _____

   _____

6. What should you do before developing the three main points? _____

_____

_____

7. What two purposes should be written for the speech? _____

_____

_____

8. Define the general purpose: _____

_____

_____

9. Define the specific purpose: _____

_____

_____

10. What is the SWOT strategy? _____

_____

_____

11. Why is it important to narrow your topic? _____

_____

_____

12. What is a good strategy for narrowing your topic? _____

_____

_____

13. What are five steps for narrowing your topic? _____

_____

_____

14. What questions should you answer when considering a topic for your next speech? _____

_____

_____

15. Why is the title of the speech important? _____

_____

_____

16. Define the process of research. _____

_____

_____

17. Why should you use credible research? _____

_____

_____

18. What are the preferred research checkpoints? _____

_____

_____

19. How can you avoid being charged with plagiarism? _____

_____

_____

20. How can you determine if the source is credible? _____

_____

_____

21. What are the four most frequently used citation styles? _____

_____

_____

22. How do you know which of the four styles of citations to use? _____

_____

_____

23. What is an example of using a signal word when verbally citing research? _____

_____

_____

24. How do you paraphrase research? _____

_____

_____

25. What research cannot be paraphrased? _____

_____

_____

26. Where do you cite pictures/photographs on PowerPoint or Prezi slides? _____

_____

_____

27. Why is it important that speeches be organized clearly and coherently? _____

_____

_____

_____

28. How many main points will your speeches usually contain? Why is it important to limit the number of

main points in your speeches?_____

_____

_____

_____

29. What are the five basic patterns of organizing main points in a speech? _____

_____

_____

_____

30. What are three tips for preparing your main points? _____

_____

_____

_____

31. What is the most important thing to remember when organizing supporting materials in the body of

your speech? _____

_____

_____

_____

32. Why is it important to outline your speeches? _____

_____

_____

_____

33. What is a preparation outline? _____

_____

_____

_____

34. What are the guidelines discussed for writing a preparation outline? _____

_____

_____

_____

35. What are the guidelines for your speaking outline? _____

_____

_____

36. Why is it important to establish your credibility at the beginning of your speech?

_____

_____

37. What are the major functions of a speech conclusion?

_____

_____

38. What are two ways you can signal the end of your speech?

    _____

    _____

39. What are four tips for your conclusion?

    _____

    _____

Shark Bites

CONDUCTING AN AUDIENCE ANALYSIS

Challenge: Learn who is in your audience and find out what they want/need to know.

Task: If you have been asked to speak for an event, contact the event manager and ask questions about the audience. If possible, get an e-mail or telephone contact list. Send a short message to welcome the potential attendees to the event and to briefly introduce yourself. Invite them to answer the following questions:

1. What is your purpose for attending this event?

2. What is it that you would like to learn?

3. How much do you already know about the subject?

4. Are there any pressing questions that you have about the advertised topic? If so, please list the questions.

Challenge Accepted: Craft your speech by including your audience in every aspect. Give your audience what they want or need to know. Answer the following questions:

1. Does your content address positive ethos, pathos, and logos?

2. Does your topic respect the diversity of audience members?

3. Did you seek to understand the audience's perspectives, backgrounds, and experiences?

4. Did you consider all aspects of the speaking event and choose a topic to add to the audience's knowledge base?

Shark Bites

PRACTICE WRITING PURPOSE STATEMENTS

Challenge: You will need to introduce yourself to the board members of a new organization that you have recently joined. Please complete the following purpose statements for this situation:

General Purpose:

_____

_____

Specific Purpose:

_____

_____

Challenge: The topic of your Informative Speech is about organ donations. Please complete the following purpose statements for this situation:

General Purpose:

_____

_____

Specific Purpose:

_____

_____

Challenge: The topic of your Persuasion Speech is about texting and driving. Please complete the following purpose statements for this situation:

General Purpose:

_____

_____

Specific Purpose:

_____

_____

Shark Bites

LET'S CHOOSE A TOPIC

To choose a topic, you first need to understand the culture of your audience and choose a topic that will interest them and add to their knowledge base. Choose a topic with which you have experience.

Make a list of possible topics and indicate reasons this topic may work well for your audience. Use this list to help make the right choice! If you can't think of a good reason why the topic may work for your audience, cross it out and go back to the drawing board!

Possible Topics	Reasons This Topic May Work Well
Example: Packing for a Trip to Italy	The audience is made of adult members who belong to a travel club.

Shark Bites

CITING RESEARCH SOURCES

Find one source of research about your topic from the following sources: newspaper, book, journal, interview. Cite the source below using MLA Guidelines for citations.

Written Citation of a Newspaper Article:

Verbal Citation of the Newspaper Article:

Written Citation of a Book:

Verbal Citation of Book:

Written Citation of a Journal Article:

Verbal Citation of a Journal Article:

Written Citation of a Personal Interview:

Verbal Citation of a Personal Interview:

Chapter Fifteen

Presenting and Rehearsing the Presentation

In this chapter:

Presentation Skills

Creating Presentational Aids

Rehearsing the Speech

Evaluating the Speech

PRESENTATION SKILLS

Are You Waiting for your Ship to Come In?

If you are sitting around waiting for your ship to come in, then you really should take another look at details involved with achieving success.

Some people think they will find success as they sit in their sturdy little rowboat, master of their own ship, and armed with a strong work ethic and perhaps a few well-chosen tools (oars would be helpful). These people believe that they will row, row, row the boat toward their goals and ultimately find success! And, they may find success eventually and with a great deal of effort! But, that is not YOU!

Other people think they can sit back on their rickety old raft in a nice comfortable lounge chair with a glass of sweet Georgia tea close by and just follow the wind until, hopefully, success finds them! These dreamers believe they are so wonderful that sooner or later someone will notice how great they are and will drag them and their raft directly into the success stream! But, that is not YOU, either!

On the other hand, YOU stand at the helm of your stately sailboat with well-chosen officers on either side and a crew of qualified mates helping you to chart a course and carefully follow the route toward success. YOU have the vision to see what is beyond the horizon. Your loyal officers are paying attention to all details required to set manageable goals and your crew is determined to help you reach those goals. Yet, all of you realize that without the "wind in the sails," your sailboat will go nowhere. The wind is the motivation that comes from within! This is the force that will move this stately sailboat toward the goal. This is the catalyst that is needed to propel you, your officers, your crew, and passengers to success! Yes, this is YOU!

How did you arrive at this type of thinking? How do we know this is YOU? We know this because YOU are the person who sees the value in making good choices regarding your support staff! YOU are the kind of person who chooses to use a great app like SpeechShark to help draft and create speeches intended to reach your goals. YOU are the kind of person who reads a speech textbook to learn about extra tools needed to help you become the speaker you want to be.

You are the captain of your ship and you don't have to "wait for your ship to come in" because YOU are the one who is navigating the ship toward success! Whether you are making a point during a speech presentation with an audience or with your co-workers and colleagues, SpeechShark can help you verbally express your dreams and share enthusiasm for things that motivate and move you! Yes, this is YOU!

Questions? Yes, you will have lots of questions, but we have the answers. In the pages to follow, we have listed your questions about presentation skills and SpeechShark answers!

Questions and Answers about Presentation Skills

What vocal cues are important for public speaking?

Paralanguage is the vocal part of speech and involves volume, rate, pitch, pace, and color. To have vocal variance, you will want to incorporate varying degrees of all these aspects. To create more emphasis or effects for your speech topic, you might choose to say some words louder or softer, some faster and others softer, some words with more emphasis showing energy for the topic, anger, or any other emotion.

Volume is the level at which a sound is heard. While it is important for the audience to hear your voice, your volume does not need to be so loud that it appears you are shouting. Speak at a volume that will allow everyone in the room to hear your message. You control this by the volume of air you project using your **larynx** or voice box. More air = louder volume. Less air = softer volume. If you normally have a softer voice, you might require a microphone to be heard comfortably by your audience. If this is the case, be sure to rehearse using the microphone prior to your speech so that you understand how to use it correctly.

Rate is the method we use to determine how fast or slow someone is speaking. Many speakers tend to speed up because their nerves often push them into overdrive. This is a normal result of adrenaline pumping through your body and causing your heart rate to rev up; resulting in faster speech. While this is not always a problem, it can cause your audience to have trouble following your message because they will not have time to comprehend everything that you say. What can you do to make sure your speech is presented at a comfortable rate? Rehearse your speech, video or audio record your rehearsal, and evaluate the rate at which you speak. Try to take notes of your speech as you listen to the recording. Do you have time to make notes? If not, then your speech rate may be too fast. Consciously make an effort to slow down your rate of speech. Is your rate too slow? Plan to speed up the speech to keep your audience sitting on the edge of their seats!

Pitch is determined by sounds produced by vocal cord vibrations. Faster vibrations result in higher pitches. Slower vibrations result in lower pitches. Typically, women and children have a higher pitch. Men normally have a lower pitch. While this is typical, it is not absolute. Women and children can slow the vocal cord vibrations to achieve a lower pitch and men can speed vocal cord vibrations to achieve a higher pitch when needed. Varying pitch is important to having good vocal variance. A constant pitch results in a monotone voice and this is truly one sure way to lose your audience because a monotone voice lacks interest, variety, and energy like the monotone teacher in Charlie Brown cartoons, "Mwa, mwa, mwa, mwa, mwa, mwa!"

Pace is the rate at which you say syllables in a word. For example, people from the southern states in America usually add a couple of extra syllables in words that folks from the northern states do not. Southerners tend to say the word, well, in two syllables. Here is an example of a typical slower pace to say, "Well, I don't think so!":

Color involves the energy, enthusiasm, feelings, and attitudes that are included in our message. It may have negative or positive implications and can extend to what we see as much as what we hear. Our voice can show color when we tell a story that describes our exhilaration about a new game or fear of the unknown. Color can also be added as we discuss our customs, habits, or describe a place or a person. We love to hear color in a speech. It is how a speaker can add a little spark to the speech!

Dialects often surface as we discuss paralanguage. Dialects are a form of language heard from people living in a particular region, but this term can also be used as we discuss language indigenous to people from specific social or cultural groups. You will hear dialects referred to as local speech, regional speech patterns, languages, linguistics, vernacular, or accents. Dialects may include variations of grammar, vocabulary, and pronunciations. For example, if someone described the man at the store as having a French accent, they would be describing the man's regional speech patterns that would lead the listener to think the man was from a French-speaking part of our world. A phonetic and/or cultural analysis can result in identifying the continent or region where the dialect is most often spoken.

Effective language skills also surface as we discuss paralanguage. It is not enough to have a great topic with research and stories to support the topic, speakers also need to use effective language skills to be a good communicator. In other words, make sure your language skills are clear, concise, and constructive! Here are some tips for using effective language skills:

- Use standard English grammar, mechanics, and language.
- Use concrete and specific language and avoid using vague or abstract language.

- Avoid using acronyms or descriptions that only select audience members will grasp. If you need to use an acronym, identify the full meaning of the acronym before going into detail.

- Create images using adjectives to describe situations or people.

- Eliminate filler words that do not serve a purpose.

- Use vocabulary and grammar that is easily understood by your audience to establish a sense of commonality with the audience.

- Use language that is on the educational level of audience members. Do not talk "above" or "below" your audience's level of understanding.

How do I avoid using "Filler Words"?

Well, you know, it is uhm, like, well, like totally the most annoying thing you can hear, you know, in some-body's well, uh, you know, their speech presentation. It's uhm, the words that people, uhm, well, you know, they add them to what they are uhm, trying to say, when well, you know what I mean, they are so darn aggra-vating, and you like, well you hear them literally all of the time. You know?

You are in good company because about six million other people have asked this question. **Filler words** are the types of phrases, sounds, or words that speakers use to fill in an awkward pause when trying to com-municate a thought or make a speech presentation. Filler words are contagious and socio-linguistically, can be a tribal form of bonding. Filler words are heard in formal speeches and in social conversations. They are "like" everywhere and add no value to the sentence or thought being communicated.

Do you use filler words? Many people use these words without ever realizing how often they use them and how distracting they might be. Once you realize you are using them, you might discover that sometimes you use them more than other times. Often people use them as a filler when they can't think of the word or thought they are trying to share. We feel that the sound helps to soften the pause while we search for the right word. Truthfully, the sound distracts the listener from hearing the full meaning we are attempting to communicate.

Speakers use filler words when:

1. Searching for the right words
2. Filling an awkward pause
3. Making a sentence sound more passive
4. Making a sentence sound more active
5. Sharing what you are thinking
6. Bonding with a friend that speaks with fillers
7. Expanding the sentence to take more time
8. Sharing the idea/experience with the listener

While it is acceptable to use an occasional filler word, it is important that you do not overuse them. Paus-ing to think of an answer or to remember your next point is a much better option than uhm, well, you know, throwing in a word or two that well uhm, like basically stretches out the moment but not the meaning.

Here are the filler words that you hear most often: Like, ya know, okay, uhm, uh, er, hmmm, so, well, literally, totally, clearly, actually, basically, seriously, really, like, I mean, just, whatever, I guess or I suppose, very, right, but, sorry, anyway, and, uh huh, uh uh, and any combinations of the above. Whew, I'll bet you thought that sentence would never end!

So, well, like, what can do you do to like, totally, get rid of all the well, you know what I mean, those annoying filler words?

Become aware of your filler word habit! Prepare and practice before speaking opportunities. Video or audio-record your speech rehearsals. Count the number of filler words you have in your presentation, speech, audition, pitch, toast, and so forth, and keep working until you eliminate as many filler words as possible.

My friend, Audrey Mann Cronin, is an acknowledged and long-time communication expert in the technology industry. She is on a mission to help us all become better speakers and created *LikeSo: Your Personal Speech Coach,* a mobile app that helps you to talk your way to success. Using voice recognition technology, *LikeSo* is a fun and effective way to practice being a more confident and articulate speaker. Speak into the microphone of your smartphone and LikeSo captures your words and helps you train and remove all of those filler words that undermine your speech, weaken your meaning, and distract your listeners. *LikeSo* also measures pacing (150 wpm considered optimal) and allows you to set goals, reminders, and track your progress over time (day/week/month/year). It is like a "Fitbit for your speech." Just search the app store: http://Apple. co/1QBuByY or the Web site: https//sayitlikeso.com and for only 99 cents you can get your own personal speech coach that will help you to be a more powerful, persuasive, and articulate speaker.

I have the app and enjoy using it with students and speakers that I coach. It is so easy! Just choose "Free-Style," your open mic for any upcoming speaking opportunity, or "TalkAbout" a conversation game to practice speaking on the fly with topics including "The Job Interview," "Debate Team," and "Small Talk." Choose your talk time, the filler words you want to train against, and receive a Speech Fitness Report. You can also follow her on Facebook, Twitter, and Instagram at @LikeSoApp. Here is a picture so that you will recognize it in the Apple Store:

Now that we know how to avoid distracting fillers, let's take a look at other important non-verbal cues.

Kinesics are physical cues we see. Following Mehrabian's research, 55% of non-verbal communication is visual and covers the majority of cues we use to read a situation. We begin evaluating and making judgments based upon what we see from the moment the speaker enters the stage area. These judgments continue until the speaker leaves the stage. As we watch the speaker, we evaluate the credibility of the speaker using his physical appearance, posture, poise, gestures, facial expressions, eye contact, smiling, and body movements. Often, we establish a judgment about the speaker before the speaker ever utters the first word. Although we would like to argue that we are not quite so petty, Albert Mehrabian's research findings prove the opposite. So, what do we need to learn from this? Take care that you are putting your best foot forward. Plan to show positive physical cues for your audience.

What type of appearance is expected during a speech?

Appearance is a non-verbal cue. Whether you are in a public speaking environment or a social arena, be very aware of the cues you are sending. The clothes and shoes you wear, the jewelry you choose, the type briefcase or bag you carry all speak to your brand. Take a look at the way you see yourself. Does your appearance reflect your own self-awareness? Do you understand your conscious and unconscious non-verbal cues through your choice of clothing and accessories?

Truthfully, there are many sides of you. There is the playful and casual side that is evident in the way you dress and behave when you are with your family and close friends. When at work, you may dress a bit more conservatively and more in keeping with the culture of the workplace. There is a romantic side when you are with the love of your life. Attitudes, beliefs, and values are often reflected in the type clothing we choose. It is appropriate to change appearances for different occasions and circumstances, but it is equally important to realize when to dress and groom in a particular manner.

Appearance is not just about the clothing, shoes, jewelry, and accessories that you choose, but also about grooming. Ask yourself the following questions:

- How does your clothing fit?
- Are your shoes polished?
- What colors do you choose?
- What styles appeal to you?
- What type hairstyle do you have?
- Are your clothes ironed or wrinkled?
- Does your clothing complement your accessories?
- Is your hair clean and styled?
- Are your fingernails manicured?

A few months ago, I had the pleasure of interviewing the Director of Talent Procurement for a Fortune 500 Company. During the interview, I asked if she looked for a particular type of clothing when she was scouting for new employees. She told me that she looks for candidates who are well-groomed and conservative and not for a particular clothing type. Different businesses reflect the culture of the business through the type clothing worn. She mentioned that for her organization, the most expensive suit was not always a bonus; however, she did want to see candidates wear clothing that was clean, ironed, and tailored to fit. As far as accessories, she said that haircuts, jewelry, and accessories often tell a great deal about the personality of the candidate. The most interesting thing she told me had to do with what the candidate was carrying! She shared that candidates who walked in with huge bags bulging with papers gave her the impression of an employee who was unorganized and messy. Instead, she preferred to see candidates walk in with a simple black folder or an iPad or tablet for note-taking. In today's technological world, anything that the employer may require can be sent with the touch of a key on the iPad or tablet. In other words, less is more!

As people prepare to make a speech presentation, they often wonder what they should wear. As a speech coach, I suggest that speakers dress according to the audience to which they will be speaking. Is it a casual or formal event? Are you speaking to people in your community or to the board of directors for your organization? In any speaking situation, it is always advisable to dress a bit more formally than the people who will be attending your presentation. Business casual or dressy business is always in good taste.

Using the SpeechShark app, you can write your speech and use the note cards available on your device.

Consequently, you will not walk to the stage with a fistful of papers; instead, you can take your device and with a well-timed swipe of the screen, you can move to your next card to stay on target with your presentation. Again, less is more!

Physical appearance sends a positive or negative message about the speaker's credibility. For most speaking occasions, it is important to dress as if you are going to a job interview. Business casual dressing for a speech is always preferred. Occasionally, speakers may dress according to the topic they are presenting. For example, if you are giving a speech about cooking, you might wear a chef's hat and apron. But for the most part, your audience will appreciate the fact that you took time to dress professionally for the speech. Blue jeans and a t-shirt that says, "BITE ME," may not be the best choice if you want your audience to take you seriously. Overly bright outfits, unusual styles or garments that do not fit properly can also be distracting. While it may be appropriate to show tattoos or piercings if your speech topic is about tattoos or piercings, it is a better idea to avoid clothing that flaunt these. Have you ever heard "You only get one chance to make a first impression"? What message are you trying to send? Dress the part, SpeechShark!

Posture sends a non-verbal cue about how you feel about yourself and your speech. Not only will good posture show self-confidence, but it has a positive effect on your breathing patterns and the way you project your message. Good posture also lends itself to effective movements and gesturing during the speech. Have you ever heard someone tell you to "Stand tall"? Hold your chin up, keep your eyes focused on your audience, and take your place among great speakers who know what it takes to deliver a strong message. As you are introduced to the stage, walk with a positive purpose to let your audience know that you are ready and prepared.

Poise is displayed with how you carry your body. Are you comfortable in your own skin? Shoulders should be up and eyes looking at your audience to display positive self-confidence. Speakers who walk to the stage looking at the floor and with shoulders drooping will send a negative non-verbal cue about themselves and their speech topic. When giving a speech, walk confidently to the lectern and pan the audience with your eyes, smiling at them and letting them know you are happy to be speaking to them. When you get on stage, avoid leaning on the lectern, shifting from one foot to the other, adjusting your clothing or hair, handling notes, or putting your hands in your pocket. All of these negative behaviors will send negative non-verbal cues to your audience and will be evidence of a poor self-image and lack of confidence in yourself and your topic. Yes, all eyes will be on you. Make sure you are showing them cues that will increase your credibility.

Gestures are the ways you use your hands, body, and facial expressions during the speech to communicate points. I've often had students ask me, "What should I do with my hands during the speech?" My advice is to get immersed in your topic and in your audience so that you do not think about your hands and body. When you do this, you will have more natural and meaningful gestures. Don't put your hands in your pockets, clench them in front of you, or hold them behind you. These movements send a negative non-verbal cue. Gestures should not seem rehearsed, but should enhance your delivery and make visual points about things you are describing. They should be natural movements. The important thing is to make sure your gestures mirror the message you are sending.

Facial expressions include eye contact, smiling, head nodding, and head tilting to send a non-verbal cue to the audience during communication. Positive facial cues send a message of your emotions and attitudes regarding the topic you are sharing.

Eye contact promotes goodwill and a connection with the audience. It also helps the speaker appear more credible and knowledgeable about the topic. As you enter the stage, establish strong eye contact and keep strong eye contact throughout the speech. I've heard people suggest looking at the back wall if you get nervous with all eyes on you; however, that will only help you to establish a connection with the back wall. Take a deep breath and establish direct eye contact to develop a connection with  the audience. Believe it or not, but the smiles and head nods of audience members will give you the strength and self-confidence to complete your speech in a positive manner. You need them and they need you.

When you have a large audience, you may find it hard to establish eye contact with each member. In this case, start with looking toward one side of your audience and pan the entire side with your strong eye contact as you move your gaze to the other side of the audience. Looking at the entire audience will help them to feel valued and included in your speech. This is how you connect with them and have them invest in your topic. Avoid gazing at any one person or group of people for too long of a time. Share your eye contact and your attention with all audience members.

Smiling is a non-verbal cue that says, "I am happy to be here!" A genuine smile will send a positive message to your audience. As you smile, you will be pleased to notice that they will also smile at you. This reciprocal smile will help you not be as nervous as you might be without positive audience cues.

Head tilting and head nodding is a non-verbal cue which lets you know if your audience comprehends your point or if they still might have questions.

Speak with Confidence: Taking a "BITE" Out of the Fear of Public Speaking

Just as a shark swims boldly forward to pursue his goal, you can also walk toward the stage with confidence and deliver your speech without hesitation! The first thing that you will want to do is to examine your own confidence level when speaking to an audience.

Here are some questions to consider:

Question	Answer Yes or No
Do you have a low level of anxiety about public speaking?	
Do you have moderate anxiety in most public speaking situations, but not so severe that you cannot cope and be a successful speaker?	
Do you have a moderately high level of anxiety and tend to avoid speaking in public when possible?	
Do you have a very high level of anxiety and will go to any length to avoid a public speaking situation?	

Unsure of whether your speaking anxiety level is low or high? Take this self-evaluation from **George L. Grice and John F. Skinner's** *Mastering Public Speaking.*

Directions: This instrument is composed of thirty-four statements concerning feelings about communicating with other people. Indicate the degree to which the statements apply to you by marking whether you **(1) strongly agree, (2) agree, (3) undecided, (4) disagree, or (5) strongly disagree** with each statement. Work quickly and record your first impression.

PERSONAL REPORT OF PUBLIC SPEAKING ANXIETY

1	2	3	4	5	Statements Concerning Feelings about Communicating with Other People
					1. While preparing for giving a speech, I feel tense and nervous.
					2. I feel tense when I see the words Speech and Public Speaking on a course outline when studying or on a job description.
					3. My thoughts become confused and jumbled when I am giving a speech.
					4. Right after giving a speech, I feel that I have had a pleasant experience.
					5. I get anxious when I think about a speech coming up.
					6. I have no fear of giving a speech.
					7. Although I am nervous just before starting a speech, I soon settle down after starting and feel calm and comfortable.
					8. I look forward to giving a speech.
					9. When the instructor announces a speaking assignment in class, I can feel myself getting tense.
					10. My hands tremble when I am giving a speech.
					11. I feel relaxed when I am giving a speech.
					12. I enjoy preparing for a speech.
					13. I am in constant fear of forgetting what I prepared to say.
					14. I get anxious if someone asks me something about my topic that I do not know.
					15. I face the prospect of giving a speech with confidence.
					16. I feel that I am in complete possession of myself while giving a speech.
					17. My mind is clear when giving a speech.
					18. I do not dread giving a speech.
					19. I perspire just before starting a speech.
					20. My heart beats very fast just as I start a speech.
					21. I experience considerable anxiety while sitting in the room just before my speech starts.
					22. Certain parts of my body feel very tense and rigid while giving a speech.
					23. Realizing that only a little time remains before a speech makes me very anxious.
					24. While giving a speech, I know I can control my feelings of tension and stress.

1	2	3	4	5	Statements Concerning Feelings about Communicating with Other People
					25. I breathe faster just before starting a speech.
					26. I feel comfortable and relaxed in the hour or so just before giving a speech.
					27. I do poorer on speeches because I am anxious.
					28. I feel anxious when I hear an announcement of a speaking assignment.
					29. When I make a mistake while giving a speech, I find it hard to concentrate on the parts that follow.
					30. During an important speech, I experience a feeling of helplessness building up inside me.
					31. I have trouble falling asleep the night before a speech.
					32. My heart beats very fast while I present a speech.
					33. I feel anxious while waiting to give my speech.
					34. While giving a speech, I get so nervous I forget facts I really know.
					TOTAL Points

To determine Your Score on the PRPSA, Complete the Following Steps:

1. Add the scores for items in purple (1,2,3,5,9,10,13,14,19,20,21,22,23,25,27,28,28,30,31,32,33,34).
2. Add the scores for items in peach (4,6,7,8,11,12,15,16,17,18,24,26).
3. Complete the following formula: PRPSA = 132 – (total points from step #1) + (total points from step #2).
4. What is your score? _____

NOTE: Your score can range between 34 and 170. There is no right or wrong answer because this report just helps you to understand if you do have speaker anxiety and the level of speaker anxiety that you may have. Understanding Your Score:

- 34–84—Very low anxiety about public speaking
- 85–92—Moderately low level of anxiety about public speaking
- 93–110—Moderate anxiety in most public speaking situations, but not too severe that the individual cannot cope and be a successful speaker
- 111–119—Moderately high anxiety about public speaking. People with this score usually tend to avoid public speaking situations.
- 120–170—Very high anxiety about public speaking. People with these scores will go to considerable lengths to avoid all types of public speaking situations.

Whether your level is low or high, it is good to realize that we ALL get nervous when speaking in public; even sharks get nervous, especially when they are swimming in waters teaming with other sharks! So, that means you are normal! Yes, I said it—you are NORMAL!

Most of us are anxious because we think that the audience is staring at us and judging us. Dry mouth, shortness of breath, sweaty palms, increased heart rate—we experience all of these! We might even think that the audience members are sitting there silently wishing that we will run screaming from the stage.

In fact, the opposite is true. Audiences WANT speakers to succeed. Audiences WANT speakers to be amazing and to wow us with their presentations! Why? Because the audience is investing their time to hear your speech. They don't want to waste time, but want to hear a message that is relevant and riveting! You can be the SpeechShark that provides what the audience WANTS!

Using the SpeechShark app will help you to do just that! The app is designed to create a speech that is geared toward your audience and is designed to satisfy the purpose for which you have been asked to speak! SpeechShark provides you with prompts that will help you maneuver through murky waters so that you, too, can swim easily and confidently toward your goal and deliver a crowd-pleasing presentation without hesitation or FEAR!

Dealing with Speech Anxiety:

How do you cope with speech anxiety? What is stage fright? Stage fright is different for everyone and speakers compensate for stage fright by using techniques that work for them.

Some people like to use **breathing exercises** before the speech to help channel the adrenaline running through their bodies. Slowing down their heart beat will also slow down the flow of adrenaline and will help calm nerves. Learning to deal with stress associated with public speaking will be your key to speaking with confidence. We all get nervous, so the best thing to know right now is that you are normal! See, doesn't that make you feel better? As you speak, you will experience good stress and bad stress.

The feeling of stress is produced as adrenaline rushes through your body. **Adrenaline** is physiological and involves increased heart and respiration rate as a result of a situation perceived to be frightening or exciting. With this adrenaline rush, you may feel more energetic, excited, sometimes stronger and happier. This is good stress and will help you to rise to the challenge. Bad stress will cause you to feel fear and anxiety. Fear is a negative emotion which truly does not help the situation at all. With this in mind, I want to show you ways to focus on the good stress and alleviate the bad stress. Try all of these different strategies and you will soon discover the strategy that works best for you.

I've discovered that the people who have stage fright the most are the people who enter the stage unprepared. The best remedy for stage fright is again—**Plan, Prepare, and Persevere!** Know what you are going to say and most of the stage fright will disappear.

We've heard from lots of speakers who say that using the SpeechShark app (www.speechshark.com) helps them to be less anxious because it helps them to know what they should say during the speech. The app also provides note cards for presenting the speech.

PLAN

KNOW your audience, understand your purpose, and know what you need to say. If you can do that, you will have less stage fright and will be a more effective communicator! The **SECRET** is to do everything and anything that will help you be more confident. It is a confidence factor, not a personality or knowledge factor.

Here is what SpeechSharks do BEFORE the speech:

- **Walk around the room before the speech.**
- **Stand by the lectern and rehearse in the room where you will be giving the speech.**
- **Rehearse with people listening to you instead of rehearsing to an empty room.**
- **Rehearse by audio or video taping yourself.**
- **Rehearse in front of a mirror.**
- **Exercise positive self-talk.**

Rehearse, rehearse, rehearse—and rehearse some more. Change wording to make sure the words are coming to you comfortably. Believe in yourself! Feel comfortable with yourself, your location, and your content. As a result, you will be more confident and you will be happier with your presentation.

PREPARE

How do you cope with speech anxiety? The **SECRET** is to do everything and anything that will help you to be more confident. It is a confidence factor, not a personality or knowledge factor. Here is what SpeechSharks do BEFORE the speech:

- **Walk around the room before the speech**, instead of sitting in a chair and waiting to be called up front. It will help you to work off some of the nervous energy, and you can greet audience members as you move around the room waiting for the event to begin.
- **Stand by the lectern and rehearse in the room where you will be giving the speech.** This is difficult when the room is full, so arrive early and spend time rehearsing in the SAME PLACE where you will be giving the speech.
- **Rehearse with people listening to you** instead of rehearsing to an empty room. Having a rehearsal audience will give you a similar experience as having the presentation audience. That will help you to feel more confident because you can see how the audience will react to certain points that you make.
- **Rehearse by audio or video taping yourself.** Be AWARE of words that you tend to "chew" up. It may mean changing the wording so that your message will have a smoother delivery.
- **Rehearse in front of a mirror.** This is awkward, but it will help you see your gestures and facial expressions as you make the presentation. It will also give you a chance to check your appearance before you meet your audience.
- **Exercise positive self-talk.** Don't let anything negative come into your brain—tell yourself, "I am going to do a GREAT job!" "This will be my BEST speech!" "The audience is really going to LOVE my topic!" "Nobody in this room KNOWS this topic like I do!" "I am an EXPERT!"

PERSEVERE

Ultimately, the main thing you can do is rehearse, rehearse, rehearse—and rehearse some more. Don't quit. Move forward. Keep your goal in mind. Change wording to make sure the words are coming to you comfortably. Believe in yourself! Feel comfortable with yourself, your location, and your content. As a result, you will be more confident and happier with your presentation.

Look forward to your next speech!

Knock out stress using the **BAM** Approach:

B = Breathing exercises can help affect your state of mind, lower heart rate ,and bring stress under control. The trick to this is to use controlled breathing exercises. As you follow the breathing exercises, you will notice that your muscle tension will relax when providing your body with much needed oxygen. The result will have a positive effect on your thoughts and feelings. The Internet is packed with breathing exercises to use before your next speech!

A = Aromatherapy involves the sense of smell and uses scents to overcome stress and improve overall mental health. Certain scents may help you to feel more calm than others, so it is important to find the scent that helps you to feel "ahhhh!" Some popular scents used to calm stress are lavender, chamomile, lemongrass, and peppermint. Diffusers are readily available online and in department stores along with vials of essential oils. There are also mixtures of various essential oils designed to bring a sense of calmness to the user. Experiment to find the oil/scent which works best for you. Diffuse the oil as you sit in your home or desk prior to giving the speech. Dab a tiny bit of oil on the inside of your wrists before a speech. There are even diffusers available that plug in to your car so that you can experience the calming scents while driving to your speech location.

M = Meditation enhanced with music will calm stress. Use imagery and positive visualization to think your way to success! Positive self-talk and imagining a successful speech are achieved as you concentrate on feeling successful while communicating to others. First, imagine yourself walking confidently to the stage, delivering the best speech of your life, and then hearing the welcomed applause of audience members! Tell yourself, "I can do this! I know my topic. I am prepared for this speech. I have a message my audience needs to hear. I am the best person to share this topic to my audience. I will do a great job and my audience will be glad they heard this speech." Do not allow negative thoughts or feelings to enter this moment. Only

concentrate on positive thoughts and visualize your success. Using calm music or sounds of nature while meditating can intensify this effect and will help you feel composed and ready to meet the challenge.

There are several strategies available, but as with anything, it is important to do what works for you and understand your stress triggers and indicators. Be sure to review the chapter covering the Speech Day Checklist. Following a checklist will help you arrive feeling prepared and ready to take the stage!

What do you need to know about entering and exiting the stage area?

Whether you know it or not, your speech begins the moment you stand and enter the stage and does not end until you have been seated or exit the stage. Audience members watch you from the very first indication that you are going to be the speaker. It is for this reason that speakers need to enter the stage confidently, acknowledging the audience while approaching the lectern. If you are using notes, place them carefully on the lectern and then move away from the lectern toward the center of the stage. Avoid standing at the lectern and spending valuable time arranging and rearranging pages of notes. Notes should be in order before you enter the stage.

Once the speech is completed, take your notes from the lectern and again make eye contact and acknowledge your audience as you move back to your seat. BIG smiles and strong eye contact will convey the non-verbal cue that you are confident to give the speech and proud of the results once the speech is completed.

What do I need to know about movement during the speech?

Sharks are known for their uncanny way of maneuvering gracefully through murky waters. You can do this, too. The only difference is that you will be maneuvering gracefully across the stage—no murky waters for you!

Movement during a speech should happen naturally as you are making the presentation, but Speech-Sharks know ways to orchestrate movements that are effective and carefully placed during the speech. It is called movement with a purpose. Use the letter W in the alphabet to help you visualize movement during your speech. There are five points in a W. Here is a numbered diagram and movements to help you walk your way to success:

Walk your way to success!

- Imagine a giant W in the middle of the stage area. Move from 1,2,3,2,1 and then from 1,4,5,4,1. This helps you move to the left side of your stage and to the right side of your stage equally.

- Begin your speech at area #1. While you are front and center of the stage area, this is where you should stand to deliver the attention step, establish relevance for the topic, establish credibility, and clearly state your thesis.

- Take two steps back and away from the middle front of the stage to area #2 as you transition to the first point.

- Then move to area #3 as you cover the first point. Use this area of the stage to cover point one.

- As you transition to the second point, take two steps back to area #2 of the diagram. Stay in this area during the transition. Move to area #1 as you cover the second point.

- After the second point has been covered and as you transition to the third point, move directly to area #4. As you lead into the third point, take two steps up to area #5. Stay in this area while you cover the third point.

- As you transition to the conclusion, move back to area #4.

- Following the transition move back to area #1 to complete the summary of three main points.

- Stay in area #1 to deliver the final Appeal to Action and end with a BANG while standing center of the stage area and close to your audience.

SpeechShark's Top Ten Tips for a Killer Presentation:

1. Start with a strong attention step.
2. Plan the speech for your audience.
3. Research the topic.
4. Add personal stories.
5. Show empathy for the audience.
6. Be conversational.
7. Move forward, even if you make a mistake.
8. Stay with your plan.
9. Use visual aids.
10. End with a BANG.

CREATING PRESENTATIONAL AIDS

Generally, an audience will find a presenter's message more effective when it is presented visually as well as verbally. If utilized properly, visual aids should enhance each aspect of the presentation. A presenter who utilizes visual aids will appear better prepared, more credible, and more professional. **Visual aids** should heighten audience interest, shift attention away from the presenter, and give the presenter greater confidence in the presentation as a whole.

Visual aids should add value to your presentation and help your audience to retain the information you share.

Let us look first at the kinds of visual aids you are most likely to use, then at guidelines for preparing visual aids, and finally at guidelines for using visual aids.

OBJECTS

Bring an object related to your presentation, it can be an excellent way to clarify your ideas. If your presentation covers information related to skydiving, why not bring the skydiving equipment to class to show your audience? Or suppose you want to inform your classmates about the art of candle making. Bring several candles to class to display and explain how they were made.

TABLE DISPLAYS

A table display should be visible to the entire audience. It is appropriate to have a table cover, and ensure the table cover is not wrinkled and placed neatly. When creating a table display, only include a collection of props that you plan to refer to in your presentation. Mishaps can be averted if you plan what to include well in advance. Make sure your audience can see everything on your table display. Avoid laying items flat on the table. Instead use easels or boxes to lift items for a clear display. Don't forget the audience members who sit in the back row. Make sure they also have a clear view of items used on your table display.

PHOTOS AND DRAWINGS

Photos make excellent visual aids if they are large enough to be seen easily by your audience. Normal-size photos are generally too small to be seen clearly without being passed around, which only diverts the audience from what you are saying.

The most effective way to show photos is to include them on a PowerPoint or Prezi slide.

GRAPHS

Your audience may have trouble grasping a complex series of numbers. You can ease their difficulty by using graphs to showcase statistical trends and patterns.

A **pie graph** can be used to show the parts of a whole. A pie graph should ideally have from two to five segments.

The **bar graph,** like the one shown on the right, is a particularly good way to show comparisons among two or more items. It also has the advantage of being easy to understand.

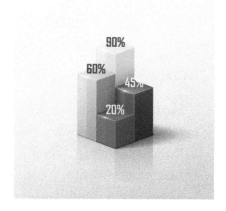

CHARTS

Charts are particularly useful for summarizing large blocks of information. By listing them on a chart, the presenter makes it easier for the audience to retain information. The biggest mistake presenters make when using a chart is to include too much information. Visual aids should be clear, simple, and uncluttered. Lists on a chart should rarely exceed seven or eight items, with generous spacing between items. If you cannot fit everything on a single chart, make a second one.

HANDOUTS

Handouts are used to help the audience retain information supplied during the speech. It is best to create your own handout rather than use a handout designed and distributed by an organization. Usually organizations design handouts for marketing purposes and their material will include company branding and contact information that is not appropriate for a speech, unless you are making a sales presentation for that organization.

Handouts can be anything from an object with a tag, to printed designed handouts that support your speech. A good handout for a cooking demonstration would be a recipe card. If your topic is to motivate your audience to spay or neuter pets, a tri-fold color brochure with information about the process may be more appropriate. If creating brochures, recipe cards, or business card handouts, be sure to use heavy card stock. Color is always a bonus, but if you find the ink costs are too expensive, try printing information on color paper instead of printing with color ink.

Since most speeches for a speech course are not sales presentations, avoid distributing handouts that market one particular company, product, or organization. However, if you are making a sales presentation, your handout should reflect the information, company, and product that you are trying to sell.

As with any visual aid, please make sure fonts and colors are consistent throughout the handout. Check for spelling and grammatical errors prior to printing and distributing the handout.

Distribute handouts before your speech if you need your audience to do something with the handout during your speech. Distribute after your speech if the purpose of the handout is to promote audience retention about the topic.

For a more professional presentation, appoint tech team members to distribute the handout for the speaker, and give clear instructions regarding the time and manner in which the handouts are distributed.

VIDEO CLIPS and MUSIC SOUNDBITES

Adding video clips or music to a speech should be conducted carefully and expertly. First, make sure the clip is not too long. While a 30–45-second video can illustrate your ideas in a memorable way, anything much longer will distract attention from the speech itself. Second, make sure the video or music is cued to start exactly where you want it. Third, if necessary, edit the video or music to the precise length you need so it will blend smoothly into your speech. The last step is to rehearse with your visual aids and with your Tech Team.

YOURSELF

Sometimes you can use your own body as a visual aid—by showing how to perform a skill, talent, and so forth. In addition to clarifying a presenter's ideas, doing some kind of demonstration helps keep the audience involved. It also can reduce a presenter's nervousness by providing an outlet for extra adrenaline. Doing a demonstration will require special practice to coordinate your actions with your words and to control the timing of your speech.

PRESENTATION TECHNOLOGY

Presentation technology allows you to integrate a variety of visual aids—including charts, graphs, photos, and videos in the same presentation. The most commonly used presentation programs are PowerPoint and Prezi.

We will look at guidelines for planning and presenting visual aids effectively. We will also look at the pros and cons to consider and the following factors when thinking about including presentation technology in your speeches.

PLANNING TO USE PRESENTATION TECHNOLOGY

If you are going to employ presentation technology effectively, you need a clear idea of exactly why, how, and when to use it. Rather than putting everything you say on-screen for the audience to read, you need to choose which aspects of your speech to illustrate. This requires careful planning.

The first step is deciding where you can use PowerPoint or some other program to your best advantage. After you have finished developing the speech, think about places where you can incorporate well-developed slides that will genuinely enhance your message.

As you plan your speeches, think about how you can use presentation technology to enhance your ideas. At the same time, remember that too many visuals—or poor visuals—can do more harm than good. Be creative and resourceful without allowing technology to overpower your entire speech.

PROS AND CONS OF PRESENTATION TECHNOLOGY

When used well, presentation technology is a great asset to presentations. Unfortunately, it is not always used well. Too often speakers allow it to dominate their presentation, attempting to wow the audience with their technical proficiency, while losing the message in a flurry of sounds and images.

At the other extreme are mind-numbing presentations that gave rise to the phrase "Death by Power-Point." In such cases, the presenter virtually reads the speech to the audience as the words appear on-screen. This is no more effective than reading dully from a manuscript. Do this and I guarantee you that your audience will be snoozing or making a grocery list, but they will not be listening to your speech.

GUIDELINES FOR PREPARING VISUAL AIDS

Whether you are creating visual aids by hand or with PowerPoint, the following guidelines will help you design aids that are clear and visually appealing.

PREPARE VISUAL AIDS IN ADVANCE

Preparing visual aids well in advance has two advantages. First, it means you will have the time and resources to devise creative, attractive aids. Second, it means you can use them while practicing your speech. Visual aids are effective only when they are integrated smoothly with the rest of the speech. If you lose your place, drop your aids, or otherwise stumble around when presenting them, you will distract your audience and shatter their concentration.

KEEP VISUAL AIDS SIMPLE

Visual aids should be simple, clear, and to the point. They should contain enough information to communicate the presenter's point, but not so much as to confuse or distract the audience. Limit your slides to a manageable amount of information, and beware of the tendency to go overboard.

MAKE SURE VISUAL AIDS CAN BE SEEN

A visual aid is useless if no one can see it. Keep in mind the size of the room in which you will be speaking and make sure your aid is big enough to be seen easily by everyone. Check your visibility by moving to a point as far away from it as your most distant audience member will be seated.

If you are using a presentation program such as PowerPoint, make sure your text and images are easy for everyone in your audience to see. By making sure your visual aid is large enough, you will avoid having to introduce it with the comment "I know some of you can't see this, but . . ."

USE A LIMITED AMOUNT OF TEXT

When displaying text on visual aids, keep it simple. Succinct phrases containing only essential key words will help audience members grasp your basic point and process the information as you're speaking.

One of the biggest mistakes people make with presentation technology is putting too much text on a single slide. A general rule for slides that contain only text is to include no more than seven lines of type. If you are combining text with images, you may need to limit yourself to fewer lines to keep the text from getting too small. If you have a number of important points to cover, spread them out over multiple slides.

USE FONTS EFFECTIVELY: Not all fonts are suitable for visual aids. Using fonts effectively can make a huge difference in your slides. Keep the following guidelines in mind when selecting fonts:

- Select fonts that are clear and easy to read.
- Avoid using ALL CAPS because they are difficult to read.
- Do not use more than two fonts on a single slide—one for the title or major heading and another for subtitles or other text.
- Stay consistent with the same fonts on all your slides.
- Place titles and headings in at least 36- to 44-point type; make subheads and other text at least 24- to 30-point.

If you use one of the built-in themes in PowerPoint, you can be confident that the fonts, which have been preselected according to the design of the theme, are clear, legible, and consistent.

USE COLOR EFFECTIVELY

When used effectively, color can dramatically increase the impact of a visual aid. Some colors do not work well together. You can use either dark print on a light background or light print on a dark background, simply make sure there is enough contrast between the background and the text so the audience can see everything clearly.

Also, stick to a limited number of colors and use them consistently. Use one color for background, one color for titles, and one color for other text throughout all your slides. This consistency will unify the slides and give your speech a professional appearance.

USE IMAGES STRATEGICALLY

One of the benefits of presentation technology is the ease with which it allows you to include photos, charts, graphs, and other images, including video. Unfortunately, some presenters are prone to adding images simply because it is easy, rather than because it is essential for communicating the message. You should never add images of any sort to a slide unless they are truly necessary. There is a great deal of research showing that extraneous images distract audience members and reduce comprehension of the presenter's point.

In addition to keeping your slides free of extraneous images, keep these guidelines in mind:

1. Make sure images are large enough to be seen clearly.
2. Choose high-resolution images that will project without blurring.
3. Keep graphs and charts clear and simple.
4. In most cases, include a title above charts and graphs so the audience knows what they are viewing.
5. Edit videos and music sound bites so they are integrated seamlessly into your slides.

GUIDELINES FOR PRESENTING VISUAL AIDS

No matter how well designed your visual aids may be, they will be of little value unless you display them properly, discuss them clearly, and integrate them effectively with the rest of your presentation. Below are guidelines that will help you get the maximum impact out of your visual aids.

Presenting Visual Aids Checklist
1. Have I prepared my visual aids well in advance?
2. Are my visual aids clear and easy to comprehend?
3. Does each visual aid contain only the information needed to make my point?
4. Are my visual aids large enough to be seen clearly by the entire audience?
5. Do the colors on my visual aids work well together?
6. Is there a clear contrast between the lettering and background on my charts, graphs, and drawings?
7. Do I use line graphs, pie graphs, and bar graphs correctly to show statistical trends and patterns?
8. Do I limit charts to no more than eight items?
9. Do I utilize fonts that are easy to read?

DISPLAY VISUAL AIDS SO AUDIENCE CAN VIEW

Check the speech room ahead of time to decide exactly where you will display your visual aids. If you are displaying an object or a model, be sure to place it where it can be seen easily by everyone in the room. If necessary, hold up the object or model while you are discussing it.

Once you have set the aid in the best location, don't undo all your preparation by standing where you block the audience's view of the aid. Stand to one side of the aid, and point with the arm nearest it. You can also utilize a pointer, which will allow you to stand farther away from the visual aid, also preventing you from obstructing the view of the audience.

AVOID PASSING VISUAL AIDS AMONG THE AUDIENCE

Once visual aids get into the hands of your audience, they will be paying more attention to the aid than to you and are likely to spend a good part of the speech looking over the handout at their own pace, rather than listening to you. Although handouts can be valuable, they usually just create competition for novice presenters.

Here is a tip to help you understand WHEN to distribute handouts:

If you plan to use the handout during your speech, please ask your Tech Team to distribute the handouts before you take the stage to speak. If you plan to use the handout as a method of helping the audience remember your speech or to use as a point of reference after the speech is over, ask your Tech Team to distribute the handout after the speech is over and you have exited the stage. This will get the handout into your audience members' hands, but will not cause a distraction.

DISPLAY VISUAL AIDS ONLY WHILE DISCUSSING THEM

Just as circulating visual aids distracts attention, so does displaying them throughout a speech. If you are using an object or a model, keep it out of sight until you are ready to discuss it. When you finish your discussion, place the object or model back out of sight.

The same principle applies to PowerPoint slides. They should be visible only while you are discussing them. You can accomplish this by adding blank slides as needed, so the audience's attention will not be diverted by the prior slide. It is also a good idea to add a blank slide at the end of your presentation, so your last content slide will not continue to be exposed after you have finished discussing it.

EXPLAIN VISUAL AIDS CLEARLY

A visual aid can be of enormous benefit—but only if the audience member knows what to look for and why. Unfortunately, presenters often rush over their visual aids without explaining them clearly and concisely. Don't just say "As you can see . . ." and then pass quickly over the aid. Tell the audience what the aid means. Remember, a visual aid is only as useful as the explanation that goes with it. It should integrate into the speech smoothly and skillfully—and you should strive to maintain eye contact with the audience when you present visual aids in your presentation.

TALK TO THE AUDIENCE, NOT THE VISUAL AID

When explaining a visual aid, it is easy to break eye contact with your audience and talk to the aid. Of course, your audience is looking primarily at the aid, and you may need to glance at it periodically as you talk. But if you keep your eyes fixed on the visual aid, you will lose your audience. By keeping eye contact, you can also pick up feedback about how the visual aid and your explanation of it are coming across.

There are many kinds of visual aids. Most obvious is the object about which you are speaking. Photos should be large enough to be seen clearly by all your audience members. Graphs are an excellent way to illustrate any subject dealing with numbers, while charts are used to summarize large blocks of information. Videos can be useful as a visual aid, but it needs to be carefully edited and integrated into the speech. You can act as your own visual aid by performing actions that demonstrate processes or ideas.

If you use presentation technology, plan carefully why, how, and when you will utilize it. Rather than putting everything you say on-screen for your audience to read, use the technology only when it will genuinely enhance your message.

No matter what kind of visual aid you use, you need to prepare it carefully. You will be most successful if you prepare your aids well in advance, keep them simple, make sure they are large enough to be seen clearly, and utilize a limited amount of text. If you are creating visual aids utilizing presentation technology, use fonts, color, and images strategically and effectively.

In addition to being designed with care, visual aids need to be presented skillfully. Avoid passing visual aids among the audience. Display each aid only while you are talking about it, and be sure everyone can see it without straining. When presenting a visual aid, maintain eye contact with your audience and explain the aid clearly and concisely. If you are using presentation technology, make sure you check the room and equipment prior to the time of delivery. Above all, practice with your visual aids so they fit into your speech smoothly and expertly.

REHEARSING THE SPEECH

You have heard it said that practice makes perfect. This is true, but only if you practice properly. You will do little to improve your speech delivery unless you practice the right things in the right ways. **Here is a five-step method that works well for presenters:**

1. Go through your outline to see what you have written.
   - Are the main points clear?
   - Do you have supporting materials?
   - Does your introduction and conclusion come across well?

2. Prepare your speaking notes. In doing so, be sure to follow the guidelines. Use the same framework as in the preparation outline. Make sure your speaking notes are easy to read. Give yourself cues on the note cards for delivering the speech.

3. Practice the speech aloud several times using only the speaking outline. Be sure to "talk through" all examples and to recite quotations and statistics. If your speech includes visual aids, utilize those as you practice. The first couple of times, you will probably forget something or make a mistake, but don't worry. Keep going and complete the speech as best as you can. Concentrate on gaining control of the ideas; don't try to learn the speech word for word. After a few tries you should be able to get through the speech extemporaneously with surprising ease.

4. Now begin to polish and refine your delivery. Practice the speech in front of a mirror to check for eye contact and distracting mannerisms. Record the speech to gauge volume, pitch, rate, pauses, and vocal variety. Most important, try it out on friends, roommates, family members—anyone who will listen and

give you honest feedback. Because your speech is designed for an audience you need to find out ahead of time how it goes over with people.

5. Finally, give your speech a dress rehearsal under conditions as close as possible to those you will face in class. Some students like to try the speech a couple times in an empty classroom the day before they actually present the speech. No matter where you hold your last practice session, you should leave it feeling confident and looking forward to speaking in your class.

If this or any practice method is to work, you must start early. Don't wait until the night before your speech to begin working on delivery. A single practice session—no matter how long—is rarely enough. Allow yourself at least a couple of days, preferably more, to gain command of the speech and its presentation.

PRACTICE WITH YOUR VISUAL AIDS

We have mentioned several times the need to rehearse using your visual aids, but the point bears repeating. No matter what kind of visual aid you choose, be sure to employ it when you rehearse. Go through the speech multiple times, rehearsing how you will show your aids, the gestures you will make, and the timing of each move. In using visual aids, as in other aspects of speechmaking, there is no substitute for preparation.

If you are using presentation technology, don't just click through casually or rush quickly over your words when you practice. Make sure you know exactly when you want each slide to appear and disappear, and what you will say while each is on-screen. Mark your speaking notes with cues that will remind you when to display each slide and when to remove it.

Rehearse with the mouse, remote, keyboard, or iPad until you can use them without looking down for more than an instant when advancing your slides. Also concentrate on presenting the speech without looking back at the screen to see what is being projected. Rehearse with your tech team, if you need one!

Given all the things you have to work on when practicing a speech with any kind of presentation technology, you need to allow extra time for rehearsal. So, get an early start and give yourself plenty of time to ensure that your delivery is as impressive as your slides.

Practicing Visual Aids Checklist	Yes	No
• Have I checked the speech room to decide where I can display my visual aids most effectively?		
• Have I practiced presenting my visual aids so they will be clearly visible to everyone in the audience?		
• Have I practiced presenting my visual aids so they are perfectly timed with my words and actions?		
• Have I practiced keeping eye contact with my audience while presenting my visual aids?		
• Have I practiced explaining my visual aids clearly and concisely in terms my audience will understand?		
• If I am using handouts, have I planned to distribute them after the speech rather than during it?		
• Have I double-checked all equipment to make sure it works properly?		
• If I am using PowerPoint, do I have a backup of my slides that I can take to the speech with me?		

CHECK THE ROOM AND EQUIPMENT

For classroom speeches, you will already be familiar with the room and equipment. Even if you have used PowerPoint on previous occasions, you need to check the setup in the room where you will be presenting.

If you are using a computer that is installed in the room, bring your slides on a flash drive so you can see how they work with that computer. If your presentation includes audio or video, double-check them using the room's audiovisual system.

Sometimes, of course, it is not possible to visit the room before the day of your speech. Never assume that everything will be "just fine." Instead, assume that things will not be fine and that they need to be checked ahead of time.

Finally, always bring a backup of your slides on a flash drive. This may seem like a lot of fuss and bother, but anyone who has given speeches with PowerPoint—or any other kind of visual aid—will tell you that it is absolutely essential.

Have a Backup Plan

No matter how much time presenters invest in mastering the technology, they can still be undermined by technological glitches. This is why experts recommend that you always have a backup plan in case the technology fails. Because we have all encountered sabotage by technology at one time or another, audiences usually have sympathy for a presenter who encounters such problems. When in doubt, be prepared to present without technology.

SPEECH DAY CHECK LIST

- Plan, Prepare, Persevere! The more planning and preparation you do before the speech, the more confident you will be.
- Think positively—YOU can do this!
- Understand what is expected of you for the speech.
- Pack all materials you need the day before your speech. Have a checklist planned to keep you on target.
- Take care of you!
  - Get a good night's sleep before the speech.
  - Eat a healthy high protein meal.
  - Stay away from milk products which can coat your throat.
  - Drink plenty of fluids before your speech, but avoid caffeine and sugar which can make you feel jittery.
- Rehearse with your tech team so they know what you need.
- Arrive early to become familiar with the speaking area.
- Rehearse using a microphone, if you need to use one.
- Rehearse using a remote for your PowerPoint, if you choose to use one.
- Visit with people as they arrive for the speech. It helps to create a bond with the audience prior to your presentation.

Consider these areas carefully and pre-pack for your presentation. Begin to pack a bag of things you will need to carry for the speech. If you need visual aids, you will also need to work with a tech team and have them rehearse with you to make sure they understand all that you will require them to do for your presentation. This means providing a script so they will know when to set up your table display for props or so they will know when to advance the slides of your PowerPoint presentation. Preparation also includes rehearsal.

First, rehearse *without* your tech team to smooth out the rough edges and to make decisions regarding the point in your speech when visual aids, sound, light changes, or PowerPoint slides should be introduced. Once you have worked through these details, then bring in the tech team.

CHECKLIST FOR A GREAT SPEECH

Before each presentation, follow this checklist to make sure every detail is in shipshape!

The Outline:
- ☐ Typed
- ✔ Correct outline format
- ✔ Header (name, company name/class name/date)
- ✔ Headings for each item is in bold letters
- ☐ Speech Category
- ☐ Title
- ☐ General Purpose
- ☐ Specific Purpose

Introduction:
- ☐ Full sentence format
- ☐ Attention Step
- ☐ Establish Need/Relevance
- ☐ Establish Speaker Credibility
- ☐ Thesis/Preview Statement (clearly states main points)

Body:
- ☐ Roman numerals (I., II., III.) Capitalized letters for sub-points (A., B., C.) and numbers for sub-sub-points (1., 2., 3.)
- ☐ Three main points (using key words or phrases)
- ☐ Transition sentences between the introduction step to the main points, between each main point, and between the last main point and the conclusion
- ☐ Each main point is covered equally

Conclusion:
- ☐ Full sentence format
- ☐ Signal to let your audience know you are concluding the speech
- ☐ Summary restates all main points clearly
- ☐ Final appeal keeps the audience thinking about the speech

Visual Aids:
- ☐ Visual aid explanation page is included with the outline
- ☐ PowerPoint/Prezi slides follow outline
- ☐ PowerPoint follows design requirements
- ☐ Handout is usable, designed by the speaker, and supplies one for each person
- ☐ Rehearse using visual aids with tech team

Research:

☐ Follow citation guidelines for the topic

☐ Include credible research sources

☐ Include the minimum number of sources required

☐ Vary types of research used

☐ Parenthetically cite research in the document

☐ Include a separate page for the Works Cited

Presentation:

☐ Rehearse using presentation notes

☐ Rehearse with the tech team

☐ Place a water bottle on the lectern

☐ Check EVERYTHING—lights, sound, computer, PowerPoint, notes folder

TECH TEAM CHECKLIST

Complete this form as you plan the use of visual aids so you are prepared for the speech. Speakers who use visual aids will need to make use of a tech team. It is the speaker's responsibility to meet with tech team members ahead of time, provide a script, and rehearse with the tech team to make sure they understand what is needed. Visual aids are an important part of the speech and a direct reflection of your credibility as a speaker.

Date: _____ **Time of Speech:** _____

Type of Speech: _____

Description of visual aids:

_____

_____

_____

_____

Note: In the area below, please list each tech team member's name and their assigned duties. Be sure to assign a member for the PowerPoint, sound, lights, setup, breakdown, and distribution of handouts. All duties may not be needed for all speeches.

Tech Team Member's Name: _____

Duties Assigned: _____

Tech Team Member's Name: _____

Duties Assigned: _____

Tech Team Member's Name: _____

Duties Assigned: _____

Tech Team Member's Name: _____

Duties Assigned: _____

_____

_____

EVALUATING THE SPEECH

SPEECHSHARKS HAVE THICK SKIN

It's no secret, SpeechSharks have thick skin. Most people who are working hard to improve their speech presentations often ask others to evaluate or critique their speeches. As speakers work to improve stage presence, they will often video and audio record presentations then play the recordings over and over again searching for ways to improve. You need thick skin for this!

Speakers welcome evaluations and critiques that recognize their strengths, but also evaluations that offer suggestions and tips for overcoming weaknesses. The purpose of an evaluation is to coach, help, build, mold, and encourage. ALL of us can improve. Not only do SpeechSharks understand this concept, but they have the thick skin needed to welcome feedback in all types of forms. Here is a strategy to help you evaluate other speakers:

I lovingly call this "The Sandwich Approach." This strategy involves building an evaluation the way that you would build a sandwich. The best part of any sandwich is the bread, but without the meat and cheese, it's just a piece of bread —a snack, but not a meal. The same is true with an evaluation. Consider the two slices of bread as the (1) Introduction Step and the (2) Conclusion Step. Consider the meat and cheese as the Body of the speech.

Start the evaluation with the first piece of bread, the Introduction Step. Do this by showing how the speaker got the audience's attention, established need for the topic, established why the speaker was credible to speak about the topic, and clearly detailed the three main points in the thesis. Also, add the strengths you noticed during the first part of the evaluation. Was the speaker prepared, did she use research effectively, was she dressed professionally, and how were her vocal skills?

Now, it is time to evaluate the message delivered. This is the meat and cheese of the sandwich and includes the content and purpose of the speech. Are the points clear, do they make sense, did the speaker use research or personal experience to clarify the points? This is also a good time to share any issues you noticed that the speaker should strengthen.

Finally, it's time for the last slice of bread. This one will cover the conclusion. How was her summary and appeal to action, did she end strong, and did her final words keep you thinking about the message she delivered. Before you finish the evaluation, be sure to add one more thing that you noticed the speaker do that was really over the top! Leave the speaker with a last word that leaves the speaker motivated to continue working on her communication skills.

It takes skill to build an evaluation that motivates, encourages, and also highlights areas to improve without making the new speaker feel defeated. Sure, SpeechSharks have thick skin. Evaluators also need thick skin, but with time and experience, evaluations can be delivered as a tender morsel to be savored, enjoyed, and appreciated!

Evaluations of presentations allow you to recognize and be prepared to capitalize on your strengths as a speaker and identify areas for improvement. Generally, a one- to two-page document is sufficient to evaluate your overall speaking strengths and areas in need of improvement.

In a learning environment, speakers may also be asked to offer written or oral speech evaluations of their peers. Written evaluations are conducted during the presentation in the form of a rubric or guideline as found below. Oral evaluations are usually presented immediately following the speech and may be delivered by a member of the audience or by the speech coach. In any case, evaluations are an excellent tool to help us become better speakers.

Consider asking a friend or colleague to video record your speech. Plan to watch the video twice before completing a self-evaluation.

The first time, watch the video without sound so that you pay careful attention to non-verbal cues that you may send. These will include the way you are dressed, movements, gestures, and facial expressions.

The second time, watch the video with sound and pay careful attention to your vocal skills and to the content delivered.

SUGGESTED GUIDELINES FOR SELF-EVALUATION

Evaluate your last classroom presentation by responding to the questions listed below. As you analyze your performance, consider your own reactions, your personal opinion of your performance, and audience reaction during your presentation. Respond to all questions:

SELF-EVALUATION

Areas to Consider	Questions to Ask
Self	Did the audience see you as a credible speaker? If yes, why? If no, why not?
Others	How well did you analyze and adapt to your audience?
Purpose	How successful was your presentation? How well did you achieve your purpose?
Context	How did you handle the logistics of your visual aids, time frame, etc.?
Content	How well did you include appropriate content substantiated with strong and valid supporting material?
Structure	What made your introduction and conclusion effective or ineffective? How well did you organize the overall presentation?
Expression	What are your delivery strengths? How will you endeavor to improve your delivery in future presentations?

Just as it is imperative to evaluate your own performance, it is critical that you have the ability to critique and evaluate your peers' presentations. Please use the Peer Evaluation Template when asked to evaluate your peers. It is not necessary to post a score, but showing a rating scale of 3–1 will help the speaker to know his/her own strengths and weaknesses. Please use the "Notes" area to acknowledge great work or to add suggestions to help the speaker.

Suggested Guidelines for Peer Evaluations

Please rate the speaker's use of each element on a scale of 3–1 as defined below:

 3 = Element was evident and very effective

 2 = Element was present, but could be revised for greater impact

 1 = Element was NOT evident or effective

Introduction:

When starting the speech, did the speaker—

 _____ 1. Gain attention through an interesting question, story, statistic, example, etc.?

 _____ 2. Clearly state thesis/purpose statement and preview the main points?

 _____ 3. Establish credibility by citation of sources and establishing speaker's own experience with the topic?

Notes:

Body:

In developing the body of the speech, did the speaker—

 _____ 1. Identify and organize main points in a manner that was easy to follow?

 _____ 2. Use well chosen examples and/or personal experience?

 _____ 3. Effectively use support materials such as statistics and quotations?

 _____ 4. Properly cite sources (verbal citations)?

Notes:

Conclusion:

When moving to finish the speech, did the speaker—

_____ 1. Clearly indicate the speech was concluding by providing a signal word?

_____ 2. Review main points?

_____ 3. End the speech with a memorable statement?

Notes:

Presentation and Visual Aids:

_____ 1. Incorporate relevant and well-designed visual aids?

_____ 2. Effectively handle presentation aids, avoiding any distraction?

Notes:

Delivery:

During the speech, did the speaker—

_____ 1. Utilize voice appropriately by varying inflection, tone, and volume?

_____ 2. Speak words clearly with proper grammar and pronunciation?

_____ 3. Physically move and gesture with purpose, avoiding distracting mannerisms?

_____ 4. Establish and maintain eye contact, while balancing use of note cards?

_____ 5. Appear confident, poised, and in control of the presentation?

Notes:

Overall Evaluation:

Considering the speech as a whole, did the speaker—

_____ 1. Choose an appropriate topic and purpose statement?

_____ 2. Meet the assignment requirements, including time limits?

Additional Comments:

Whether you are completing the speech for a grade in a class or working toward a personal goal, you may want to know how you will be evaluated and what your audience expects. Here are two more evaluation rubrics. These can be adapted to any type of speech. When Research and Visual Aids are not required, add the extra points to the Introduction and Conclusion steps.

SPEECH EVALUATION RUBRIC

Speech Performance 100 possible points	Excellent 5 points	Good 4 points	Average 3 points	Fair 2 points	Poor 1 point	N/A 0 points
Introduction Step: Attention Step: Establish Need/Relevance: Establish Credibility: Thesis:						
Body: Point #1						
Body: Point #2						
Body: Point #3						
Transitions (4) To first point To second point To third point To conclusion						
Conclusion Step: Summary: Appeal to Action:						
Use of Research Verbal Citations: Number Sources Used: Research Supported Topic:						
Visual Aids Types: _____ _____ Setting up Handling of Aids (Use) Design Visibility						

Speech Performance 100 possible points	Excellent 5 points	Good 4 points	Average 3 points	Fair 2 points	Poor 1 point	N/A 0 points
Language Skills Vocabulary Sentence Structure Grammar Usage						
Vocal Delivery Skills Voice Volume Rate Vocal Variance						
Enthusiasm for Topic Energy/Passion						
Gestures						
Eye Contact						
Poise and Confidence						
Appearance						
Movement: Entrance to Stage Exit from Stage Stage Movement						
Time of Speech						
Management of Tech Team						
Professionalism						

Additional Comments for the Speaker:

OUTLINE RUBRIC

Outline	Possible Points = 100	Points Earned
Standard Outline Format	20 points	
Typed	5	
Roman Numerals I, II, III	5	
ABC	5	
123	5	
Introduction Step:	20 points	
Attention Step:	5	
Establish Need/Reliance:	5	
Establish Credibility:	5	
Thesis:	5	
Main Points	15 points	
#1	5	
#2	5	
#3	5	
Transitions (4)	10 points	
#1	2.5	
#2	2.5	
#3	2.5	
#4	2.5	
Conclusion:	10 points	
Summary:	5	
Appeal to Action:	5	
Research	25 points	
Required Sources Used	5	
Parenthetical Citations	5	
Works Cited Page	5	
Follows Citation Guidelines	5	
Copy of Research Included	5	

You won't fear a shark attack when you keep your eyes open and are prepared for whatever comes your way! Some refer to shark movements as a feeding frenzy. Truthfully, it is no frenzy at all, but a graceful ballet in which the sharks are fast and swim confidently toward their goal. You can do this too! Be a Communication Shark! Use this section to test your skills and understanding.

Presenting and Rehearsing the Presentation

1. What is the definition of volume? _____

_____

_____

2. What is a larynx? _____

_____

_____

3. What is the definition of rate? _____

_____

_____

4. What is the definition of pitch? _____

_____

_____

5. What is the definition of pace? _____

_____

_____

6. What is the definition of color as used to describe a voice? _____

_____

_____

7. What type dialect do YOU have? _____

_____

_____

8. What are filler words? Do you use them? _____

_____

_____

9. What non-verbal cues do you send about yourself with your posture and pose? _____

_____

_____

10. What gestures send negative non-verbal cues? _____

_____

_____

11. What is a benefit of using strong eye contact throughout the speech? _____

_____

_____

12. What is the definition of adrenaline? _____

_____

_____

13. What is the BAM Approach for speaking with confidence? _____

_____

_____

14. What strategy works best for you when you need to deal with speech anxiety? _____

_____

_____

15. Why do most of us experience speech anxiety in some form? _____

_____

16. What symptoms are evident with speech anxiety? _____

_____

17. Does the audience want you to succeed? _____

_____

18. How do breathing exercises help with speech anxiety? _____

_____

19. What can you do before the speech to calm your nerves? _____

_____

20. What are the major advantages of using visual aids in your speeches?

_____

_____

21. What kinds of visual aids might you use in a speech?

_____

_____

22. What factors should you consider when planning to use presentation technology in a speech?

_____

_____

23. What will help you to be more confident the day of your speech? _____

_____

_____

24. What should you do before the speech to take care of YOU? _____

_____

_____

25. What should your outline include? _____

_____

_____

26. What should you check prior to the presentation? _____

_____

_____

27. What are the characteristics of effective speakers? _____

_____

_____

28. Why does the audience want YOU to succeed? _____

_____

_____

29. What are the benefits of good communication skills? _____

_____

_____

30. Why is it important to evaluate your own presentation?

_____

_____

Shark Bites

IMPROVING PRESENTATION SKILLS

Practice Eye Contact: Work in a group of four or five people. Put your chairs in a circle. Take turns speaking impromptu (Suggested Topic: Your favorite vacation). As you speak, make sure you are making direct eye contact with each person in your group. Spend two or three seconds looking directly at each person and then move your gaze to the next person. Continue doing this until your story is finished and you have held direct eye contact with each person in the group.

Practice Good Posture: Stand next to your chair. Place an object on your head (iPad or phone). Count to twenty slowly and keep your head balanced so that your device does not fall off your head.

Practice Good Gestures: Using your arms, hands, head, and face, practice gestures for the following: saying "no," saying "yes," showing how many numbers, showing how large or small something is, showing locations, showing you understand, and showing you do not understand.

Practice Using Note Cards: If you are using the SpeechShark app, note cards will be on your phone or tablet. Practice using them and swiping to move from one point to the next point.

Practice Using Different Verbal and Non-Verbal Cues: Make up hypothetical situations with a friend and respond using the following:

1. Angry response
2. Happy response
3. Confused response
4. Submissive response
5. Assertive response

Peer Evaluate each other to make sure verbal words and the responses aligned with non-verbal cues. Are there things you need to improve? What are they?

Shark Bites

TAKING A BITE OUT OF THE FEAR OF PUBLIC SPEAKING

List five things that cause you to have presentation anxiety:

1.

2.

3.

4.

5.

Rank these fears from 1–5. Assign 1 to the fear that causes the most anxiety.

Draw a line through the fear and add a positive thought beside each one.

Use BREATHING Exercises to help you feel calm:

Sit in a chair with both feet on the floor and your hands in your lap. Close your eyes. Breathe in and count 1, 2, 3, 4 and out 1, 2, 3, 4. Do this for one full minute (timing yourself with the timer on your phone).

Do this exercise again, but this time try to take only six to ten breaths per minute.

Take your hands out of your lap and let them hang loosely by your sides. Shake your hands as hard as you can for three seconds. Then drop your hands by your side and imagine all of your anxiety dripping out from your fingertips and landing on the floor. Stay in this position for ten seconds.

Return your hands to your lap. Again repeat breathing in and count 1, 2, 3, 4 and breath out 1, 2, 3, 4.

Think positive thoughts and tell yourself—I've got this! I'm a SpeechShark!

Shark Bites

CHECKLIST FOR THE VISUAL AIDS AND RESEARCH!

Complete the following Task Checklist:

The Task	Completed	Needs More Work
Visual Aid ☐ Include a Visual Aid Explanation Page with Outline ☐ PowerPoint/Prezi follows Outline ☐ Handout is Usable ☐ Handout is Designed by Speaker ☐ One Handout for Each Audience Member ☐ Rehearse Visual Aids with Tech Team		
Research ☐ Follow Citation Guidelines for the Subject ☐ Use Credible Sources ☐ Include Minimum Required ☐ Vary Types of Research ☐ Parenthetically Cite Sources in the Outline ☐ Include a Works Cited or Bibliography Page with the Full Citation		
Presentation ☐ Rehearse, Rehearse, Rehearse ☐ Rehearse Using Presentation Notes ☐ Rehearse with Tech Team ☐ Double-Check EVERYTHING—lights, sound, computer, PPT, notes, water		

This human communication guide book is unique from other texts because it was written as a companion book for SpeechShark, the textbook published by Kendall Hunt, and also for the SpeechShark app, available for Android and IOS phones and electronic devices.

Visit GooglePlay or Apple Store using your phone or electronic device and search SpeechShark to download the app. Let us know how you enjoy using it!

Visit our Web site at www.SpeechShark.com and download the SpeechShark app for iOS and Android phones and devices!

Works Cited

Adkins, Reginald. *Conflict Management Styles Assessment.* Elemental Truths. IREM, 2006.

Adkins, Reginald. "How Do You Respond to Conflict? Conflict Management Styles Assessment." Elemental

Truths. IREM, http://irem.org/File%20Library/ChapterServices/ConflictManagementWS/

ActivityConflictManagementStylesAssessment.pdf. Accessed February 2018.

Altman, Irwin, and Dalmas Taylor. *Social Penetration Model: The Development of Interpersonal*

Relationships. Holt, 1973.

"Authoritarian, Democratic, and Laissez-Faire Leadership": Leadership Styles Diagram. Research Starters

eNotes.com, Inc. 29 March 2015, https://greatleadersgrow.wordpress.com/2015/03/29/leadership-styles-

pros-cons/. Accessed February 2018.

Burgoon, Judee. *Applying a Comparative Approach to Nonverbal Expectancy Violations Theory.* Sage,

1992, pp. 53–69.

Dewey, John. *How We Think: A Restatement of the Relation of Reflective Thinking to the Educative Process.*

Heath, 1933.

Eklund, Andy. Conflict Resolution Workshop. 2018, http://www.andyeklund.com/conflict-resolution-

workshop/. Accessed 5 February 2018.

Frymier, Ann Bainbridge, and Gary M. Shulman. "What's in It for Me?": Increasing Content Relevance to

Enhance Students' Motivation. *Communication Education Journal*, vol. 44, no. 1, 1995, pp. 40–50.

Hofstede, Geert. *Attitudes, Values, and Organizational Culture: Disentangling the Concepts.* Sage Journals,

1 May 1998.

Janis, Irving L. *Groupthink: A Psychological Study of Policy Decisions and Fiascoes.* 2nd ed., Houghton

Mifflin Company, 1982.

Kilmann, Thomas. "Conflict Mode Instrument," http://www.andyeklund.com/conflict-resolution-workshop/

Accessed, May 2016.

Knapp, Mark L., and Anita L. Vangelisti. *Relationship Stages: A Communication Perspective. Interpersonal

Communication and Human Relationships.* 5th ed., Pearson Education, 2005, pp. 36–49.

Kotter, John. "Leading Change: Why Transformation Efforts Fail." *Harvard Business Review*, March–April

1995, http://foresightlearning.com.au/leadership/john-kotter-on-leading-change/. Accessed February

2018.

Luft, Joseph, and Harrington Ingram. Einfuhrung in die Gruppendynamik. *Johari Window.* Klett. p. 2971.

Mehrabian, Albert. *Silent Messages: Implicit Communication of Emotions and Attitudes.* 2nd ed.,

Wadsworth Publishing Company, 1980.

Mittelman, W. "Maslow's Study of Self-Actualization: A Reinterpretation." *Journal of Humanistic

Psychology*, vol. 31, no. 1, 1991, pp. 114–35.

National Association of College and Employers. *Job Outlook.* 2018, http://www.naceweb.org/career-

development/trends-and-predictions/job-outlook-2016-attributes-employers-want-to-see-on-new-

college-graduates-resumes/.

Neuliep, James W., and James C. McCroskey. *The Development of a US and Generalized Ethnocentrism

[GENE] Scale.* Communication Research Reports. 2009, pp. 385–98, https://www.google.com/search?q

=GENE+scale&oq=GENE+scale&aqs=chrome..69i57j0l5.2630j1j7&sourceid=chrome&ie=UTF-8.

Accessed February 2018.

Newman, Gabriela, et al. *Leadership Theories: Leadership Styles Words.* Virtual Business Solutions Ltd.

2018, http://www.vbsl.co.nz/leadership-theories/. Accessed February 2018.

Schaubhut, Nancy A. *Technical Brief for the Thomas-Kilmann Conflict Mode Instrument: Description of the Updated Normative Sample and Implications for Use.* CPP. 2007, http://www.cppasiapacific.sg/wp-content/uploads/2016/09/TKI_Technical_Brief.pdf. Accessed. February 2018.

Snyder, Mark. *Who Should Survive. Test.* Oklahoma Association of Youth Services. 2018, http://www.oays. org/images/toolbox/5/who_should_survive.pdf. Accessed February 2018.

Team Roles of Group Members: Communication and Distributed Leadership Form. Assessment 4.1. http:// www.pathways.cu.edu.eg/subpages/training_courses/teams/chapter4.htm.

Tuckman, Bruce W. "Group Development Model. Developmental Sequence in Small Groups." *Psychological Bulletin*, 1965, pp. 384–99.

Vicky. *Trait Theory of Leadership Diagram: Leadership: Types, Importance, and Theories.* 2018, https:// difengsun88.wordpress.com/2016/05/22/blog-3-most-effective-leadership-management-styles-approaches/ .

Wilson, Gerald L. *Groups in Context: Leadership and Participation in Small Groups.* 6th ed., McGraw Hill, 2018.

Index

Accommodation, 104
Action language, 66
Active listening, 55, 165
Adaptation, 31
Adaptor, 67
Affect displays, 67–68
Albert Mehrabian's Communication Model, 40
Altman, Irwin, 91, 92
American Psychological Association (APA) citation style, 248
Anger, 104
Announcement speech, 204
Anxiety, 284–290
APA citation style, 248
Appeal to action, 133
Appearance, 68, 281–284
    eye contact, 283–284
    facial expression, 283
    gesture, 283
    head nodding, 284
    head tilting, 284
    physical, 282–283
    poise, 283
    posture, 283
    smiling, 284
Appreciative listening, 55
Aromatherapy, 289
Artifactual language, 66, 72
Attention step, 162, 163, 164, 171
Audience, 159, 257, 298
    conversational quality and, 219
    demonstration speech and, 189
    informative speech and, 183
    introduction speech and, 177
    persuasion speech and, 196, 197
    public speaking and, 164–165
    questioning, 257
    speaker responsibilities and, 161
    special occasion speech and, 203
Audience analysis, 228–229, 231, 269
Auditory signal, 54
Authoritarian leader, 117

Authority rule strategy, 134
Autocratic leader, 117
Avoidance, 104
Award acceptance speech, 204
Award presentation speech, 204

Backup plan, 300
Bar graph, 292
Barrier, 41–42
Behavior, 176, 195, 196
Bias, 22
Bibliography, 254
Bing, 246
Blog, 245, 246
Blush, 31, 32
Body language, 40, 67
Body of speech, 254, 301
Book, 247
Brainstorming, 119, 123–125, 133, 223
Breadth, 92, 99
Breathing, 289
Bruce Tuckman Model, 114–115
Burgoon, Judee K., 70

Category, 233, 236
Causal order, 252
Central idea speech, 183
Ceremonial speech, 203, 204–205
    award acceptance, 204
    award presentation, 204
    commemorative, 205
    commencement, 205
    dedication, 205
    eulogy, 205
    installation, 204
Channel, 7, 8
Chart, 293, 294, 296
Chicago Manual of Style (CMS) citation, 248
Chronemics, 71, 72
Chronological order, 252, 253

Citation, 248–249, 250, 251, 275
   APA style, 248
   CMS style, 248
   CSE style, 248
   MLA style, 248
Closer phrases, 212
Closing statement, 259
Closing strategies, 212
CMS citation style, 248
Co-culture, 28
Code, 7
Collaboration, 104
Collectivism, 29
Color, 279, 295–296
Commemorative speech, 205
Commencement speech, 205
Commitment, relationship, 87
Communication
   competence, 12
   defined, 4, 159
   functions of, 9–10
   importance of effective skills in, 4
   social media and, 11, 12, 13
   technology and, 10
   as transactional process, 159
Communication barrier, 42
Communication function
   identity needs, 10
   physical needs, 9
   practical needs, 10
   social needs, 10
Communication interactive stages, 86–87
Communication model, 7–8
   linear, 7
   transactional, 7–8
Communication Model (Mehrabian), 40
Communication skills
   evaluation sheet, 5
   in workplace, 4
Communication technology, 10
   pace of, 10
Communication type
   dyadic/interpersonal, 9
   group, 9
   intrapersonal, 8
   mass, 9
   public, 9
Competency, in communication, 12
Competent communicator, 12
Competition, 104
Compromise, 104
Conclusion, 162, 254, 258, 301
   checklist, 259
Confidence, 284
Conflict, 104–110
Conflict approach styles, 104
Conflict management styles activity, 109–110

Conflict resolution, 105
Connective, 260
Connector, 162
Connotative language, 40
Consensus strategy, 134
Constructive conflict management, 104
Context, 8
Conversational quality, 219
Conversational tone, 161
Copyright, 245, 250
Council of Science Editors (CSE) citation style, 248
Credibility, 162, 164, 258
Critical listening, 55
Cronin, Audrey Mann, 281
Cry, 31
CSE citation style, 248
Cultural awareness checklist, 35
Cultural Dimension, 29
Culture, 28–35
   co-culture, 28
   defined, 28
   dimensions of, 29–30
   intercultural communication strategies, 31
   language and, 42, 43
   subsets, 28
   traits we share, 32
Curiosity, 256

D

Decision, 132
Decoder, 7
Decoding, 52, 53, 159
Deconstructive conflict management, 104
Dedication speech, 205
Delivery, practice and, 298
Delivery cue, 255
Delivery methods, 217–219
   extemporaneous, 219
   impromptu, 218–219
   manuscript, 217–218
   memorization, 218
   practice and, 217
Delivery skills improvement, 225
Democratic leader, 117
Demonstration speech, 189–194
   audience and, 189
   brainstorming worksheet, 191–193
   outline template, 194
   plan, 189
   purpose of, 235
   rehearsal, 190
   topics, 189, 239
Denotation and connotation worksheet, 47
Denotative language, 40
Depth, 92, 99
Dewey, John, 133

Dialects, 279
Digital technology, 10, 11
Discrimination, 28
Distance, proxemics and, 69
Distraction, 56, 165
Diverse audience, 233
Diversity, 28, 232–233. *See also* Culture
Drawing, 292
Dress, 68, 144–145, 282–283. *See also* Appearance
Dyad, 9, 86
Dyadic/interpersonal communication, 9

E

Effective group meeting, 118
Effective language skills, 279–280
Email, 10, 40
Emblem, 68
Empathetic listening, 55, 165
Empathy, 163
Encoder, 7
Encoding, 52, 53, 159
Engagement, 31
Entertaining speech, 176
Environment, 8
Equipment check, 300
Esteem, 9
Ethics, 232
Ethnicity, 28
Ethnocentrism, 28
Ethos, 232
Eulogy, 205
Evaluation form, communication skills, 5
Evaluation, of message, 55
Evaluation of speech, 305–315
    outline rubric, 315
    peer evaluation guidelines
    self-evaluation guidelines, 307
    speech evaluation rubric, 313–314
Evaluation rubric, 313–314
Expectancy Violation Theory, 70–71, 79, 81
Extemporaneous delivery mode, 219
Extemporaneous speech, 217, 218, 219
External noise, 8
Extraneous noise, 56
Eye contact, 68, 75, 219, 283–284

F

Facebook, 11, 40
Face-to-face communication, 10, 40
Facial expression, 283
Family relationship, 86, 89
Farewell speech, 206
Fear of public speaking, 167–168, 284–290, 323
Feedback, 7–8, 52, 53, 159
Feminine, 29, 43
Fetal position, 31, 32

Filler word, 280–281
First impression, 260
Font, 295
Forming stage of group development, 114, 115
Friendship, 86, 89
Frown, 31, 32

G

GALILEO, 247
Gallup Polls, 247
Gender, 42, 43–44, 76
General appearance, 68
Generalization, 28
General purpose, 233, 234
Gesture, 67, 219, 283
Goals of speech, 234–235
Goodwill, 256
Google, 246
Google Scholar, 246
Graph, 292, 294, 296
Group, 114–130
    characteristics of, 114
    cohesion in, 115–116
    defined, 114
    development, 114–115
    leadership in, 116–117
    meetings, 118
    member roles in, 116
    norms, 115
    presentation, 119, 120, 121–122, 123–124
    problem solving in, 132–138
Group cohesion, 115–116
Group commercial activity, 129–130
Group communication, 9
Group conflict exercise, 137–138
Group development model (Tuckman), 114–115
Group goals, 114, 116
Group norms, 115
Group presentation, 119–125
    advantages of, 119
    brainstorming in, 119, 123–125
    checklist, 120
    plan, 121
    PREP model, 122
    topics, 240
Group problem solving, 132–138
    decision-making strategies, 134
    Groupthink and, 134
    Monroe's Motivated Sequence, 132–133
    stages of, 133–134
Group roles, 116
Groupthink, 134

H

Handout, 293
Haptics, 71–72, 72

Head nodding, 68, 284
Head titling, 68, 284
Hidden agenda, 114
High context, 30
    vs. low context, 30
High power, 29
Hofstede, Geert H., 29

I

I Am Legend, 10
Identity management, 22
Identity needs, 10
Illustrator, 68
Image, 296
Imagery, 164
Impression management, 22
Impromptu delivery mode, 218–219
Impromptu speech, 218–219
Indentation, 254
Individualism, 29
    vs. collectivism, 29
Information gathering interview, 141
Informative listening, 55
Informative speech, 176, 183–188
    audience and, 183
    brainstorming worksheet, 185–187
    outline template, 188
    purpose of, 235
    topics, 184, 239
    visual aids in, 184
Ingham, Harringham, 91, 93
Installation speech, 204
Internal noise, 8
Internal summary, 260
Internet, research, 246
Interpersonal communication, 9, 86–101
    defined, 86
    intimacy and, 91
    patterns of, 86–89
    self-disclosure and, 91, 92–93
    types of, 86
Interpersonal conflict, 104–110
Interpersonal skills, in workplace, 4
Interview, 141–146, 247
    after, 143
    basic questions, 145
    before, 142
    closed questions for, 141
    closing, 142
    defined, 141
    dress for, 144–145
    during, 143
    face-to-face, 142
    illegal questions, 146
    information needed for, 140
    post interview do's and don'ts, 146
    PREP model and, 144

probing questions for, 141
process, 145–146
questions to ask, 146
recording and, 142
skills, 141–142
Skype, 142
tips for, 140–141, 144
tough questions, 145
Intimacy, 91
Intimate distance, 69, 70
Intimate space, 69, 70
Intrapersonal communication, defined, 8
Introduction, 254, 256, 258, 301
    checklist, 257
Introduction speech, 177–182
    audience and, 177
    brainstorming worksheet, 179–181
    outline template, 182
    past, present, future and, 177
    purpose of, 235

J

Janis, Irving, 134
Jargon, 42
Job interview, 141. *See also* Interview
Johari Window, 91, 93
Journal, 247

K

Key idea speech, 183
Keynote address, 203–204
Key word, 247
Kinesics, 67, 72, 281
Knapp, Mark, 86

L

Laissez-Faire leader, 117
Language, 40–44
    culture and, 42, 43
    gender and, 42
    power of, 40–41
Language barrier, 41
Larynx, 278
Laughter, 31, 32
Leadership, 116–118
    defined, 116
    trait theory of, 117
Leadership styles, 117
Library, 247
LikeSo: Your Personal Speech Coach app, 281
Linear Model of Communication, 7
Line graph, 296
Linguistics, 40
Listener evaluation sheet, 57
Listening, 52–63, 75, 164–165

active, 55
appreciative, 55
challenges in, 54–55
critical, 55
distractions to, 56
empathetic, 55
evaluation sheet, 57
vs. hearing, 53–54
informative, 55
misconceptions of, 53–54
process of, 52–53
strategies, 56
types of, 55
value of, 52
Listening challenge, 63
Logos, 232
Long-term time, 30
Love and belonging needs, 9
Low context, 30
    vs. high context, 29
Low power, 29
    vs. high power, 29
Luft, Joseph, 91, 93

M

Magazine, 247
Mail, 10
Main point, 252–253, 256
Maintenance/relationship, 116
Manuscript delivery mode, 217–218
Manuscript speech, 217–218
Masculine, 29, 43, 44
    vs. feminine, 29
Maslow, Abraham, 9
Maslow's hierarchy of needs, 9–10
Mass communication, 9
Meaning, 4, 21, 40, 56, 75
Meditation, 289–290
Meeting agenda, 118
Mehrabian, Albert, 11, 40, 69, 281
Memorization delivery mode, 218
Memorized speech, 218
Message, 7
Messenger, 40
Mindfulness, 31
Mindlessness, 31
Miscommunication, 41–42
MLA citation style, 248
Mock interview, 149, 151–152
Moderator, 121, 122
    Q & A session and, 122
Modern Language Association (MLA) citation style, 248
Monroe, Alan H., 132, 196
Monroe's Motivated Sequence, 132–133, 196
Motivational speech, 176
Movement during speech, 290, 291
Multicultural environment, 28

N

Narrowing of topic, 236
National Association of Colleges and Employers (NACE), 4
National Communication Association, 160
National Speaker's Association, 160
Newspaper, 247
Noise, 8, 52, 53, 56, 159
Nomination speech, 204
Nonverbal communication, 40, 49, 66–81
    characteristics of, 66
    competency in, 75
    context and setting in, 76
    cultural context, 76
    defined, 66
    functions of, 69
    influences of, 67–68
    professional context, 76
    proxemics, 69–72
    relational context, 76
    types of, 72, 73
Non-verbal cue, 165, 281
Nonverbal language, 40
Norming stage of group development, 114, 115
Norms, 20, 22
Notes/note taking, 165, 255, 298

O

Object language, 66
Olfactory communication, 72
Opportunities, 234
Organization, 21
Outline, 210, 298, 301
    conclusion, 258–259
    connectives, 260
    constructing, 256–261
    credibility and, 258
    demonstration speech, 194
    internal summary, 260
    introduction, 256–257, 258
    introduction speech, 182
    main points, 252–253, 256
    organization of, 252
    persuasion speech, 202
    preparation, 253–254
    presentation, 165
    sales presentation, 216
    signpost, 261
    speaking, 255
    special occasion, 210
    topic, 257
Outline rubric, 315

P

Pace, 279
Paralanguage, 278

Paralinguistic, 72
Paraphrase, 249
Pathos, 232
Peer evaluation guidelines, 309–311
Perceived self, 22
Perception
    defined, 21
    factors influencing, 22
    process of, 21
Perception checking, 22
Performance review, 141
Performing stage of group development, 115
Personal distance, 69, 70
Personal space, 69, 70
Personal story, 251
Persuasion, 41, 132–133
Persuasion speech, 195–202
    audience and, 196, 197
    brainstorming worksheet, 199–201
    Monroe's Motivated Sequence, 196
    motivation and, 195
    outline template, 202
    purpose of, 235
    topics, 197, 240
Phone, 10, 40
Photo, 292, 294, 296
Physical appearance, 68
Physiological needs, 9
Pie graph, 292
Pitch, 279
Pitch Perfect, 42
Plagiarism, 245–246
Point, 236
Poise, 67, 283
Posture, 31, 67, 283
PowerPoint, 190, 294
Practical needs, 10
Practice, 298
    delivery methods and, 217
    public speaking and, 160, 168
    visual aids, 299
Prejudice, 28
Preparation outline, 253–254
PREP model, 122, 144
Presentation, 302
    appearance and, 281–284
    confidence and, 284–285
    filler words, 280–281
    group, 119–125
    movement during, 290, 291
    sales, 211–216
    skills for, 321
    stage entering and exiting, 290
    text in, 295
    vocal cues, 278–280
Presentation aids, 292–293
    chart, 293
    citing, 250

drawing, 292
graph, 292
handout, 293
music soundbite, 293
photo, 292
table display, 292
video clip, 293
yourself, 293
Presentation outline, 253–254
Presentation technology, 294
    planning for use of, 294
    pros and cons of, 294
Presented self, 22
Prezi Slide Presentation, 190, 294
Primary territories, 70
Probing question, 141
Problem analysis, 133
Problem identification, 133
Problem-solution order, 252, 253
Problem solving, 4, 132–138. *See also* Group problem
    solving
    defined, 132
Problem-solving interview, 141
Professional communication, 140–152
    job interview, 141–146
    resume, 140, 141
Professional relationship, 89
Proxemics, 69–72, 72
    defined, 69
Public communication, 9
Public distance, 69, 70
Public domain, 250
Public relations speech, 204
Public self, 22
Public space, 69, 70
Public speaking, 158–171
    anxiety and, 285–290
    audience responsibilities, 164–165
    common mistakes speakers make, 233
    vs. communication, 159
    communication tips for, 166–168
    defined, 159
    effective speaker characteristics, 166
    fear of, 167–168
    perseverance and, 164
    plan, 163
    practice and, 160
    preparation for, 163–164
    speaker responsibilities in, 161
    speech introduction, 164
Public territories, 70
Purpose of speech, 233–234
Purpose statement, 271

Q

Q & A session, 122
Questions of fact, 197

Questions of policy, 197
Questions of value, 197
Quotation, 257

R

Race, 28
Racism, 28
Radio, 10
Rate, 279
Receiver, 7, 8, 53, 159
Reflective Thinking Process, 133–134
Regulator, 68
Rehearsal
    demonstration speech and, 190
    great speech checklist, 301–302
    room and equipment, 300
    speech day checklist, 300
    visual aids practice, 299
Relational context, 76
Relevance, 162, 164, 171
Remember, message, 54
Report speech, 204
Research, 245–250, 302
    citations and, 248–249
    defined, 245
    guidelines, 246
    key words and, 247
    methods for, 246–247
    online, 246
    paraphrasing and, 249
    plagiarism, 245–246
    presentation aids citation, 250
    search engines for, 246–247
    verbal citation of interview, 251
Research methods, 246, 246–247
Response, 55
Resume, 140, 141
    computer-friendly, 141
    headings, 140
Retirement speech, 206
Rhetorical question, 257
Roast speech, 206
Roles, in group, 116
Romantic relationship, 86, 89

S

Sadness, 32
Safety needs, 9
Sales closer phrases, 212
Sales closing strategies, 212
Sales presentation, 211–216. *See also* Persuasion speech
    brainstorming worksheet, 213–215
    closer phrases, 212
    outline template, 216
    sales success strategies, 211–212
"Sandwich approach," 305

Search engine, 246–247
Secondary territories, 70
Self-actualization, 9
Self-centered, 116
Self-concept, defined, 20
Self-concept and perception exercise, 25
Self-confidence, 67
Self-disclosure, 91, 92
Self-distortion, 21
Self-esteem, 20
Self-evaluation guidelines, 307
Self-expression, 20
Self-fulfilling prophecy, 21
Self-perception, 20
Self-presentation, 22
Semantics, 40
Sender, 7, 8, 159
Sex, 43
Shark Bites
    audience analysis, 269
    citing sources, 275
    conflict management, 109–110
    cultural awareness checklist, 35
    delivery skills, 225
    denotation and connotation, 47
    Expectancy Violation Theory, 79, 81
    fear of public speaking, 323
    group commercial, 129–130
    group conflict, 137–138
    intimacy, 99
    listening challenge, 63
    mock interview, 149, 151–152
    nonverbal communication, 49
    presentation skills, 321
    purpose statement, 271
    self-concept and perception, 25
    self-disclosure analysis, 97
    social media detox, 17
    social penetration model, 101
    speech preparation, 171
    topic, 273
    topic brainstorming, 223
    visual aids and research, 325
Shark-o-licious speech, 162–164
    introduction to, 164
    perseverance, 164
    planning, 163, 171
    preparation, 163–164
Shark-o-licious Treat, 162
Short-term time, 30
    vs. long-term time, 30
Shrug, 31
Sign language, 66
Signpost, 261
Skype, 40
Slang, 42
Slump, 31
Smell, 72

Smile, 31, 32, 67–68, 284
Smith, Will, 10
Social distance, 69, 70
Social loafer/slacker, 116
Social media, 10
    communication and, 11
    competent communication and, 12
    evaluation sheet, 13
    pace of, 12
    reasons for using, 11
Social media detox, 13
Social needs, 10
Social occasion speech, 203
Social penetration model, 91, 92, 101
Social space, 69, 70
Solution evaluation, 134
Solution follow-up, 134
Solution implementation, 134
Soundbite, 293
Spatial cue, 69
Spatial order, 252, 253
Speaker, 53, 121, 159
Speaking outline, 255
Special occasion speech, 176, 203–210, 205–206
    brainstorming worksheet, 207–209
    ceremonial, 204–205
    farewell, 206
    outline template, 210
    retirement, 206
    roast, 206
    special occasion, 205–206
    toast, 205
    welcome, 206
    work-related, 203–204
Specific purpose, 233, 234
Speech, 176–212, 298–299
    delivery methods for, 217–219
    demonstration, 189–194
    entertaining, 176
    goals of, 234–235
    informative, 176, 183–188
    introduction, 177–182
    motivational, 176
    persuasion, 195–202
    purpose of, 176, 233–234
    rehearsal, 298–299
    special occasion, 203–210
    strategies, 235
    time and, 235–236
    types of, 176–177
Speech anxiety, 284–290
Speech day checklist, 300
Speech evaluation, 305–315
SpeechShark app, 71
    how to use, 173
    time and, 236
Stage area, 290

Stages of coming apart, 88
Stages of coming together, 88
Stages of relational development (Knapp and Vangelisti),
    86–87, 88, 89
Standard outline, 177
Startle, audience, 256
Startling statement, 163
Stereotype, 28, 43
Stimuli, 21
Storming stage of group development, 114, 115
Storytelling, 10, 176, 251, 257
Strategic organization, 252
Strength, 234
Sub-point, 254
Summarization of speech, 259
Supporting material, 253
SWOT analysis, 234
Symbolization, 254

T

Table display, 292
Task, 115, 116, 119, 120, 121
Taste, 72
Taylor, Dalmas, 91, 92
Team, 114. *See also* Group
Technology
    communication and, 10
    presentation, 294
Tech team, 190
Tech team checklist, 303
TED Talks, 232
Telegraph, 10
Television, 10
Termination, of relationship, 87
Territoriality, 70, 72
Text, 40, 295
Thesis, 258
Threat, 234
Time, 235–236
Time restraints, 71
Toastmasters International, 160
Toast speech, 205
Topic, 257, 273
    category, 236, 237, 238
    choosing, 243
    narrowing, 236–238
    point, 236, 237, 238
    search, 236
    suggestions for, 239–240
    type, 236, 237, 238
Topical order, 252, 253
Traits, 31, 32
Trait Theory, 117
Transactional Model of Communication, 7–8
Transition, 162, 254
Tuckman, Bruce, 114

Twitter, 40
Type, of topic, 177

U

Uncertainty avoidance, 29, 30
Understand, message, 54

V

Vangelisti, Anita, 86
Verbal citation, 248–249
Verbal communication
    language and, 40
    in workplace, 4
Verbal cue, 165
Verbal language, 40
Video clip, 293, 294, 296
Visual aids, 184, 301. *See also* Presentation aids
    displaying, 297
    explaining, 297
    practicing with, 299
    preparation guidelines, 294–296
    presentation guidelines, 296–298
Visual aids and research, 325

Vocal cue, 278–280
Voice, 158
Volume, 278
Voting strategy, 134

W

Wave, 31, 68
Weaknesses, 234
Welcome speech, 206
Wikis, 245, 246
Work-related special occasion speech, 203, 203–204
    announcement, 204
    keynote address, 203–204
    nomination, 204
    public relations, 204
    report, 204
Works cited page, 254
Written communication, in workplace, 4

Y

Yahoo, 246

Photo Credits

UNIT 5:

From *Speech Shark: A Public Speaking Guide,* Second Edition, by Penny Joyner Waddell, Ed. D. and Travice Baldwin Obas, M. Ed. © 2018 Kendall Hunt Publishing Company. Reprinted by permission.

Front Matter
iii   © Urupong Phunkoed/Shutterstock.com
vii   Waddell Photo; Source: Dr. Penny Joyner Waddell
vii   Obas Photo; Source: Travice Baldwin Obas
viii   Source: Dr. Penny Joyner Waddell

Unit 1
1   © Triff/Shutterstock.com

Chapter 1
3   © garetsworkshop/Shutterstock.com
5   Source Waddle & Obas
7   Source Waddle & Obas
     © George Rudy/Shutterstock.com
8   Source Waddle & Obas
8   © Foxy burrow/Shutterstock.com
9   © Plateresca/Shutterstock.com
10   Source Waddle & Obas
11   Source Waddle & Obas
11   © M-SUR/Shutterstock.com
12   © Maslowski Marcin/Shutterstock.com
12   Source Waddle & Obas
12   © stoatphoto/Shutterstock.com
13   Source Waddle & Obas
13   © rvlsoft/Shutterstock.com
13   © solomon7/Shutterstock.com
13   © tanuha2001/Shutterstock.com
13   © Evan Lorne/Shutterstock.com
13   © Mary_ART_S/Shutterstock.com
13   © tanuha2001/Shutterstock.com
13   © Rose Carson/Shutterstock.com
13   © Zoa-Arts/Shutterstock.com

13   © Ramisclao/Shutterstock.com
13   © Evgeniya Mukhitova/Shutterstock.com
13   © FOOTAGE VECTOR PHOTO/Shutterstock.com
15   © pockygallery/Shutterstock.com

Chapter 2
19   © metamorworks/Shutterstock.com
20   © Tashatuvango/Shutterstock.com
21   Source Waddell & Obas
21   Source Waddell & Obas
22   © StunningArt/Shutterstock.com
23   © pockygallery/Shutterstock.com
25   Source Waddell & Obas

Chapter 3
27   © Rawpixel.com/Shutterstock.com
29   Source Waddle & Obas
30   Source Waddle & Obas
30   © Kheng Guan Toh/Shutterstock.com
32   © FGC/Shutterstock.com
32   © mimagephotography/Shutterstock.com
32   © CREATISTA/Shutterstock.com
32   © View Apart/Shutterstock.com
32   © wavebreakmedia/Shutterstock.com
32   © rustycanuck/Shutterstock.com
33   © pockygallery/Shutterstock.com
35   Source Waddell & Obas

Unit 2
37   © Triff/Shutterstock.com

Chapter 4
39   © mindscanner/Shutterstock.com
40   © Daisy Daisy/Shutterstock.com
41   © Lemon Tree Images/Shutterstock.com
42   © avh_vectors/Shutterstock.com
43   © Fabrik Bilder/Shutterstock.com
45   © pockygallery/Shutterstock.com

47   Source: Waddell & Obas

Chapter 5

51   © Rido/Shutterstock.com
52   © Voronin76/Shutterstock.com
53   Source Waddell & Obas
      Source Waddell & Obas
54   Source Waddell & Obas
55   © DeeaF/Shutterstock.com
56   © Monkey Business Images/Shutterstock.com
      © crazystocker/Shutterstock.com
57   Source Waddell & Obas
59   © pockygallery/Shutterstock.com

Chapter 6

65   © Kopytin Georgy/Shutterstock.com
      © Kopytin Georgy/Shutterstock.com
      © Kopytin Georgy/Shutterstock.com
      © Kopytin Georgy/Shutterstock.com
67   © Syda Productions/Shutterstock.com
      © WAYHOME studio/Shutterstock.com
68   © michaeljung/Shutterstock.com
69   Source Waddell & Obas
      Source Waddell & Obas
70   © blvdone/Shutterstock.com
71   Source Waddell & Obas
72   © Minerva Studio/Shutterstock.com
      Source Waddell & Obas
73   Source Waddell & Obas
76   © Rido/Shutterstock.com
77   © pockygallery/Shutterstock.com

Unit 3

83   © Triff/Shutterstock.com

Chapter 7

85   © Dmytro Zinkevych/Shutterstock.com
86   © Photographee.eu/Shutterstock.com
      Source Waddell & Obas
87   © BOULENGER Xavier/Shutterstock.com.
      Adapted by Kendall Hunt Publishing Company.
89   Source Waddell & Obas
91   Source Waddell & Obas
92   © Amero/Shutterstock.com. Adapted by Kendall
      Hunting Publishing Company.
93   © mtlapcevic/Shutterstock.com. Adapted by
      Kendall Hunting Publishing Company.
95   © pockygallery/Shutterstock.com
97   Source Waddell & Obas
99   Source Waddell & Obas
101   Source Waddell & Obas

Chapter 8

103   © worradirek/Shutterstock.com
104   Source Waddell & Obas
105   © catwalker/Shutterstock.com
107   © pockygallery/Shutterstock.com
109   Source Waddell & Obas

Unit 4

111   © Triff/Shutterstock.com

Chapter 9

113   © pixelheadphoto digitalskillet/Shutterstock.com
114   Source Waddell & Obas
115   Source Waddell & Obas
116   Source Waddell & Obas
      Source Waddell & Obas
117   Source Waddell & Obas
      Source Waddell & Obas
119   © Pressmaster/Shutterstock.com
122   Source Waddell & Obas
121   © racorn/Shutterstock.com
122   Source Waddell & Obas
123   © Ellagrin/Shutterstock.com
127   © pockygallery/Shutterstock.com

Chapter 10

131   © pixelheadphoto digitalskillet/Shutterstock.com
132   Source Waddell & Obas
133   © Rawpixel.com/Shutterstock.com
134   Source Waddell & Obas
135   © pockygallery/Shutterstock.com

Chapter 11

139   © Monkey Business Images/Shutterstock.com
140   © Neomaster/Shutterstock.com
141   Source Waddell & Obas
141   © iQoncept/Shutterstock.com
142   Source Waddell & Obas
143   Source Waddell & Obas
145   © Monkey Business Images/Shutterstock.com
147   © pockygallery/Shutterstock.com
151   Source Waddell & Obas

Unit 5

153   © Triff/Shutterstock.com

Chapter 12

157   © Rawpixel.com/Shutterstock.com
158   © Minerva Studio/Shutterstock.com
159   Source Waddell & Obas
160   © Rawpixel.com/Shutterstock.com

161 © Sergey Nivens/Shutterstock.com
162 Source Waddell & Obas
164 © Monkey Business Images/
      Shutterstock.com
165 © Vjom/Shutterstock.com
166 © Hermann Eske/Shutterstock.com
168 Source Waddell & Obas
179 © pockygallery/Shutterstock.com
171 Source Waddell & Obas

Chapter 13
175 © Rawpixel.com/Shutterstock.com
176 Source Waddell & Obas
177 © ESB Professional/Shutterstock.com
179 © Marketa Kuchynkova/Shutterstock.com
183 © Rawpixel.com/Shutterstock.com
185 © BeautyLine/Shutterstock.com
190 © Volodymyr Tverdokhilib/Shutterstock.com
191 © MaDedee/Shutterstock.com
195 © Jacek Dudzinski/Shutterstock.com
196 © Kendall Hunt Publishing Company
197 © Kheng Guan Toh/Shutterstock.com
199 © ibreakstock/Shutterstock.com
203 © Rawpixel.com/Shutterstock.com
204 © ESB Professional/Shutterstock.com
205 © Heinrich Knoetze/Shutterstock.com
207 © Skovoroda/Shutterstock.com
211 © Raisa Kanareva/Shutterstock.com
213 © Happy Art/Shutterstock.com
217 © Sergey Nivens/Shutterstock.com
218 © Erce/Shutterstock.com
221 © pockygallery/Shutterstock.com
223 Source Waddell & Obas

Chapter 14
227 © Rawpixel.com/Shutterstock.com
228 © Sergey Nivens/Shutterstock.com

231 Source Waddell & Obas
234 © prizma/Shutterstock.com
235 Source Waddell & Obas
237 Source Waddell & Obas
238 Source Waddell & Obas
241 Source Waddell & Obas
246 © Sashkin/Shutterstock.com
250 Source Waddell & Obas
      © TORWAISTUDIO/Shutterstock.com
253 © Halfpoint/Shutterstock.com
259 © Monkey Business Images/
      Shutterstock.com
260 © Aakruthi Vishwa/Shutterstock.com
263 © pockygallery/Shutterstock.com
269 Source Waddell & Obas
271 Source Waddell & Obas
273 Source Waddell & Obas

Chapter 15
277 © Rawpixel.com/Shutterstock.com
279 © Andrea Danti/Shutterstock.com
282 © michaeljung/Shutterstock.com
283 © SvetlanaFedoseyeva/Shutterstock.com
284 © ESB Professional/Shutterstock.com
      © bazzier/Shutterstock.com
289 © OPOLJA/Shutterstock.com
      © GraphicsRF/Shutterstock.com
290 © Andrea Agrati/Shutterstock.com
291 © Sergey Nivens/Shutterstock.com
292 © Jack1e/Shutterstock.com
317 © pockygallery/Shutterstock.com
321 Source Waddell & Obas
323 Source Waddell & Obas
325 Source Waddell & Obas
326 © Rawpixel.com/Shutterstock.com

CPSIA information can be obtained
at www.ICGtesting.com
Printed in the USA
LVHW05s0857070818
585701LV00002B/2/P